# Political Self-Sacrifice

Over the last decade the increasing phenomenon of suicide terrorism has raised questions about how it might be rational for individuals to engage in such acts. This book examines a range of different forms of political self-sacrifice, including hunger strikes, self-burning and non-violent martyrdom, all of which have taken place in resistance to foreign interference. Karin Fierke sets out to study the strategic and emotional dynamics that arise from the image of the suffering body, including political contestation surrounding the identification of the victim as a terrorist or martyr, the meaning of the death as suicide or martyrdom and the extent to which this contributes to the reconstruction of community identity. *Political Self-Sacrifice* offers a counterpoint to rationalist accounts of international terrorism in terrorist and security studies, and is a novel contribution to the growing literature on the role of emotion and trauma in international politics.

K. M. FIERKE is Professor of International Relations in the School of International Relations at the University of St Andrews. Her books include *Changing Games, Changing Strategies: Critical Investigations in Security* (1998), *Diplomatic Interventions: Conflict and Change in a Globalizing World* (2005), *Critical Approaches to International Security* (2007) and an edited collection with Knud Erik Jorgensen, *International Relations: The Next Generation* (2001). She has also published widely on topics related to constructivism and security as well as trauma, memory and political violence in a range of internationally recognized journals, including *International Studies Quarterly*, the *European Journal for International Relations*, *International Theory*, the *Review of International Studies* and *Millennium – Journal of International Studies*.

*Cambridge Studies in International Relations: 125*

# Political Self-Sacrifice

*Cambridge Studies in International Relations* is a joint initiative of Cambridge
University Press and the British International Studies Association (BISA). The
series will include a wide range of material, from undergraduate textbooks
and surveys to research-based monographs and collaborative volumes. The
aim of the series is to publish the best new scholarship in International Studies
from Europe, North America and the rest of the world.

*Cambridge Studies in International Relations*

*Series list continues after index*

# Political Self-Sacrifice

## Agency, Body and Emotion in International Relations

K. M. FIERKE
*University of St Andrews*

CAMBRIDGE UNIVERSITY PRESS
Cambridge, New York, Melbourne, Madrid, Cape Town,
Singapore, São Paulo, Delhi, Mexico City

Cambridge University Press
The Edinburgh Building, Cambridge CB2 8RU, UK

Published in the United States of America by
Cambridge University Press, New York

www.cambridge.org
Information on this title: www.cambridge.org/9781107029231

First published 2013

Printed and bound in the United Kingdom by the MPG Books Group

*A catalogue record for this publication is available from the British Library*

*Library of Congress Cataloging in Publication data*
Fierke, K. M. (Karin M.)
    Political self-sacrifice : agency, body and emotion in international
relations / K. M. Fierke.
        p.   cm. – (Cambridge studies in international relations: 125 political self-sacrifice)
    ISBN 978-1-107-02923-1 (Hardback)
    1. International relations–Psychological aspects.   2. Self-sacrifice–Political aspects.
I. Title.
    JZ1253.F54 2012
    327.101'9–dc23
                                                                        2012023307

ISBN 978-1-107-02923-1 Hardback

*In memory of Mateo Castrillon (1993–2012)*

# Contents

# Figures

# Acknowledgements

This project began with an observation regarding the use of the labels 'suicide' terrorism and 'martyrdom' to refer to the human bomb. While the language of 'martyrdom' is often dismissed as the mere propaganda of terrorists, I questioned what was being communicated in the use of these two terms and the dynamics generated by these different meanings for the same phenomenon. After presenting the paper 'Agents of death: the structural logic of suicide terrorism and martyrdom' at a workshop in honour of Professor Raymond Duvall at the University of Minnesota, Professor Kathy Hochstetler suggested that I look at other forms of bodily self-sacrifice, such as self-immolation. My first thanks must go to her, since, without her suggestion, I might not have taken the project in this particular direction.

I would also like to thank a few people who played a significant role in the research. A second inspiration for this work was an article I co-authored with Khaled Fattah (Fattah and Fierke 2009). Khaled also provided research assistance on the article arising from the workshop mentioned above (Fierke 2009b), as well as comments on Chapter 7. Janina Skrzypek did a tremendous job organizing our research trip to Poland, and guiding me through the cities and archives with unceasing insights into Polish culture. My niece, Johanna Fierke, deserves thanks for taking time from her busy university schedule to carry out archival research of documents from Vietnam that I was unable to access in the United Kingdom. I would also like to thank the Linenhall Library in Belfast and the Charta Institute in Warsaw for allowing me access to their archives.

Several people have read major portions of this book at different stages of its production and have provided valuable feedback, including Ian Austin, Tarak Barkawi, Robert Burgoyne, Richard English, Nick Rengger, Janina Skrzypek and, last but certainly not least, Mary Jane Fox, who waded through the almost final text before it was sent off to the publisher, and Beatrix Futak-Campbell, who prepared the index. I also would like to thank the co-editors of the BISA *Cambridge Studies in International Relations* series, Nick Wheeler and Chris Reus-Smit, for their enthusiasm for the book, as well as John Haslam, the politics editor for Cambridge University Press, Carrie Parkinson, the politics, sociology and psychology editor, and the reviewers, who provided very helpful feedback. This project has developed over a six-year period, during which various chapters have been presented at workshops or conferences and many individuals have raised insightful questions and provided comments. These have included, among others, Emanuel Adler, Kenneth Booth, Naomi Head, Chris Brown, Neta Crawford, James Der Derian, Faye Donnelly, Rick Fawn, Caron Gentry, Lene Hansen, Christoph Humrich, Kimberley Hutchings, Marcus Kornprobst, Ron Krebs, George Lawson, Richard Ned Lebow, Jennifer Mitzen, Cerwyn Moore, Jeffrey Murer, Nicholas Onuf, Taryn Shepperd, Duncan Snidal, Jens Steffek, William Thomson, Alexander Wendt, Antje Wiener, Tim Wilson and Maja Zehfuss.

# Introduction

The world is a big place, and those who seek to study it have struggled with the question of whether to focus their analysis at the level of individuals, states or the international system. Scholars of international relations (IR) have traditionally emphasized the latter two 'levels', defined by a distinction between foreign policy analysis and international relations theory. The importance of the individual has, however, been highlighted in more recent debates regarding human security, which were in part inspired by statistics that 90 per cent of the casualties in contemporary wars are civilian.[1] On the other side of the spectrum, the international focus on terrorism, and 'suicide terrorism' since 11 September 2001, has represented individuals as a threat to the state. The targeting of civilians is a breach of the laws of armed conflict. 'Suicide terrorism' represents a problem of a different kind, given that non-state actors have not been written into the rules of war and their status remains ambiguous. The latter was most evident in Guantanamo Bay, where detainees were categorized as 'unlawful combatants', which, according to the administration of President George W. Bush in the United States, excluded them from protection by the Geneva Conventions. Historically, the rules, institutions and customs of international relations have placed individuals outside the boundaries of war, except as soldiers of the state or representatives of institutions of other kinds, such as diplomats. The individual has primarily been constructed as a subject within discourses of the

---

[1] Adam Roberts (2011: 357; see also Roberts 2010) argues that the 90 per cent statistic, which since the early 1990s has become an 'urban myth', is flawed, as is the view that civilians are much worse off than in earlier periods. These statistics have increasingly been questioned. In the academic literature, the shift of focus to human security was reinforced by the development of critical security studies, which highlighted the individual as the referent object of security. See, in particular, Booth (1991); Krause and Williams (1997); Fierke (2007).

state – a subject with rights, duties and obligations whose death in war may be memorialized as a glorification of the state.[2]

The sacrifice of the soldier in war is tragic yet has 'sense' given that the larger values of a sovereign community are at stake. The recent phenomenon of 'suicide terrorism' has proved to be far more difficult for Western observers to comprehend, raising the question of how it could be rational to undertake voluntarily an act that would result in the loss of one's own life. Indeed, much of the early literature on this subject focused on the psychology of the individuals involved, assuming that the agent had to be irrational or psychologically disturbed (see Kramer 1990; Merari 1990; Post 1990).[3] Use of the word 'suicide' implies that the bodily death is more individual than political. If one looks more closely, however, and from a somewhat different angle, the assumption of the purely individual nature of the act has to be called into question.

The terminology of 'suicide' terrorism is at odds with the terminology of 'martyrdom' used by the agents themselves and those who identify with them. Martyrdom more explicitly embeds the actor in a social world in which the death is a witness to injustice on behalf of a community. As I began to look beyond the human bomb, to other contexts that involved some form of self-sacrifice, such as hunger strikes, self-burning or non-violent martyrdom,[4] two striking patterns became evident. The first was the recurring contestation over the identity of the agent as a criminal or terrorist, on the one hand, or a martyr, on the other, as well as the meaning of the act as a suicide or martyrdom. The second was a contestation over the reason for the act – that is, whether the agents were perpetuating crimes against the state, or whether they were witnessing to human rights violations by an 'occupying' power.[5]

---

[2] Recently, the individual has begun to occupy a more distinct place in international law, in reference both to human rights and to potential culpability before the International Criminal Court.

[3] Many scholars have argued subsequently that suicide bombers are indeed rational, viewing the benefits of the tactic as outweighing the costs (Sprinzak 2000; Cronin 2003; Moghadam 2003; Bloom 2005; Pedahzur 2005; Hronick 2006).

[4] Non-violent martyrdom is not a fate inflicted by the agents themselves, and in this respect is not voluntary. It is a predictable consequence of a refusal to conform, however, and this non-violent witness is in fact more consistent with the meaning of martyrdom than the act of the human bomb.

[5] I place 'occupying' in quotation marks as I am not using it in the formal, legal sense of the term but, rather, highlighting the claims being made by the agents.

The patterns raised several questions that challenge the tendency to draw fixed boundaries around bodies, whether individuals or states. The first question is one of identity in relation to a social world and whether the agent is outside community, a criminal or terrorist who is violating the norm, or a martyr who suffers on behalf of a community and is therefore an integral part of it. The second is a question about the strategic choices available to those whose sovereignty has been denied, as distinct from citizens inside the state or sovereign agents outside it, in the international realm. The third question regards the role of violence or nonviolence in transforming the boundaries between the individual and the 'body politic'. A central claim of this book is that the individual, state and international levels cannot be neatly separated in an era of globalization. Acts of political self-sacrifice provide a fascinating site for exploring how the three interact.

## Inside/outside

Since 11 September 2001 the question of why individuals would sacrifice their lives in a suicide mission has been a central theme of the burgeoning literature on suicide terrorism. Scholars have high-lighted several types of causal explanation for the phenomenon, including personal motivation (Lachkar 2002; Sarraj and Butler 2002; Berko 2007), group organizational factors (Bloom 2005; Pape 2003; Pedahzur 2005), socio-cultural causes and multiple levels of analysis (Moghadam 2006a; Hafez 2007; Singh 2011). This study is a departure from these debates in several respects. First, although some have acknowledged the role of a language of 'martyrdom' in garnering local support (Hafez 2006, 2007; Moghadam 2008), this study goes further to analyse the signifi-cance of the *contestation* over the meaning of acts of bodily destruction as a 'suicide' or 'martyrdom' (see also Fierke 2009b). The question of cause thereby shifts to one of the constitution of meaning. Second, I examine a class of actions, including not only the human bomb but also hunger strikes, self-burning and non-violent martyrdom, that share a family resemblance as more or less voluntary acts of bodily destruction with a political end, or what I refer to as 'political self-sacrifice'. Third, the book explores the strategic dynamics that arise from the various forms of political self-sacrifice, including the role of violent or non-violent resistance, in shaping the emotional dynamics surrounding the body and the context to which authorities must respond.

Suicide and martyrdom usually rely on different ontological assumptions. The former is often assumed to be a framework of individual action. Maurice Halbwachs (1978 [1930]: 10) argues that solitude is common to all types of suicide, stating: 'People only kill themselves following or under the influence of an unexpected event or condition, be it external or internal (in the body or in the mind), which separates or excludes them from the social milieu and which imposed on them an unbearable feeling of loneliness.' Suicide also violates a social code. As Naim Ateek (2000: 11) points out, in Christianity the person who commits suicide has been considered the only true atheist, as he or she has no faith or hope in God and has totally given up on life. The word for 'suicide' in Arabic is *intihar*, which means killing oneself for personal reasons. In both traditions, ending one's life with suicide brings an end to earthly life, and, given the religious prohibition, is not generally tied to an afterlife.

Suicide is taboo in most religious traditions, and is regarded as the act of the non-believer who has given up all hope. It is also the act of the isolated individual who is alienated from any human or divine community. In the more secular world of the West, the association of suicide with criminalization and the moral responsibility of the individual is a product of modernity and the principle that life at any cost is preferable to death (Minois 1999: 328). Suicide is defined in opposition to Western notions of rationality, which focus first and foremost on a self-interest in survival. To call an act a suicide is to depoliticize it and to place the agent outside community.

Martyrdom, in contrast to suicide, is associated with an act of witness to truth or injustice. Martyrdom requires a martyr, who is a person who on some level chooses suffering and death in order to demonstrate absolute commitment to a cause (Cook 2007: 1). David Cook refers to this witness as one of the most powerful forms of advertisement, insofar as it communicates personal credibility and experience to an audience, which locates the act in a social world. Mark Juergensmeyer (2003: 167) highlights the performative nature of martyrdom as a religious act of self-sacrifice. As Lindsey Harlan (2001: 121) states:

Frequently a martyr is someone who dies and is willing to die, but is always understood as being forced to choose to die, contradictory as that may seem. A martyr defends a principle, a notion of truth, which he or she cannot surrender. The idea that a martyr chooses to defend truth until death, but does not choose death itself, makes the martyr heroic and denies the accusation that the martyr embraces suicide, for the martyr's death serves and is effected by a compelling cause. Such a martyr sees no other way to affirm, defend, and propagate truth. Whereas suicide is selfish – it represents a failure of nerve, endurance, or patience and often an inability to go on despite grief, pain, dissatisfaction or deprivation – martyrdom is selfless.

Aside from a few examples of cult suicide, the word 'suicide' highlights the choice of the individual to take his or her own life, and the problem thus fits within a model of individual preference, if not rational choice.[6] Suicide, no less than martyrdom, is a socio-cultural phenomenon, however, which has varied in meaning across historical and cultural space (Durkheim 2006 [1897]).[7] As Georges Minois (1999: 2) notes, actors in other historical periods or cultural contexts, and philosophers from Cato to Seneca to Bruno Bettelheim, to name just a few, regarded an act of voluntary death as 'the supreme proof of liberty and of the freedom to decide one's own being or non-being'. Martyrdom is more directly recognizable as a social phenomenon, insofar as one does not martyr the self for the self's own sake but for a cause, whether this be religious, political or humanitarian.

Suicide and martyrdom are central to the political contestation revealed in the empirical analyses of this book. The theoretical exploration revolves around a concept of political self-sacrifice, however. 'To sacrifice' is a verb, which points to an agent, an act and an outcome. The word suggests a relationship between the individual who is sacrificed and a community that is the beneficiary of that sacrifice. Sacrifice is a rite of destruction that, according to Juergensmeyer (2003: 167), is found in virtually every religious tradition. The spiritual process of

[6] As Domenico Tosini (2009) notes, rational choice theory continues to be the dominant paradigm of terrorism studies.
[7] Émile Durkheim emphasized the importance of understanding the social world in which suicide takes place and cautioned us to be wary of explanations that focus on individual psychology. Durkheim's main point was that we tend to think of suicide as a supremely individual and personal act, but it also has a social and non-individual aspect, as shown by the fact that different types of society produce different rates of suicide. Suicide is not a purely individual phenomenon (Bloch and Parry 1982: 2) but a social category.

destroying, which comes from the Latin word *sacrificium*, means 'to make holy', which suggests the transformation of death into something positive.

There are several reasons for choosing political self-sacrifice as the key analytical concept. First, given that suicide and martyrdom are at the heart of the contestation explored in the various cases, 'self-sacrifice' is a more neutral and less politically loaded term. Second, political self-sacrifice approaches the problem from a different angle. The question of how it can be rational to give up one's life voluntarily rests on an assumption that individual survival is the ultimate rational end. A concept of political self-sacrifice, like martyrdom, shifts the focus away from the individual to a social space, raising the question of 'Survival for whom?'. Sacrifice points to something outside the self, insofar as one cannot meaningfully sacrifice the self for the self's own sake but only for others. Third, sacrifice is an ancient human practice that is modified by a more modern concern with 'self'. In Chapter 1 I argue that contemporary forms of self-sacrifice share a family resemblance with older practices, while finding distinct expression in the context of the modern state and a globalizing media. Finally, the word 'political' points to the objective of the sacrifice, which is the restoration of sovereign community.

## Inside/outside states

Sovereignty and non-interference have been defining principles of the inter-state system in the period since Westphalia. Survival has been the priority of the sovereign state; but survival has had two sides in Western thought, depending on whether one is looking inside the social contract or outside to the world of international relations. Rational choice begins with a concept of humans as self-seeking egoists, an idea that goes back at least to Thomas Hobbes and the idea that society could be organized around selfish motives. Hobbes' *Leviathan* (1968 [1651]) sketches a world of permanent 'war of all against all' in which life was 'solitary, poore, nasty, brutish and short'. The social contract was a way out of the perpetual fear of death and involved relinquishing a degree of individual sovereignty to an authority that, in return, would provide protection. Hobbes asks a question as to why, having agreed to the contract, humans would necessarily abide by it. He provides two possible reasons: '[E]ither a Feare of the consequence of breaking their word; or a Glory or Pride in not appearing to break it.' Pride, he argues, was seldom sufficient to ensure that individuals would keep to the contract, so fear had to be the dominant motive.

Inside the social contract, conformity or compliance arise out of a fear of sovereign authority, although this also presumes sovereign protection. Outside, in the international 'state of nature', states need to conform with the competitive logic of self-help in order to survive (Waltz 1979).[8] International relations theories often emphasize the rational constraints imposed on sovereign states by the condition of anarchy. For those who have historically been situated outside sovereignty – that is, those whose sovereignty has been taken away or never been formalized – the logic is quite different. To conform to the rules of a hegemon from this position is to lose one's separate identity, and the compelling challenge is to salvage some notion of community when the material and ideological forces of the world are pushing against this. Survival thus comes to rest on an interesting dialectic between existence and non-existence, inside and outside. It is not merely that collective being is existentially threatened. Sovereignty has already to some degree been denied, devalued or eliminated. Communities that have historically been victims of the state system or balance of power politics fall within this category, their sovereignty and security sacrificed for the sake of the sovereignty or wealth of another people.

The focus of IR theory has been on the security and sovereignty of those states that are in a position to securitize others by virtue of their successful constitution as states. We can also ask a question, however, about those communities that have fallen between the cracks. The problem of rationality, self-interest or self-sacrifice looks different in a situation in which sovereignty has *already* been lost or severely curtailed. In this case, the context cannot be approached in terms of bounded insides and outsides, or a single rational and autonomous actor, because it is the boundaries themselves and the structure of authority that are drawn into question. This book approaches the central problem of international relations, sovereignty and non-interference from a different angle, focusing on communities that have been victims of the practices of international politics.

---

[8] The way in which IR theory defines the distinct worlds inside and outside the state was the theme of R. B. J. Walker's (1992) classic work.

## *Inside/outside violence*

Fighting from the boundary is inherently paradoxical. The sovereign agent fights in order to survive. The defeated or occupied community exists only by virtue of their conformity with someone else's rules, which may define them as second-class citizens. In these circumstances, to live by their own rules, almost by definition, means nonconformity. International law defines who has a legitimate right to use violence and who does not. In this respect, the rules define the agency of violence in two distinct ways. On the one hand, sovereigns have the legal authority to use violence, which has been buttressed by the moral authority of 'just war' theory. On the other hand, those who belong to defeated, occupied or marginalized communities do not have this right, although since World War II, based on the experience of the French resistance, this rule has been somewhat modified (Walzer 1977: 177–8).[9] In using violence, members of these communities are likely to be labelled 'terrorists', or, in refusing to comply with the rules of a hegemon in other ways, may be branded as criminals.

If material power and force are what primarily drive international politics, as argued by realists and neo-realists, then actors in the second category can only step into the position of moral authority, such that they have a legitimate monopoly on the use of violence, by defeating and replacing the existing powers that be. By virtue of their position, however, they play with a weak hand and are unlikely to be successful in any attempt to overpower without assistance from outside, which carries risks of its own, given that sovereignty is the objective. There is also a danger that an attempt to overpower without the strength or conditions to do so may result in a further loss of legitimacy, which could be used to justify the elimination of violent resistance, as happened in 2009 with the Tamil Tigers in Sri Lanka.

The anti-colonial literature on resistance in the period since World War II emphasized overpowering the enemy in order then to impose a

---

[9] Michael Walzer notes that, if the citizens of a defeated country attacked the occupation authorities, the act once carried the charge of 'war treason', which was punishable by death. After the experience of the French partisans and other guerrilla fighters in World War II, however, 'war treason' has disappeared from the law books. He states: 'We have come to understand the moral commitment [that individuals] may feel to defend their homeland and their political community, even after the war is officially over.'

new set of sovereign rules. Frantz Fanon (2001 [1963]: 27), writing in the context of Algerian resistance to France, states:

[N]ational liberation, national renaissance, the restoration of nationhood to the people...decolonization is always a violent phenomenon. At whatever level we study it – relationships between individuals, new names for sports clubs, the human admixture at cocktail parties, in the police, on the directing boards of national and private banks – decolonization is quite simply the replacing of a certain 'species' of men by another 'species' of men. Without any period of transition, there is a total, complete and absolute substitution.

Non-violent campaigns, such as Mohandas Gandhi's independence movement in India, shifted the balance, making nonconformity with the rules of the dominant power a major site of political contestation rather than violent conflict. By eliminating violence from one side of the equation – that is, the action of the resistance – Gandhi highlighted the questions 'Whose rules, whose sovereignty, and whose security?' while resolving the question of 'Whose violence?', since this was left to the forces of authority. This represents agency in a pure sense, which goes against the dominant structure, while recognizing that the failure to conform will bring certain suffering and perhaps death. For the non-violent campaign, principled mobilization replaces military mobilization. Arguably it is harder to persuade a population to remain calm and disciplined, without hitting back, in the face of government retaliation to resistance than to persuade a minority to pick up arms, even in largely unequal conditions. It is arguably easier to make sense of killing someone else in the context of violent exchange than to make sense of sacrificing one's own life without hitting back. The latter defies not only rational concerns for self-preservation but the natural impulse to retaliate in self-defence.

Although the choice between violent and non-violent resistance is in theory clear-cut, in practice they usually combine in different ways during the course of an extended campaign, and self-sacrifice is not the territory exclusively of non-state resistance. The soldier on the battlefield who fights in defence of the state also potentially sacrifices his or her life to be hailed as a martyr. The idea of martyrdom is often firmly attached to the honour of warriors. Farhad Khosrokhavar (2005: 6–10) makes a distinction between two types of martyrdom: offensive and defensive. Offensive martyrdom arises from a desire to destroy the enemy but relies on violence that has been sanctioned by religion and is thus legitimate. This strand, which has focused on military confrontation, can be found in a variety of religions and has often inspired nationalism. He provides several examples, including the patriotism of World War I or the revolutionary phenomena of 1789. With offensive martyrdom, one bears witness in sacrificing the self in a battle against injustice.

Defensive martyrdom can be traced back to Christian martyrdom during the Roman Empire. The first martyr, according to Eusebius of Caesarea, was Procopus, who refused to make a sacrifice to the gods in the presence of the emperor, stating that he recognized only one god and was ready to sacrifice himself to Him (Khosrokhavar 2005: 6). His head was then cut off. Christian martyrdom was characterized by a refusal to obey Caesar in matters of religion, and subsequent death at the hands of the authorities.

Many contemporary acts of political self-sacrifice, while often informed by religious meaning, are directed to secular ends and, in the cases explored here, the sovereignty of a community. The agent who 'acts as if' a different set of rules is in place, but without violence, may be no less engaged in defence of a community and no less likely to sacrifice the self for a political end than the agent who uses violence. The most troubling combination of violence and self-sacrifice is to be found with the suicide terrorist. The suicide terrorist deliberately takes his or her own life, while killing innocent victims in the process. The recent spread of this tactic has raised questions about how rational human beings can take their own life in this way. The Romans also asked this question of the Christian martyrs, however, and they were all the more perplexed because they did so without fighting back. As Khosrokhavar (2005: 6) notes, the Romans viewed these acts of martyrdom with incomprehension, asking how a rational being could commit 'irrational suicide', especially when he or she caused the fatal blow to be struck by others.

## The international and the global

Political self-sacrifice remains exceptional. On the surface, cases of voluntary death or suffering would appear to have little to do with questions of international relations. In several respects, though, when approached from a different angle, the relevance is clear to see. I have adopted the term 'international relations' in the title to highlight the fact that the organizing principle of sovereignty has resulted in a loss of sovereignty for some. This use further highlights Sanjay Seth's (2011: 182) claim that '"the international" is a realm where endless and seemingly irresolvable contests – over meanings and morals as much as resources and power – testify to the fact that few things have become so naturalised that they are not potentially subject to contestation, few presumptions so stabilised that they are not period-ically destabilised'. Against the backdrop of globalization, 'the inter-national' is itself an object of contestation. Cases of contemporary political self-sacrifice reveal the tension between 'the international' and the more transversal processes that characterize a globalizing world.

There are several dimensions to this tension. First, two concepts at the heart of the contestation surrounding acts of political self-sacrifice draw on two potentially conflicting principles of international law, namely the sovereignty of the state, on the one hand, and a more cosmopolitan conception of human rights, on the other. The latter highlights the tension between the legitimacy of the state to use force by virtue of its sovereignty and the potential human rights problem for people who, through historical processes of intervention or the draw-ing of boundaries, have found themselves second-class citizens, denied the right to define the rules by which they live. The tension between sovereignty and human rights is a tension between the international and the global, between notions of the individual as a citizen of the state and a more cosmopolitan understanding of the human.

Second, political self-sacrifice takes on a different meaning in an age of globalization, particularly of the electronic media. Images of violence against the body – from Thich Quang Duc, the Vietnamese Buddhist monk who set himself on fire in 1963, to the suicide bomber – have become iconic. All the following cases were dependent on forms of international media for communicating the emotions and thus the power of the sacrifice. Political self-sacrifice can be a means to focus attention in a world characterized by a shortage of attention, given the bombardment of information and images. An image of self-sacrifice evokes emotions that go beyond words, to something more primal. It is not only that the image captures the attention; it also causes a disruption or a rupture, insofar as it is so perplexing, so contrary to ideas of self-preservation, that the audience has to stop and ask questions about what is happening and why. Given the almost daily images of 'suicide' bombings on the news, these acts have become almost routine and thus less likely to invoke these questions. For this reason it is useful to look back at a period when actions belonging to this 'family' set a precedent. There is nothing new about self-sacrifice. Buddhist practices of self-burning (Benn 2007) or Hindu practices of sati go back centuries. The Christian martyrs during the Roman Empire engaged in non-violent self-sacrifice and the Assassins were a precursor to modern forms of suicide terrorism.[10] The precedent in this case relates to the use of self-sacrifice in a context of globalizing media, in which its potential use as a political weapon, for attracting the attention of a much larger audience, across national boundaries, has expanded.

The spread of globalized forms of communication has transformed the space within which acts of political self-sacrifice take place, turning them potentially into international and global phenomena rather than a purely domestic one. What has come to be referred to as public diplomacy is usually associated with the attempt by states to influence populations beyond their own borders (see, for example, Nye 2005; Melissen 2005; Cowan and Cull 2008). While state propaganda has always played an important role in war, the soft power of public diplomacy involves more of a conversation between states and populations, and the attempt to 'win over' and attract (Nye 2004, 2005). The development of a global media has also meant, however, that states have greater difficulty excluding alternative narratives or blocking images from view. The abuse of Buddhist monks in Burma or protesters in the Arab Spring was captured on mobile phones and transmitted via the internet and other electronic means, despite government efforts to constrain media access. The circulation of images of human suffering may create pressure on governments to act or may result in a loss of soft power, as governments find

---

[10] The Assassins (Arabic: *Hashishin*) were an order of Nizari Ismailis, located in Syria and Persia in particular, from about 1092 to 1265, who relied on a method of assassination, namely the selective elimination of prominent officials, usually carried out in public spaces. Members used daggers to kill their victims and deliberately sought martyrdom in the execution of the act. The most feared of the Assassins were the Lasiqs, who were referred to as *fida'i* (self-sacrificing agents). The *fida'i* were famed for their public missions, during which they often gave their lives in the process of eliminating adversaries.

themselves circumscribed in their attempt to communicate the one 'true' story. Indeed, use of military power that appears disproportionate can, in these circumstances, lead to a loss of soft power, as was evident with the loss of soft power by the United States in the context of its War on Terror (Nye 2004, 2008; Smith 2007).

The third dimension relates to the initial claim that we can no longer limit the focus to discrete levels of analysis, or treat states as fixed entities; rather, given the processes of globalization, we have to be attuned to the relationship between transformations of individual, community and global identity. While self-sacrifice is only one expression of this relationship, it is an important one for analysing how these different 'levels' are co-constituted. Just as the global and state levels constitute the individual, more individual acts of self-sacrifice can transform the state and have effects that reverberate throughout the international system.

Suicide terrorism in Lebanon in the early 1980s resulted in a withdrawal of US forces. The hunger strikes in Northern Ireland and Solidarity's campaign in Poland both took place around the same time. Although hunger strikes and non-violence have earlier precedents and later antecedents, the coincidence of these three types of political self-sacrifice, at the height of the Cold War, raises a question about their role in producing what Victor Turner (2008 [1969]) refers to as 'liminality', or the confrontation between structure and anti-structure, which shakes up the system and opens up a slow process of transformation. Given that these practices were precursors of those that constituted the processes of dialogue that developed with the end of the Cold War, the non-violent and coloured revolutions[11] of the early twenty-first century or, in the case of suicide terrorism, the global logic of the War on Terror, the analysis raises a question about the relationship between these more localized 'micro'-practices and larger transformations that later cascaded across state borders. The claim is less one about cause than about how practices of 'acting as if' a new game was in place provided a set of rules for others in different times and/or places to imitate and follow.

---

[11] The term 'coloured revolution' is one widely used by the media to refer to the primarily non-violent revolutions that developed in the states of the former Soviet Union and in the Balkans, including, for instance, the Rose Revolution in Georgia (2003) and the Orange Revolution in Ukraine (2004).

Political self-sacrifice in various forms has, in the context of the increasing globalization of the media since World War II, contributed to processes of resistance to historical patterns of imperial power. This implies turning the 'game' of anarchy on its head. Rather than approaching anarchy as a function of states, and the distribution of power between them – that is, a top-down approach – we start from 'below', with the agency of self-sacrifice, in order to observe its inseparability from a social process of articulating an experience of social suffering and, with it, definitions of community against a background of dominant international power. The insides and outsides of international relations are explored from the boundaries or intersections between them. The focus is on people who have 'fallen through the cracks' of the state system or otherwise been its victim. This positioning shapes considerations of rationality and survival or strategic questions regarding the use or avoidance of violence. These questions take on added significance with the emergence of a global media and its dramatization of human suffering.

## The approach

This book does not pose the normative question regarding the right of communities that have lost their sovereignty to resist, particularly with violence. Instead, my focus is on the empirical observation that communities in this position often do resist, and that political self-sacrifice can be an important component of this resistance. The theoretical objective is to analyse the dynamics of political self-sacrifice, particularly as they relate to different violent or non-violent expressions. The word 'non-violent' may seem a misnomer in relation to acts that involve violence against the body and death. I use the term to refer less to an absence of violence than to a choice by agents of resistance to remain non-violent themselves, which implies that the violence is inflicted by others. The central question is how actors and audiences have made sense of more or less deliberate acts of political self-sacrifice and why these acts would have a power and logic that can be distinguished from, for instance, the sacrifice of soldiers in war. I argue that the power and the logic of political self-sacrifice are different if one's starting point is outside sovereignty, rather than within it, and that therefore they are deserving of separate analysis.

On one level, the two cannot be distinguished. Whether in conflicts between states or between states and sovereign-less communities, two different ideas or sets of rules regarding how to govern sovereign life are in conflict, and the bodily sacrifice of the combatant represents a materialization of these ideas. Elaine Scarry (1985) makes this argument about the contest of war, claiming that what is at stake in war is less a question of outnumbering the other than maintaining morale. Her analysis raises a question about the point at which a community will decide that the cost of fighting outweighs the benefits of continuing the war. Indeed, during the Vietnam War, the Vietnamese suffered twenty deaths for every one American soldier, but they were willing to continue to fight indefinitely because their independence was at stake. As Robert McNamara, the US secretary of defense from 1961 to 1968, admitted upon meeting the former foreign minister of Vietnam twenty-five years after the war ended (Morris 2004), American assumptions about why the Vietnamese were fighting and how long they would continue before surrendering did not acknowledge this possibility. The United States had placed the conflict in the framework of the Cold War and communist expansionism rather than a history of colonial influence – that is, in the context of great power politics rather than resistance to external interference and a desire for independence.

This example points to the nature of the rules at the heart of contestation in cases of this kind, which are distinct from but related to other types of rules at the international level. In the neo-realist model, states have to conform with the rules of the international system in order to survive. These rules are not regulative rules in the way that international law is. They are more constitutive and a function of the organization of the international system into sovereign states, which implies the absence of any international police force or authority to step in to save a state that is under attack. As participants in a self-help system, states, first and foremost, have to be concerned about their survival, and therefore need to be prepared to protect their sovereignty if need be (Waltz 1979). Neo-realists might point to a pattern that can be evidenced throughout time, harking back to Thucydides' (1951 [431 BCE]) claim that the strong do what they will and the weak what they must. Whenever distinct communities with separate interests engage with one another there is a potential for conflict, and a need to manage that conflict such that it does not result in a loss of sovereignty for one or the system of sovereign states as a whole. The balance of power has historically been the mechanism by which equilibrium within the system has been maintained.

It is less the accuracy of the neo-realist claim that is problematic than the assumption that the pattern is universal across time or that the global map of states is a fixed field of objective entities. There have been periods of history when the sovereignty of particular states has been sacrificed for the sake of the balance of power between great states. The various partitions of Poland, which was eliminated as a state for extensive periods of time, are a case in point, as are large portions of the world that have been shaped into states on the basis of the competitive needs of imperial powers. Most state-based models of international relations fail to acknowledge that the development of 'stateness' is a process that, even in the context of more developed industrial states in Europe, is relatively recent (Milliken and Krause 2003). They ignore the extent to which populations have continually been uprooted, relocated or redefined as the boundaries of their identity and territory have been constituted and reconstituted, with many 'peoples' falling through the cracks, not necessarily eliminated by genocide, but with their traditional practices and identities devalued in the process. Sovereignty has been the defining feature of the international system since the Treaty of Westphalia, and since World War II it has been more or less universalized. The codification of the sovereignty rule has, however, created a problem for diverse communities whose historical identity has been subsumed by the creation of formal state boundaries with decolonization, such that one hegemony, often formed as a part of the 'divide and rule' politics of colonialism, has replaced another.

The rule of sovereignty in international law competes with a host of other rules, codified in humanitarian and human rights law. The result, against the backdrop of globalization, is a field of contestation in which the sovereign rights of states often come head to head with the rights of the subordinated communities and individuals within them. On the one hand, external intervention in conflicts often comes to be defined by the question of which rule will have priority, namely sovereignty versus human rights – a question that has been a focus of the literature on humanitarian intervention (see, for example, International Commission on Intervention and State Sovereignty 2001; Wheeler 2002; Holzgrefe and Keohane 2003; Welsh 2004).

This project shifts to contestation over rules at a more micro-level – that is, contestation over the constitutive and regulative rules that govern the day-to-day life of a community in the absence of sovereignty: the rules of the state or the rules of the subordinate community. I examine how actors bring arguments about sovereignty or human rights to bear in making claims for the legitimacy of their own actions.

The analysis is further narrowed by a focus on the dynamics of political self-sacrifice and strategic engagement in an asymmetrical relationship. A question about the spectacle of terrorism could be raised in this context but, given the existence of an extensive literature on the topic, it has not been included here. Conventional forms of terrorism, such as those carried out by Euskadi ta Askatasuna (ETA), the Irish Republican Army (IRA) or the Red Army Faction,[12] did not generally involve the deliberate sacrifice of the self, as violence was directed at others.[13] The hunger strikes by IRA prisoners in the early 1980s deviated from this rule outside the prison, and they are the focus of Chapter 4. I am also not looking at non-violent forms of protest more generally.[14] While all the cases emerge out of contexts of resistance, which often rest on an ethos of sacrifice, my focus is on the sacrifice of the human body. The central question is one of political self-sacrifice in its violent and non-violent forms, as a form of communication with both domestic and more global audiences. A focus on the self-sacrifice of the body raises significant questions about the approach of this study to religion, agency and emotion.

## Religion and political self-sacrifice

Robert Pape and James Feldman (2010) argue that the central cause of suicide terrorism is foreign occupation (see also Pape 2003, 2006; Tosini 2009). In focusing on occupation, they also challenge widely held assumptions, prevalent during the Bush administration's War on

[12] Several members of the Red Army Faction, otherwise known as the Baader-Meinhof Gang, did, according to official accounts, commit collective suicide in their prison cells. To the extent that there was contestation surrounding these suicides, it had more to do with questions of whether they had in fact been murdered, given that some of the evidence was not consistent with suicide.

[13] For a recent discussion of the concept of terrorism, see English (2009).

[14] For a recent collection of studies of non-violent resistance in the post-World-War-II period, see Roberts and Garton Ash (2011).

Terror, about the causal role of religious fundamentalism. After 11 September 2001 many Americans came to assume that Islamic culture has a propensity for violence (Smidt 2005: 249). Arguments of this kind fail to recognize the extent to which other religious traditions have been drawn on to justify or give meaning to forms of political self-sacrifice, and that, as the Irish example demonstrates, more or less secular examples can also be found. The tendency to claim a specific relationship between a religion, such as Islam, and a proclivity for violence rests on methodological assumptions that Islam is a fixed and unchanging framework of meaning. I instead approach political self-sacrifice as a 'form of life', visible across cultures and/or religious traditions yet, within any one, subject to varying types of argumentation and justification that have, across time, been changeable and shaped by historical conditions. As such, it is necessary to 'look and see' how meaning is put to use, how different historical forms of argumentation and memory combine to constitute contextually specific forms of action and interaction.

Traditions that in one historical context have justified violent action may in another be drawn on to construct non-violence. Claims that Islam breeds violence have been challenged by a growing body of Islamic scholars, who argue the scholarly basis for non-violence (Abu-Nimer 2003) and point to any number of real-world examples, from a twenty-year non-violent campaign against the British by Pashtuns in what is now Pakistan to the extensive non-violent campaign by Albanian Muslims in Kosovo, to the non-violent elements of the Palestinian struggle or the non-violent campaigns in protest at the re-election of Mahmoud Ahmadinejad as president in Iran, or more recently the uprisings of the Arab Spring in Tunisia and Egypt. Likewise, while Christianity provides some of the oldest historical examples of non-violent martyrdom, it has often been the banner carried by states going into war. As the Polish case demonstrates, what constitutes martyrdom is a function of the meaning attached to it. The Catholic pope John Paul II was instrumental in transforming the more violent tradition of Polish romanticism into a message of non-violence (Zagacki 2001: 690).

A question about the relationship between religion and political self-sacrifice is important from the perspective of non-violent resistance as well as violent resistance. Roland Bleiker (2000) has constructed a genealogy of resistance, which emerges from ideas that power and government rest on popular consent. He argues that the articulation of theories of dissent corresponded with the 'death of God'. The humanist idea that people are their own masters and able to change themselves and the world required the dislodging of the theory of divine right and the central place of God in guaranteeing political order and legitimacy. His larger point is the need to accept the contingent character of foundations, rather than seeking grand theories. Given the increasingly transversal nature of dissent in a globalizing world, 'ahistorical and spatial modes of representation' are inadequate, he argues (117). Interactions between domination and resistance thus have to be analysed in specific historical and geographical contexts. Although this book does precisely that, it diverges from Bleiker's account in two respects. First, while agreeing that modern notions of agency are central to political *self*-sacrifice, I argue that religious frameworks of meaning often play a constitutive role. Second, while recognizing widespread dissent as the contextual back-drop, this book shifts attention to the specific problem of self-sacrifice in relation to modern secular state structures, in which appeals to the divine often provide an alternative basis for the legitimacy of marginalized communities, but are also, arguably, important for giving meaning to acts that involve sacrifice of the self. Pape and Feldman (2010) challenge the idea that religion is the main cause of suicide terrorism. Bleiker argues that dissent has grown out of a notion that 'God is dead'. The present analysis approaches religion not as a necessary condition but often an important one for shaping the meaning of an act that involves bodily sacrifice.

The cases that follow are informed by different religious trad-itions, from Catholicism to Islam to Buddhism. I do not approach these traditions with the expertise of the comparative theologian or with the subsequent intention of rendering the most theologically sound understanding of political self-sacrifice. My focus instead is directly related to the political nature of the analysis: to explore how religious traditions were drawn on by actors in various contexts to give meaning to practices of political self-sacrifice. It is not my place to judge the accuracy of their use, only to analyse meaning *in* use and its political consequences. This is, therefore, less an engagement in the comparative study of religions than an analysis of how con-textually situated actors grounded the meaning of their actions in religious structures that had a wider resonance to potential agents and audiences.

## Strategy and agency

Pape and Feldman (2010) argue that foreign occupation is the main cause of suicide terrorism. They do not, however, sufficiently address the question of why or how suicide terrorism, as distinct from other tactics, might achieve the objective of removing foreign occupiers, aside from a perception that it works (Pape 2006: 61). The primary mode of thinking about the success or failure of suicide terrorism has been quantitative – that is, how often these acts have achieved their goals – and thereby causal: to what extent did suicide terrorism result in independence? In his earlier work, Pape (2003) points out that campaigns of this kind have been successful in achieving only limited goals. His argument that suicide terrorism has a 54 per cent success rate has been challenged by Assaf Moghadam (2006b: 713), who argues that it has been successful in only 24 per cent of the cases, and has thus more often resulted in failure than success. Success is measured by the extent to which the target states make significant policy changes towards the terrorists' major political goals. This poses a question about the relative success of non-violent campaigns. In an analysis of violent and non-violent campaigns between non-state and state actors between 1900 and 2006, Maria Stephan and Erica Chenowith (2008) found that major non-violent campaigns have achieved success 53 per cent of the time, compared with 26 per cent for violent resistance campaigns, while terrorist campaigns fare worse.

This analysis approaches the equation from a different angle. Instead of asking whether 'suicide terrorism' is successful – however success is defined – the focus shifts to the role of different forms of political self-sacrifice in constructing the agency of marginalized communities. Pape and Feldman (2010), as well as Emanuel Adler (2010), point to a 'dilemma' faced by authorities confronted with suicide terrorism. The analysis of a 'family of actions', including non-violent as well as violent forms of political self-sacrifice, provides useful insight into the strategic dynamics of different members of this family and their relationship to what I refer to as the 'warden's dilemma'. The warden's dilemma provides a framework for exploring how the use of violence or non-violence by the agents of self-sacrifice shapes the space within which authorities respond. I argue that any association of political self-sacrifice with violence by the agent is likely to contribute to a security dilemma, which justifies retaliation against 'terrorists'. By contrast, if the source of violence and death is attributed to the authorities, the result is more likely to be a 'warden's dilemma', which raises questions about the legitimacy of the powers that be.

## The body and emotion

There is a substantial literature within IR that draws on Michel Foucault's (1979 [1975]) argument about the way that power shapes and disciplines the body. Giorgio Agamben, who builds on Foucault, has introduced the concepts of 'bare life' (1998) and the 'state of exception' (2005). Both scholars suggest that the management of bodies and their disciplining is more characteristic of Western societies than democratic deliberation. Sovereign power, in this type of argument, refers to more than superiority over territory and the law of the state. It relates to the ability of sovereign power to draw lines that distinguish different types of subjectivity, determining their place inside or outside community, and thus whether they possess political rights (Edkins and Pin-Fat 2005).

These works are part of a larger shift within anthropology and sociology away from understanding the body first and foremost as a physiological and anatomical object, or part of a Cartesian dualism.[15] Alexandra Howson (2004: 8–11) identifies three points of agreement that have come to define this literature. First, bodies are more than a physical and material frame; they are inseparable from culture and society. While forms of human embodiment tend to be taken for granted, they are products of complex social and political processes and actions. As they are woven into history and the social fabric, they are potentially subject to change. Second, in the context of modernity, the body has increasingly become the target of political control, rationalization and discipline, with the state managing the movements of populations in time and space. Finally, it is not only that social and political processes shape the body, but the body also forms the basis of social experience and action. On the one hand, we attribute meaning to bodies and use the

---

[15] René Descartes (1596–1650) formulated the distinction between mind and body, including the mental versus the material and the soul versus nature. He privileged the former over the latter. While bodily experiences might impact on processes of thinking, thought was to have greater value in that it was disembodied (Fraser and Greco 2005).

body as a symbol for social objects and worlds. On the other hand, bodies create meaning by acting within and upon their environment.

These approaches to body and emotion also share some themes with the 'aesthetic turn' in international relations, which has highlighted the role of sensation and affect, visual perception, and questions of emotion and meaning. Cerwyn Moore and Laura Shepherd (2010) use the term 'global politics' to 'signal a form of resistance' to the dominant paradigms of mainstream IR, moving beyond the focus on states and power politics to an agential and pluralistic approach that recognizes the fluidity and multiplicity of a multidisciplinary and innovative global politics. This involves drawing out emotional themes related to, for instance, humiliation and dignity, while examining questions of cultural meaning, belonging and self-sacrifice as a reflection on authentic human being (Moore 2009: 71).

Vikki Bell (2005) argues that 'suicide terrorism' operates through the aesthetic reaction it produces, provoking a response and mobilizing further responses. A similar claim can be made about the various forms of political self-sacrifice examined here. The act of bodily destruction communicates and prompts a search for meaning, transforming it into a discursive phenomenon. It raises questions about the relationship between the body and our common humanity and the inhumanity by which the death occurred (Bell 2005: 249). A key question is whether the various performances of political self-sacrifice differ in the way they communicate and in terms of the conclusions reached by various audiences and the subsequent political impact. The goal is to examine the extent to which the relationship between violence and non-violence relates to the creation of alternative forms of identity and belonging, such that members of marginalized communities are transformed from criminals or deviants into political subjects, able to engage in dialogue over the conditions in which they live. This necessarily acknowledges the difficulty of identifying a community that has ceased to exist in any formal sense, when the institutional mechanisms by which collective identity is constructed and reproduced – or 'imagined', to use Benedict Anderson's (1983) terminology – may have been severely curtailed, given the destruction of archives, constraints on the political use of language (and even the speaking of a native language) or engagement in public rituals. The 'body politic', like any community, is a construction that is always in the process of being produced; it is not a fixed category (Mattern 2005).

## Methodology

A study of this kind necessarily shifts away from quantification and cause to a question of meaning and the production of legitimacy. An examination of meaning requires a more in-depth enquiry into the cultural symbols and memories by which acts of political self-sacrifice are constituted, as well as the political contestation surrounding the legitimacy of the deviant/subject. It thus goes beyond the emphasis in the securitization literature on the speech act of naming an existential threat (see Wæver 1995; Buzan, Wæver and de Wilde 1998), to a *process* by which the political landscape comes to be defined by the question 'Security for whom?'.

The subject matter is by definition critical, in that this framing of the question creates a space for those who play with a weak hand to have a voice within the analysis, given that they tend to be written out of more conventional accounts of 'terrorism' or international relations.[16] Locating the analysis at the intersection of pre-modern notions of sacrifice, modern notions of agency and the postmodern circulation of emotion raises some further methodological issues, however. Modernity has tended to discount the role of religious meaning, which is associated with the pre-modern. Postmodernism has included a critique of modern assumptions related to science. Modern notions of science exclude the role of emotion as too messy. In this respect, these are 'levels' of another kind, which represent less a categorization of distinct 'eras' than qualitatively different assumptions about the meaning and nature of being in the world. Rather than the one cancelling out the other, we can instead examine how they mutually constitute contemporary practice. Science may discount the role of religious meaning, but religious meaning continues to shape how agents give meaning to their actions. Acts of political self-sacrifice, which have no 'sense' within modern frameworks of rationality, can provide some understanding of another realm of experience. Insofar as the postmodern global environment rests on an acceptance of difference and multiplicity, it provides an opening for the examination of the relationship between these three different assumptions about being in the world.

---

[16] This is, of course, more of a focus for critical approaches to terrorism. See, for instance, Jackson (2005) and the journal *Critical Studies on Terrorism*.

The intent is to construct a form of dialogical analysis. I, as analyst, engage in a conversation with the texts of the diverse agents in each of the contexts examined here. Rather than giving preference to a particular subject of analysis, such as the state, as is common in much IR scholarship, I reconstruct a dialogue between the central subjects of contestation, to examine their assumptive world and how this was shaped and transformed through a conversation between them over time. Given the central place of the material body, the analysis is not merely about language, however. The case studies employ a form of constitutive process tracing, which can be distinguished from the more positivist assumptions that usually underpin this method (see, for example, George and Bennett 2005; Bennett and Elman 2006). Process tracing, as generally conceived, revolves around the identification of intervening connections between independent and dependent variables. The focus is on events that intervene between agents with causal capacities and outcomes. This may involve physical, social or psychological processes that cannot be directly observed and an attempt to make imperfect inferences about them on the basis of observed data. A more *constitutive* approach to process tracing instead identifies shifts in meaning as part of a process that establishes the parameters of a new game (see, for instance, Fierke 1998). The focus is on the meaning attached to identity, action and bodily materiality, rather than events per se, and the relationship between the changing boundaries of identity and policy-making. Rather than being inferred from unobservables, the process is observed in the assumed language, the shared and conflicting categories of those engaged in political contestation, to the end of tracing changes in these 'language games' over time, including changes in forms of identity, action and material practice.

With one exception, I have chosen cases that are sufficiently in the past to ensure the availability of extensive documentation. Given that people often remember differently in hindsight from how they do at the time of action, I focus on written documents and other cultural artefacts from the time in question rather than contemporary interviews with participants. When possible, I have relied on texts in the native language, as well as English texts, and in these cases I have worked closely with a native-speaking research assistant. The biggest constraint on the analysis is one of space, given the difficulty, when dealing with several cases in a book-length manuscript, of saying all that could be said about the numerous sources that have been drawn on and the cultural, political and other complexities of each case.

A further reason for going back to earlier cases is to analyse these processes from a greater distance, in order to avoid either engaging with contexts that are still unfolding or becoming caught up in ongoing political battles. The one exception is Chapter 7, in which I explore several forms of political self-sacrifice in the contemporary Middle East. Given the current fascination with suicide terrorism, the book attempts to stand back and ask larger questions about the dynamics of political self-sacrifice, in the hope that this will have some reflexive value for actors on both sides – state or non-state – who find themselves confronted with choices. Given the importance of locating these practices in historical, cultural and political context, the number of cases is necessarily limited, and any conclusions from specific cases do not represent a claim that the same dynamics would be present when transferred to another time and place. The trends identified in the historical cases have more recent expressions, and the potentials have expanded with the development of electronic technologies, such as the internet and mobile phones, not to mention the competition between multiple global networks in different geographical locations.

However imperfect, what follows is an attempt to examine the culturally, historically and politically specific meanings that shape acts of political self-sacrifice. The focus on multiple cases makes it possible to identify rudimentary patterns that tie the cases together – thus making the comparison useful – while identifying the distinct dynamics of each. Political self-sacrifice can be understood as what the philosopher Ludwig Wittgenstein (1958: paras. 19, 23, 241) refers to as a 'form of life', which can be accessed only through an analysis of the culturally specific 'language games' by which these social acts are expressed.

The choice of cases began with variations between them. After an initial study relating to human bombs (Fierke 2009b), I began to explore a number of other types of voluntary destruction of the body, from hunger strikes to self-burning to non-violent martyrdom. After identifying rudimentary patterns across cases involving non-state actors, I decided to focus on this angle and not to include, for instance, the Japanese Kamikazis, who were soldiers of the state. A number of similarities across cases emerged from this initial analysis. First, the sacrifices related to communities that framed their resistance in terms

of occupation or interference by a foreign power. Second, the language
of humiliation and dignity had a central place. Third, each involved
contestation over the identity of the agent and the meaning of the
sacrifice. Fourth, in all cases the agent was hailed as a martyr,
although audiences were more or less divided over this depiction.

Conscious of the tendency to associate humiliation with Arab culture,
I wanted to look at a cross-section of Western and non-Western cultures.
I have included Northern Ireland, as a more secular case, even though it
is connected to Catholicism; Poland, where the role of Catholicism was
significant; Vietnam, as a context influenced by Buddhist thought; and
Islam, in the Middle East. Moreover, in order to examine assumptions
about how violence or non-violence works, or doesn't work, in different
types of more or less open political structures, and to avoid suggesting
that one historical power is responsible for the world's ills, I also tried to
identify cases that involved different dominant powers, including the
United States, Israel, the United Kingdom and the former Soviet Union.
In summary, the similarities or patterns that tie the cases together
emerged out of a pilot study, which began without a clear idea of what
I would find. As I began to examine further cases, the differences
became as important as the similarities.

One suspects that, beyond the desire to become a science, international relations theory has adopted the types of methodology it has
in the past precisely because it is so difficult to approach analysis of
the world from multiple cultural perspectives. In the process, it has
failed to acknowledge that what is often claimed as scientific truth is
heavily influenced by the position of gazing at the world through
the lens of imperial power, given the origin and foundation of IR as
a field in the United States and United Kingdom. Wittgenstein alluded
to the difficulty of grasping the structures of meaning within which
different cultures operate without 'going native', although the more
salient point may be the difficulty of grasping human activities in the
absence of language (see, for instance, Wittgenstein 1958: para. 207).
Indeed, having lived in several Western cultures, I am struck by the
extent to which, to use Bernard Shaw's phrase, we are often 'divided
by a common language', given that differences, even here, run very
deep. The task of gaining some understanding of Arab, Asian or Slavic
cultures would seem to be even more beyond reach. At the same time,
this can all too easily become an excuse for avoiding the attempt to
be reflexive, given that the imposition of Western understandings

on different cultures has historically been part of the problem. This journey is like any attempt at conversation, in that it is based on the hope that some kind of understanding will become possible through the exchange, and that I, and any readers, will be transformed through the process.

In sum, we are not dealing at the level of pure facts or fixed 'bodies', whether individual or collective, but with the processes by which the meaning and boundaries of identity and human value are defined. We are not dealing at the level of structure, by which rationality relates purely to survival, but look to an agency of suffering and even death. A structural logic and the subsequent pressure to conform with the rules of the dominant game do, however, provide a point of departure for understanding the dynamics of this agency.

## Structure of the argument

The first section of the book establishes the framework of analysis through an examination of self-sacrifice, agency, body and emotion. Building on an anthropological literature, Chapter 1 argues that contemporary political self-sacrifice shares a family resemblance with more ancient forms of sacrifice but has a distinct expression in the context of the modern state and globalization. Rather than constituting a form of substitution or sacrifice to the gods, modern self-sacrifice communicates a political message. The sacrifice gives rise to a process of contestation surrounding the identity of the injured or dead body, raising questions about whether the death represents a suicide or martyrdom. In the liminal state surrounding the death, the body of the martyr has the potential to expand through the identification with it of a nascent *communitas*.

Chapter 2 shifts to a question of rationality associated with the modern self and the strategic dimensions of an act of self-sacrifice. An analysis of the problem presented by political self-sacrifice for the rational choice literature is followed by an argument about the need to shift away from the individual ontology of the rational choice and game theory literature towards a social ontology, in which knowledge of the underlying rules of the game is the prior condition for understanding the rationality of an act. The logic of the prisoner's dilemma is turned on its head by approaching the prison as a metaphor for a context of hierarchy, in which the sovereignty of the occupants is constrained. The 'warden's dilemma', mentioned earlier, provides a framework for thinking about the strategic dynamics of agency in a context in which, through some form of external occupation or intervention, the sovereignty of a people is denied.

Chapter 3 examines a further dimension of this strategic dynamic, taking the analysis beyond the interaction between agents and warden to explore how emotions attached to the injured or dying body circulate, moving outwards towards a nascent community that, potentially, is restored and expands through its identification with the martyr. The focus of this chapter is the various audiences that are witness to the act – a potential that is expanded by the existence of a global media. It explores further the role of historical memory in the negotiation of meaning by these audiences and the potentially transformative effect on the boundaries of community or, through imitation, the spread of practices internationally.

The second section of the book engages in a form of constitutive process tracing of a range of contexts since World War II relating to different forms of political self-sacrifice. Chapter 4 examines the hunger strikes of 1980 and 1981 in the Long Kesh Prison in Northern Ireland, following on from a four-and-a-half-year campaign of non-cooperation by IRA prisoners. The analysis traces the shift from contestation surrounding the identity of the prisoners as criminals or prisoners of war (POWs) to a question regarding the identity of the criminal, given the inflexible response of Margaret Thatcher, the British prime minister, to the hunger strikers, even as they were dying, and widespread identification with them as martyrs. This case is of particular interest as it is a context most closely related to the prison metaphor explored in Chapter 2. It is also interesting because of the specific dynamics that arose from the coincidence of a violent campaign of IRA 'terrorism' outside the prison and the 'non-violent' campaign within. Although significantly different from contemporary forms of suicide terrorism, this case does combine, in a different way, a politics of self-sacrifice with a politics of violence towards others.

Chapter 5 examines the role of martyrdom in the campaign of Polish Solidarity, and in particular the martyrdom of Father Jerzy Popiełuszko, Solidarity's priest, at the hands of the Polish security service in 1984. The completely non-violent nature of this campaign provides an interesting contrast to the Northern Irish case, and raises a question about how Solidarity managed to remain non-violent, through successive stages of government brutality and suppression, culminating with the death of Popiełuszko. The chapter analyses the politics of talk, and how a history of more violent martyrdom in Poland was translated into a message of non-violence. In the context of martial-law Poland and the criminalization of Solidarity, Popiełuszko's 'Masses for the fatherland' played a significant role in keeping Solidarity alive, drawing on memories of past martyrs for the nation, and translating people's desires for vengeance into calm non-violence. His death, which was proclaimed a martyrdom worldwide, played a role in paving the way for Solidarity's reappearance as a political agent and its negotiations with the government. It was arguably an impetus for the 'velvet revolutions' that spread, a few years later, across central and eastern Europe as others began to 'act as if' they were free.

Chapter 6 explores the self-burning of Buddhist monks and nuns in Vietnam in the early 1960s and the imitation of this form of political self-sacrifice by Quaker and Catholic Americans, situating them against the backdrop of the fall of the regime of Ngo Dinh Diem in South Vietnam, as well as shifts in the United States' Vietnam policy. While self-burning has a long history of meaning within Mahāyāna Buddhism, it is far more problematic within a Christian framework. In addition to exploring a concept of 'imitation' in practice, this chapter examines the relationship between acts in the two contexts as a global conversation over the meaning of self-immolation as suicide or martyrdom.

Chapter 7 explores various forms of political self-sacrifice in the contemporary Middle East. The objective is to apply insights from the older cases to this context, which is still evolving, and to engage in some comparison across time and in relation to the various types of political self-sacrifice. The 1983 Shia suicide mission in Lebanon, which led to a withdrawal of American troops, was viewed as a success, and later became the inspiration for the suicide terrorism of militant Sunnis such as al-Qaida,[17] which was employed most dramatically on 9/11. The success of the earlier action is contrasted with the security dilemma that developed in the context of the War on Terror, and particularly in Israel/Palestine. The 'martyrdom' of Turkish humanitarian aid workers after Israeli soldiers boarded the *Mavi Marmara*, which was en route to Gaza in the summer of 2010,

---

[17] It was also the inspiration for the Tamil Tigers (Cronin 2003).

turned into a diplomatic crisis, revolving around questions of whether the aid workers were terrorists, on the one hand, or the Israeli acts were criminal, on the other. There is far less precedent within Islam for acts of self-burning, such as that of Mohammed Bouazizi in Tunisia, which triggered the protests that led to the resignation of President Ben Ali. The chapter investigates how Islamic conceptions of martyrdom were drawn on to give meaning to the three types of self-sacrifice, while examining the larger themes of the book.

Chapter 8 draws out the theoretical and empirical conclusions of the different studies while also raising questions about the relationship of the cases to more global processes of transformation and the importance of this subject matter for the study of international relations. This introduction has highlighted some of the theoretical, methodological and empirical issues raised by a concept of political self-sacrifice. The next chapter goes into much more depth regarding more ancient forms of sacrifice as a backdrop for distinguishing the characteristics of contemporary forms of political self-sacrifice.

# PART I

# The Framework

# 1 | *Political self-sacrifice*

Sacrifice is usually associated with pre-modern, tribal practices that are considered to be primitive and barbaric. The idea of humans or animals being killed in the context of a ritual ceremony is disturbing to modern sensibilities. The purpose of this chapter is to explore the relationship between contemporary self-sacrifice and these earlier practices. One clear difference is the adjective 'self', which suggests individual agency in bringing about an act of bodily destruction – a topic that is explored in more depth in Chapter 2. Here I argue that sacrifice and self-sacrifice are not the same but share a 'family resemblance'.[1] The contrast provides insight into the distinct character of the more recent expressions and their relationship to a larger context of inter-state relations. I examine four themes from the anthropological literature on sacrifice: substitution, ritual, the dialectical relationship between the criminal and the sacred, and the cyclical regeneration of life after death.

Sacrifice can be understood as what Wittgenstein (1958: paras. 19, 23, 241) refers to as a 'form of life', or a practice that is visible across cultures, albeit embedded in very different systems of meaning. Approaching the analysis in terms of a 'form of life' suggests a different approach to patterns from what has been typical in the social sciences more broadly or international relations in particular. While the introduction placed this study in a post-World-War-II context of emerging human rights law and the globalization of the media, the notion of a 'form of life' points to the continuation of more ancient practices in contemporary forms. As Derek Hughes (2007: 9) notes:

---

[1] Regarding family resemblances, Wittgenstein (1958: para. 66) states that 'we see a complicated network of similarities overlapping and criss-crossing: sometimes overall similarities, sometimes similarities of detail... I can think of no better expression to characterize these similarities than "family resemblances"; for the various resemblances between members of a family: build, features, colour of eyes, gait, temperament, etc., etc. overlap and criss-cross in the same way...'

Ever since Frazer's Golden Bough and the work of Freud, we have been fascinated with seeing ineradicable survival of primitive patterns in our own culture. Burkert gives new life to a question that is powerfully present from Greek times onwards: that of the relationship between man (*sic*) the sacrificer and man the hunter.

Human sacrifice has reflected the concerns of particular eras, including changing views of the significance of the body, individual rights, the social or sacred value of the individual and the relation between home and foreign cultures.

A 'form of life' cannot be operationalized, given that differences are of as much interest as the identification of 'family resemblances' across cultures. Sacrifice is not a label for a singular observable phenomenon but is embedded in culturally and historically specific systems of meaning. According to Diego Gambetta (2006b: 270), suicide missions, which include the human bomb and other forms of self-immolation, represent a 'family of actions' that grows out of the 'belief that [self-sacrifice] will best further the interests or the cause they care about and identify with'. Here lies the conceptual confusion. Suicide is the act of an isolated individual, who in 90 per cent of the cases has psychological problems (Gambetta 2006b: 269), which contrasts with the agents of suicide missions, who, it has been shown, generally do not. In this respect, the actions of the latter belong to a different category that focuses on the interests of the group. A notion of sacrifice points to a subject or community that is the beneficiary of the act. Gambetta, and others in the volume (Gambetta 2006a), refer to self-sacrifice but do not adequately problematize the difference between suicide and sacrifice. Although this book shares a focus on a 'family of actions', I highlight a concept of political self-sacrifice as the point of departure for exploring the dynamics of contestation surrounding the deaths as suicide or martyrdom.

If self-sacrifice fits more comfortably with a notion of group interest, then the spectrum of actions belonging to this 'family' is marked less by self-inflicted violence than by self-sacrifice on behalf of a cause. Indeed, as suggested in the introduction, the early Christian martyrs did not inflict violence on themselves or others and were viewed by the Romans as no less irrational or suicidal than contemporary suicide bombers. Sacrifice has taken many different forms across human history and cultures. I now explore four characteristics of a concept of self-sacrifice in relation to themes from the anthropological literature on sacrifice. This more established literature from another discipline provides a framework for analysing the distinct qualities of political self-sacrifice and its significance for contemporary international relations. I approach the analysis as an anthropologist seeking understanding in the Wittgensteinian sense of the term, who sets out to uncover the practical understanding of the ritual acts and discourses that are being performed in order to 'restore their meaning, to grasp their logic' (Bourdieu 1990: 18).

## Substitution

A sacrificial lamb is someone or something that is put forward to the authorities with the understanding that it will be removed or destroyed, usually in order to prevent someone or something else from being removed or destroyed (Procter 1995: 1247). In his classic study of human evil, René Girard (2008 [1972]) argues that substitution is the core of sacrifice – that is, fury felt towards one party is redirected towards a surrogate victim or scapegoat, who was chosen only because of his or her vulnerability and dispensability and because he or she is close at hand. The sacrificial object is thus an innocent who pays the debt for a guilty party, as society attempts to defeat the violence that would otherwise be vented on its own members, whom it seeks to protect.[2] The vitality of substitution as an institution rests on its ability to conceal the displacement upon which the rite is based. It nonetheless must not lose sight entirely of the original object or cease to be aware of the act of transference from the object to the surrogate victim, as this awareness is necessary for the substitution to take place.

Girard argues that modern societies have replaced this mechanism for dealing with vengeance with criminal systems, in which institutionalized vengeance prevents further violence. He warns, however, that the elimination and demystification of vengeance may lead to increasing and unlimited violence. War crimes tribunals and the International Criminal Court are in part a response to the emergence of genocide, which is an intentional act that, in the spirit of Girard's concept of sacrifice, presents not an individual victim but a social

---

[2] Girard's view of the sacrificial ritual as the controlled displacement of chaotic and aggressive impulses is also a theme of Walter Burkert (1996).

group for sacrifice, a social victim that is understood by the perpetrator to be expendable and whose elimination is said to purify the community. The foremost example, the Holocaust, arose not in a tribal society but a modern European state.[3] Genocide, or unlimited violence against a people as vengeance for a perceived injustice (in this case Germany's defeat and humiliation in World War I[4]), was facilitated by mass industrialization and modern technology.

While there is a family resemblance between pre-modern notions of substitution and Hitler's sacrifice of European Jews, substitution is in many respects diametrically opposed to the contemporary forms of political self-sacrifice explored here. Contemporary examples, whether in the form of self-burning by Buddhist monks and American Quakers during the Vietnam War, the hunger strikes of IRA prisoners in the Maze Prison in Northern Ireland, the martyrdom of Polish Solidarity's priest, Jerzy Popiełuszko, or the phenomenon of the human bomb, do not, in several respects, fit with Girard's depiction of sacrifice. First, in each case, the person or persons who were sacrificed identified with a community, and their acts of sacrifice were on behalf of that community. In this respect, the sacrificed was more an agent than a marginalized scapegoat. Having said this, each of the cases emerges from the experience of marginalization or the scapegoating of one *community* vis-à-vis another, due to foreign occupation or interference, although the application of these labels was also often a subject of contestation. Thus, it is less that a community chose an expendable scapegoat for the sake of substantiating and legitimating the powers that be (Bloch and Parry 1982); rather, members of subordinated and marginalized communities sacrificed themselves on behalf of justice for these communities. Even though the selection of human bombs in the Middle East, for instance, is based on an institutionalized policy of recruitment, the recruits are by no means scapegoats but, instead, are viewed as heroic members of the community.

Second, in the contemporary examples the existence of a legal system does not necessarily ameliorate further conflict or satisfy the

---

[3] Hughes (2007: 240) argues that the Holocaust became synonymous with sacrifice, although the metaphor is derived less from the its original sacrificial sense – that is, the burning of the single lamb in the temple – and more from the mass destruction implied in journalistic descriptions of categories in which 'holocaust' became synonymous with 'inferno'.

[4] See, for instance, Fierke (2004).

need for vengeance, as in Girard's argument. Indeed, criminal systems may facilitate definitions and distinctions, for example of ethnic minorities or occupied territory, that codify and reinforce a separate and, in practice, subordinate status. Interpretations of law may become bound up in political contestation (see Burgis 2008, 2009); for instance, authorities may accuse 'terrorists' of crimes against the sovereign state, while the agents of sacrifice, as 'martyrs', may seek to witness to human rights violations by the government. The act of self-sacrifice takes place within a context of ongoing conflict and resistance. Although these conflicts may be fuelled by a desire for vengeance that has not been satisfied by official structures, the relationship between political self-sacrifice and vengeance is paradoxical insofar as the self is the object of harm rather than the Other, who is said to be the source of injustice.[5] This suggests a transference, as in Girard's argument, but in a distinct configuration of relationships, which is examined in Chapter 3.

I argue that self-sacrifice, rather than being a substitution, is an 'act of speech' in which the suffering body communicates the injustice experienced by a community to a larger audience. In the theory of speech acts, saying something is doing something (Austin 1962). For instance, promises or threats are not mere words but acts with words, which are part of a conversation with others. The speech act is illocutionary, or an act *in* saying something, which has a certain *force* in the act of saying, given its dependence on social, historical and cultural convention (Austin 1962: 121). By contrast, the sacrifice of the material body is an act that communicates but without words. This represents an inversion of the speech act. In both formulations the act and the communication are inseparable, but the relationship is reversed. The main point is that the self-sacrifice communicates to an audience and produces consequential effects. The act is perlocutionary, in that it will often produce effects in the feelings, thoughts or actions of the audience. As John Austin (1962: 101) states, a perlocutionary act is viewed at the level of its consequences in persuading, convincing, enlightening, inspiring or otherwise getting someone to do something. A perlocutionary act can achieve these effects without words. For instance, intimidation can be achieved by waving a stick or pointing a gun, and hurling a tomato may communicate protest non-verbally.

---

[5] Suicide terrorism is distinct in that it targets both.

Self-sacrifice as an act of speech is bound up in more culturally specific systems of meaning that connect the act to a long history of sacrifice on behalf of the community, which is part of the emotional resonance. The self-sacrifice is not a purely individual act. It emerges from a social context of resistance, and, as discussed in Chapter 2, is not an expression of individual self-interest. The latter is nonsensical in relation to an act that may result in the self ceasing to exist. Sacrifice in a political context implies a community for which the sacrifice is made and an audience to which it speaks. The self-sacrifice, while leading to the injury or death of individuals, is about the restoration of the nation in circumstances in which sovereignty has been curtailed.

While Girard's argument rests on a distinction between pre-modern practices of sacrifice and their elimination in modernity, given the emergence of legal institutions to deal with vengeance, contemporary self-sacrifice is a political weapon that crosses the boundary between the two and, given the context, takes a different form. On the one hand, the frameworks for attributing meaning to the act are, in all the cases that are examined here, at least in part religious, but also refer to international laws relating to human rights. On the other hand, the use of self-sacrifice as a political weapon has been facilitated by the development of a global, and particularly a visual, media. Acts in this category take place in opposition to the practices of modern states, whether occupation, imperialism or repression – practices that have silenced the voice of particular communities along with culturally specific modes of expression.[6] In this respect, acts of political self-sacrifice are situated across three different ways of organizing life: the pre-modern religious; the rationalized modern state, which is part of the inter-national system; and the globalizing postmodern culture of the media. Against this background, political self-sacrifice may play a role in bringing alternative forms of community into being. The impact may also spread abroad through the rapid transmission of text or visual images and through subsequent practices of 'imitation'.

---

[6] One strand of literature argues that Islamic radicalism and terrorism, including suicide terrorism, are a response by traditional societies to modernity in a context of globalization (Friedman 2000; Kaplan 2000). The focus of this argument is less on globalization as a cause of suicide terrorism than on the globalized media as a facilitating condition for acts of political self-sacrifice. In this respect, the argument is more constitutive than causal.

We can see remnants of more traditional forms of sacrifice in contemporary expressions of political self-sacrifice, yet the latter take place in a much different context and can be distinguished from the former as well. Contemporary self-sacrifice is not for the purpose of giving a gift to the gods (Hughes 2007: 10), through the sacrifice of a scapegoat, but, rather, is about *communicating a political message*. The sacrifice does not authorize the powers that be but, instead, potentially delegitimizes dominant power structures in favour of alternative forms of community. In addition, sacrifice may be a *by-product* of contemporary criminal systems, which have located sovereign decision-making in the hands of some agents at the expense of others, rather than having been replaced by criminal systems, as argued by Girard. It is also an *expression* of the conflict between contemporary forms of international law, and sovereignty and human rights in particular. There are remnants of traditional sacrifice that are evident in the more contemporary manifestations, however. The first is the ritual nature of acts within this 'family'. The second is the tension between a criminal and a sacralizing act. The third related feature is the transformation of the profane into the sacred and the transfer of the divine qualities of the sacrificed victim to the marginalized community.

## Ritual action

The last section presented self-sacrifice as an act of speech that communicates a political message. Anthropologists, such as Stanley Tambiah (1990), have emphasized the social dimension of the speech act as part of a ritual mode of action, which means that the act has to conform to established social conventions and be subject to judgements of legitimacy. Ritual communicates and thereby indirectly affects social realities and perceptions of those realities. The notion of a language game relies on similar premises as the speech act – or act of speech, in this case – but further highlights the underlying social conventions and ritual aspects (see Wittgenstein 1958: paras. 23, 83).[7]

---

[7] There is a tension between the importance of social convention in the construction of ritual, on the one hand, and Austin's claim that perlocutionary acts, as distinct from illocutionary acts, are non-conventional, on the other hand. The performance of the self-sacrifice is bound up in ritual. Nevertheless, the *effect* that may be achieved, far from being conventional, is one of contestation,

While the speech act suggests a singular move, the game metaphor points to a larger rule-bound space within which a variety of moves are possible. In this respect, the act of speech is one move within a language game, which brings a conversation into being. As Bleiker (2000: 90) notes, *satyagraha*, which was the framework for Gandhi's understanding of self-sacrifice, had a profound psychological effect as 'a conversation with the consciousness of the opponent'.

Sacrifice is the most prominent of all Indo-European rituals. Bruce Lincoln (1986: 41) argues that sacrifice is a 'rich, complex, polyphonic act', open to a variety of interpretations by participants and analysts, whether indigenous or foreign. In the West, ritual tends to be viewed as a type of special activity linked to sacral tradition and organized religion, as distinct from daily routine action. From this perspective, ritual is an archaic practice that is at odds with modernity, having more to do with other times and places. Ritualization, as distinct from ritual, is the term often used to refer to studies focused on technologically advanced societies (Bell 2009a [1992]). Catherine Bell (2009b [1997]: 138–69) examines six categories of ritual-like activity, as understood more traditionally, and their relevance to contemporary practice. Ritual-like activities invoke more than one, but not necessarily all, of these features. They highlight the importance of the body and its movement in space and time, in an environment that shapes bodily responses but that is, at the same time, created and organized by the ways people move within it.

The first and most frequently cited characteristic of ritual is formality, although formality is not restricted to ritual per se. Generally, the more formal a series of movements or activities, the more ritualized they are likely to seem. 'Formality' refers to the use of limited and rigidly organized expressions or codes. Formalized activities can communicate complex socio-cultural meanings in an economical way, particularly messages relating to social classification, hierarchical relationships and the negotiation of identity and position within a social web. Erving Goffman (1967) analyses human

in which the audience is confronted with questions about the meaning of the act and its legitimacy, as well as the source of the death. The effect of convincing, persuading or inspiring will be a function of how this contestation is resolved. The ritual nature of the act may thus be more or less comprehensible to various audiences, depending on their cultural locations – that is, the closeness or distance of the encounter.

interchange in terms of ordered sequences of symbolic communication, which he refers to as 'interaction rituals' or 'ritual games', the significance of which becomes clearer in the next chapter. He argues that humans construct their identity, or 'face', as a type of sacred object that is constituted by the ritual of social exchange. The organization of social encounters into various formal acts and events trains people to be 'self-regulating participants', who live by a set of moral and social rules that define what it means to be human in a particular culture.

Gestures of greeting or parting, for instance, can be formal conventions that convey symbolic information. While rituals of this kind do not communicate factual information, they do communicate. Ritual can express the existence of a positive social relationship rather than, for instance, one that threatens aggression. The formalism of political self-sacrifice may relate to the constitution of patterned activity surrounding the death of the 'martyr', such as the creation of videotapes prior to a suicide mission or the institutionalized practices that surround the burial of martyrs.

A second aspect of ritual activity is its traditionalism, which involves the repetition of activities from an earlier period, the adaptation of action to a new setting or the creation of practices that evoke an identification with the past (Bell 2009b [1997]: 145). Rituals appeal to custom and the repetition of historical precedents.[8] All the cases explored here evoke a memory of past sacrifice on behalf of the nation. Polish Solidarity, for instance, developed a range of symbols, from stamps to postcards to statues, that displayed images of past martyrs and powerful cultural symbols, such as the Black Madonna. The symbols added to the emotional resonance of the suffering experienced by those who resisted the Polish regime.

A third aspect of ritual-like action is invariance, which is usually understood as a disciplined set of actions involving precise repetition and physical control. Although traditionalism harks back to the authority of the past, invariance evokes the timeless authority of the

---

[8] Court proceedings in the United Kingdom are often ritual-like, with the adoption of judicial regalia dating from the seventeenth century, in the requirement that judges and lawyers wear wigs, robs, buckled shoes, breeches, lace neck ruffs (the jobs) and a hood or cape (tippets). Likewise, the use of academic robes, which was once the everyday dress of scholars and clerics, fosters an ethos of the scholarly community as the custodians of timeless truths.

beliefs and practices of a group. Routinized actions that are concerned with precision and control fit this category.[9] Socialization transforms regulative rules, which define what is required or permitted, into something taken for granted. In the precise duplication of action, the individual and the contingent are subordinated to that which is understood to be enduring. Actions such as the salt march during Gandhi's 'Quit India' campaign involved a tremendous amount of discipline, both to maintain the formation of an army going into battle and to ensure that participants remained non-violent. Suicide missions also rely on institutionalized processes of grooming potential 'martyrs', which are an important part of their socialization.

Rule governance is a further element of ritual activity, which is most evident in contests that involve complex codes of orchestration with the aim of limiting the potential for violent chaos (Bell 2009b [1997]: 153), as is most evident in various forms of sport or war. Joyce Carol Oates once observed, in commenting on the boxing career of Mohammed Ali, 'Though highly ritualized, and as rigidly bound by rules, traditions, and taboos as any religious ceremony, [boxing] survives as the most primitive and terrifying of contests' (Oates 1992). The rules of war play a role in channelling, constraining, and simultaneously legitimating the violent interaction of opposed groups (Bell 2009b [1997]: 154). Interactions involving political self-sacrifice evoke rules relating to human rights rather than to war, or the cultural meaning of symbols, which channel emotions surrounding the sacrifice into the construction of the nation. The ancient Brehon Laws in Ireland, for instance, constituted one backdrop of rules by which the hunger strikes in Northern Ireland have been understood and given meaning.

A further example of ritual is the appeal to supernatural beings. For instance, the president of the United States, when taking the oath of office, places his left hand on the Bible and swears to uphold the duties and responsibility of the presidency. The act is derived from Christian ritual and represents the Christian values of American civic religion. Activities that generate and express the sacred significance of key symbols, such as the flag, or the repetition of the pledge of allegiance

---

[9] The emphasis in the educational process on, for example, disciplined routines for moulding and socializing individuals has been compared to ritual, quite distinct from the more explicit rituals, such as commencement, that are incorporated within the social world of the school (Bell 2009b [1997]: 152).

in US schools, are ritual-like. Even in the absence of a specific claim to religion, there is a sacred quality to acts of this kind, insofar as they are set apart as important and having extra meaning. Subsequently, they are able to evoke emotion-filled images and experiences that point to something beyond the self (Bell 2009b [1997]: 157). Most expressions of political self-sacrifice examined here rely on a larger system of cultural or religious meaning to attribute meaning to acts of 'martyrdom' as something beyond the self, which binds the martyr to a community, both earthly and divine.

Finally, ritual shares features with theatrical performance, in that there is a deliberate, self-conscious 'doing' of a highly symbolic act in public. Performances communicate on 'multiple sensory levels, usually involving highly visual imagery, dramatic sounds, and other forms of stimulation' (Bell (2009b [1997]: 160). The performance is powerful because the heightened experience of the audience goes beyond that of merely being told or shown something. The dynamics of framing the performance may invoke distinctions between the sacred and profane, the special and the routine, transcendent ideals and concrete realities, thereby communicating that what is being observed is different and significant, which has the effect of capturing attention. In this respect, performance is something other than routine reality. The globalizing media is an important contextual background for the spectacularization of acts of political self-sacrifice. Images of, for instance, the Buddhist monk who set himself on fire in 1963, in the context of the Vietnam War, have become iconic, as have images of suicide terrorists. The extraordinariness of the action disrupts routine reality, raising questions about what could be so important that an agent would sacrifice his or her life for it.

Bell (2009a [1992]: 67) emphasizes the primacy of ritual as a social act in which strategies are embedded in the doing of the act. In this respect, ritualization is a strategic way of acting in specific social situations. Ritualization invokes oppositions that, through a series of movements, gestures and sounds, are acted in space and time (140). In this respect, ritualization is a strategy for the construction of a certain type of power relationship (198). Building on Foucault (1979 [1975]), Bell argues that the analysis of power is, at one and same time, an analysis of resistance to power.[10] 'Ritual' is one of several words used

---

[10] See also Zevnik (2009).

by Foucault to refer to the formalized, routinized and often supervised practices that mould the body. The body is 'the place where the most minute and local social practices link up with the large scale organization of power' (Dreyfus and Rabinow 1983: 111). The body is a political field disciplined by power relations, which 'invest it, mark it, train it, torture it, force it to "carry out" tasks, to perform ceremonies, to emit signs' (Foucault 1979 [1975]: 28). His analysis of the body and the close workings of power demonstrate the strategies by which power relations constitute the social body.

The strategic role of sacrificial ritual invokes oppositions, and a transformation of the profane into the sacred. In this light, Bell (2009b [1997]: 116) argues that ritualization is the most effective form of action in two types of overlapping situations: when the 'relationships of power being negotiated are based on indirect rather than direct claims to power, and when the hegemonic order has to be rendered socially redemptive in order to be personally redemptive'. For example, she states 'ritualization is the way to construct power relations when the power is claimed to be from God, not from military might or economic superiority; it is also the way for people to experience a vision of community order that is personally empowering' (116). Sacrifice of the body, as explored in the cases here, fits, to different degrees, these criteria. The power of resistance does not appeal to military or economic power; it is, rather, about empowering individuals to 'act as if' they are free in the hope of restoring sovereign community.

The different elements of sacrificial ritualization are relevant for the examination of contemporary forms of political self-sacrifice. The latter are more or less formalized, involving interaction rituals that range from ceremonies surrounding death, such as the preparation of media tapes, to the embedding of reasons for sacrifice in religious ritual. Traditionalism is expressed in the frequent reference to past martyrs who have sacrificed themselves for the nation. Invariance takes the form of a discipline that socializes individuals into a set of practices, whether related to violent or non-violent forms of action, which facilitates a complex code of organization that is rule-guided. Many of these appeal to a supernatural or religious point of reference for the act. Finally, the spectacular form of the self-sacrifice before a globalizing media makes it akin to a theatrical performance, insofar as it is a deliberate and highly symbolic act in public.

## Criminals and martyrs

Girard highlights the dialectical relationship between the legitimacy and illegitimacy of the act of sacrifice, which is central to its power, while Bell refers to the centrality of invoking oppositions as a part of ritual activity. In a contestation between communities, this may find further expression in conflict between a practice accorded the highest form of honour, to those who practise it, and the highest form of impiety, to those who do not (Hughes 2007: 12). The dialectic at the heart of pre-modern forms of sacrifice was one of criminalization and sacralization. In their classic work on sacrifice, Henri Hubert and Marcel Mauss (1964 [1898]) argue that the dialectic expresses the tension between a victim who it is criminal to kill because he is sacred, but who becomes sacred only as a result of the killing. Sacrifice always implies consecration. In every sacrifice an object passes from the common into the religious domain; it is consecrated. In sacrifice, the consecration extends beyond the thing consecrated. The 'sacrifier' is the subject who benefits from the sacrifice or who undergoes its effects (Hubert and Mauss 1964 [1898]: 9–10). Sacrifice is defined as a religious act that, through the consecration of a victim, modifies the condition of the moral person who accomplishes it or that of objects with which it is concerned. The tension between criminality and sacralization remains evident in contemporary forms of political self-sacrifice, but in a somewhat different form. In each of the cases the sacrifice results in a consecration of the martyr, which then extends to the community as 'sacrifier'. The main difference between the criminal and the martyr hinges on the question of the source of the death – that is, whether the agent has been killed or has taken his or her own life (and perhaps the life of others), both of which acts are in conflict with modern or religious notions of the dignity and sanctity of human life. How this question is resolved – that is, whether or not the body is consecrated as sacred – is a matter of whether the audience 'writes' the death as a suicide or as martyrdom.

The case studies reveal that the specific categories of contestation vary from context to context and culture to culture. The community surrounding the agents of political self-sacrifice is more likely to politicize the act, by placing it within a conceptual framework of martyrdom, regardless of whether the form was violent or non-violent. The powers that be, by contrast, are more likely to depoliticize the act, through the use of the labels 'suicide', 'terrorism' or 'crime'. While both concepts – suicide and martyrdom – imply injury to the body and the strong possibility of death, suicide more directly suggests self-inflicted violence, whereas martyrdom is more often associated with harm inflicted upon the agent by others. The terms 'terrorism' and 'crime' imply that the agent has inflicted violence on others.

The attribution of meaning, as either criminal or sacred, is not a matter of applying a label to an objective phenomenon that exists independent of language; the language constitutes the meaning and identifies the source of the bodily destruction, whether from the agent or the state. In each of the cases, what begins as a question about the identity of the agent – that is, as a criminal or a political subject – is transformed as each context unfolds, into a question about the possible criminality of the state. For instance, during the hunger strikes in the Maze Prison in Northern Ireland, what began as a contest over the identity of the hunger strikers as criminals or prisoners of war evolved, as they began to die, into a contest over whether the hunger strikers were martyrs and the British prime minister, Thatcher, was a criminal. Political self-sacrifice may unsettle the power of dominant authority if it raises a question about the meaning of the act: whether the agent has committed suicide, and therefore is an isolated individual, who is outside the community, or is a martyr, who has sacrificed all on behalf of a community and social cause. The dialectical tension is the heart of the process. This does not represent a mere contest over two different labels; rather, each category – criminal or martyr – evokes a different world of action and attributes a different meaning to the injured or dying body. The injured or dying body 'speaks' to an audience, and various audiences respond as they enter into a conversation regarding the meaning of the act.

The attribution of meaning is not merely descriptive but, as Wittgenstein (1958) says, like making a move in a game that is underpinned by a set of rules. In articulating the identity of the agent, a further set of entailments, related to this identity, are brought into play. In the various cases explored here, the political self-sacrifice gave rise to a contestation over the meaning to be attached to the suffering body – that is, whether the agent was a criminal/terrorist or a martyr – regardless of whether the act involved violence or was non-violent. Each of the identities was attached to further entailments, as illustrated in Figure 1.1.

(a) The resistance

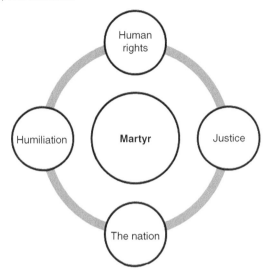

(b) The state

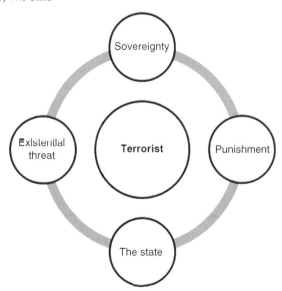

**Figure 1.1** The body of self-sacrifice: contesting games (a) The resistance
(b) The state

The first language game of martyrdom provides a structure of rules within which the resistance gives meanings to acts of political self-sacrifice. The martyr is a witness to injustice, which refers to the humiliation of a population vis-à-vis what is defined as an occupying power, as distinguished from the historical but oppressed community that the resistance seeks to restore. This draws on a larger international discourse of human rights, which prohibits humiliation and highlights the dignity of all people. The martyr sacrifices the self on behalf of a community, which politicizes the suffering or dead body and plays a role in regenerating the nation of resistance. The second language game expresses the meaning structure employed by state authorities, which depoliticizes, by identifying the actor as a criminal or terrorist,[11] whose death may be attributed to 'suicide'. The naming of the criminal or terrorist is part of a securitizing move that identifies an existential threat to the state, which links to a larger international discourse of sovereignty and justifies the punishment or elimination of this extremist element. Which set of rules one draws on to make sense of the act of self-sacrifice is largely a function of one's position in relation to the object of contestation. The naming in either case has resonance with particular audiences, both domestic and international.

## The construction of *communitas*

The dialectical tension between criminality and martyrdom, and the contestation surrounding it, relate to a further theme in the anthropological literature on sacrifice, which is the channelling of emotion to the end of strengthening social bonds. In ritual, norms and values become saturated with emotion (Turner 1967: 29). Ancient forms of sacrifice, though diverse, were situated within a religious framework and established a means of communication between the sacred and the profane, through the mediation of a victim, who during the course of the ceremony was destroyed (Hubert and Mauss 1964 [1898]: 97). The social function of the sacrifice, in the form of joint participation in acts of prayer, killing, butchering and eating, also served to bind the participants in a cohesive community (Lincoln 1986: 41). It is less a

---

[11] While the categories of 'criminal' and 'terrorist' are by no means the same, they do both refer to identities that are situated outside political subjectivity and community as abject Others.

question of the truth of the beliefs within this framework than an observation that these religious ideas were believed by populations. They existed as social facts, and the investment of persons or objects with a sacrificial meaning was a social and ritualized process. As Hubert and Mauss (1964 [1898]: 102) state, 'Sacrifice is a social function because sacrifice is concerned with social matters,' and can, among others, have the function of investing authority in society or re-establishing an equilibrium that has been upset. All forms of sacrifice contain an element of redemption (Hubert and Mauss 1964 [1898]: 99), or a restoration of that which has been lost. Lincoln (1986: 42) likewise argues that sacrifice in the Indo-European traditions was a performance that was believed to recreate the world.

According to Maurice Bloch and Jonathan Parry (1982: 5), sacrifice, and the death it produces, is part of the rebirth of community, which is given meaning through the rituals that surround it. Within these rituals, the deceased was not only a biological individual but a 'social being grafted upon the physical individual', whose destruction was tantamount to a sacrilege against the social order (Hertz 1960 [1907]: 77). Funerary rites had the function of disaggregating the individual from the collective and re-establishing society, which required a reallocation of the roles that the deceased once occupied (Bloch and Parry 1982: 2). In this respect, every life cycle ritual includes a death and a rebirth (Hertz 1960 [1907]: 81). As Bloch and Parry (1982: 5) state, 'The rebirth which occurs at death is not only a denial of individual extinction but also a reassertion of society and a renewal of life and its creative power.' The reassertion of social order is thus a *product* of ritual rather than its cause, as the death becomes an occasion for creating 'society' as an external force.

The dialectical tension between killing or suicide and sacrifice revolves around a distinction between the 'good' and the 'bad' death. Suicide is often viewed as the supreme example of a bad death because it represents surrender to the disappointments of life. The agent of suicide acts for him- or herself alone and thus lacks the restorative power for others. The 'good' death, by contrast, involves a transfer of the vitality of life through its recycling and thereby evokes the 'supreme altruistic gift of the martyr by whose death life is renewed' (Bloch and Parry 1982: 16–17). Despite this clear distinction, the categorization is not unambiguous; the authorities may criminalize an act that is viewed by the agents as sacred. Nonetheless, this tension is an important element of the dialectic in which, given a similarity between the good death and bad death, the one becomes a parody of the other. In this respect the 'good' regenerative death is constructed as the antithesis of the image of 'bad' death, which it implies (Bloch and Parry 1982: 18).[12] The 'good' death has restorative power though its legitimation of a social order and its authority structures. The social group thereby becomes anchored, not only by political power but by some of the deepest emotions, beliefs and fears shared by a people.

While the authority of a community is reclaimed through the 'good' death, it is not, in the contemporary cases, the authority of the powers that be that is reaffirmed but, potentially, that of the subordinate and marginalized community. In this respect, the dialectical tension between criminality and the sacred is expressed in a confrontation between structure and anti-structure, which produces, in the confrontation, a liminality that is productive of alternative forms of community, or what Turner (2008 [1969]) refers to as *communitas*.[13] The liminal transition is marked by three phases: separation, margin (or limen) and regeneration or reincorporation as the passage is consummated. The symbolic behaviour of separation detaches an individual or group from an earlier and more fixed relationship to a social structure, whether this is a set of cultural conditions, the political 'state' or both. In the liminal period the identity of the ritual subject is ambiguous, as he or she passes through a cultural realm that shares little with either the past state or the coming state. During reaggregation the individual or corporate subject returns to a relatively stable state once again.

Liminality is an ambiguous state in which the network of classifications that normally locate status and positions in cultural space no longer function. Liminal entities are neither here nor there but 'betwixt and between' the positions defined by law, custom, convention and ceremony. A rich variety of symbols express the indeterminacy and ambiguity as the social and cultural transition is ritualized.

---

[12] Andrew Louth (1997), who focuses on the body in Catholicism, and Paul Williams (1997), who looks at Mahāyāna Buddhism, highlight the tension between the bad body (related, for instance, to decay, pleasure, the ego) and the good body (related to asceticism, transcendence, benefit to others), which would seem to link to these conceptions of the bad death and the good death.

[13] The idea of a 'liminal' phase of a rite of passage was framed by Arnold van Gennep (1909), which, he argues, accompanies every change of place, state or social position.

Liminality is frequently likened to death, to being in a womb, to invisibility and to darkness, representing a 'moment in and out of time' and in and out of secular social structure (Turner 2008 [1969]: 95), which reveals some recognition, if primarily symbolic, of a generalized social bond that has ceased to exist.

In the liminal phase two 'models' for human interrelatedness are juxtaposed and alternate. The first is that of the dominant structure of a society that is a differentiated and often hierarchical system of politico-legal positions, which distinguish people in terms of 'more' or 'less'. The second, which emerges during the liminal period, is that of society as a rudimentary structure and relatively undifferentiated *communitas*, community and even communion of individuals. Many of the binary oppositions that characterize the tension between a status system and liminality have been institutionalized in modern religions, of which the most relevant to the analyses that follow are the avoidance of pain and suffering, in relation to the former, and the acceptance of pain and suffering – that is, martyrdom – in the latter (Turner 2008 [1969]: 106–7). For those involved in the maintenance of 'structure', any manifestation of *communitas* will appear to be dangerous or anarchical, which is evident from the response of the authorities.

Interaction usually presupposes the existence of two discrete identities. This raises a question about the nature of interaction in a situation such as political self-sacrifice, in which the identities of those involved – that is, individual agents and the audience that is affected or influenced by the act – are not static. I argue that the interaction occurs first and foremost between structure and anti-structure – that is, between the dominant structure of authority in each context, and the rudimentary anti-structure of those who resist. Given the relative formlessness of the latter, the visual performance, as well as the language surrounding the sacrifice, becomes key to the constitutive power of *communitas*. The transformative power of the political self-sacrifice lies precisely in the reconstitution of the boundaries surrounding the individual body that is sacrificed and a larger 'body politic'. Thus, what can be said to begin at the level of the individual – although one that is in all the cases linked to social and institutional structures – expands into an interaction between identities that, to use Anderson's (1983) language, are 'imagined' or constituted in language, thereby making possible a common identity between people who may never meet. The methodological problem, explored in Chapter 3, is how this works.

The purpose of the case studies is to describe this process 'thickly' – to the extent possible, given space limitations – in several contexts. This can be understood as providing an explanation of how the constitution of a community of resistance was facilitated or made possible by an act or acts of self-sacrifice, though this is not an explanation in the way that this term is usually understood within the social sciences. Explanation usually rests on a covering law derived from repeated correlations that establish a basis for stipulating causality. In this case, the pattern, a 'form of life' involving self-sacrifice, is played out in a number of culturally and historically specific locations, which share a family resemblance yet are distinct. What these distinct cases reveal is something universal about the power of self-sacrifice, while acknowledging the specific dynamics that accompany various violent and non-violent forms. The 'generalization', which places the study more firmly in the category of international relations – rather than comparative politics – is the focus on a category of self-sacrifice that expresses resistance to some form of occupying or imperial presence.

The other generalization relates to the emotional structure of these contexts, which grows out of an ongoing experience of humiliation by a population at the hands of an outside power and a desire to restore dignity. The external power places constraints on the sovereignty of a community, which represents a lowering of their status, and thus a humiliation, insofar as they are unable to engage in defining the rules by which they live. This involves a lack of recognition as political subjects, which is often accompanied by an attempt to criminalize and depoliticize acts of resistance. In this respect, the humiliation is not just a physical experience, although interrogation, bodily searches, harassment or violence may be the daily experience of a subordinated population. The humiliation, the status lowering and the lack of recognition represent a form of silencing. One set of memories, practices, beliefs and a way of being are either subordinated or 'written over', and replaced by other structures of meaning. This was perhaps most dramatic in countries where the communist experiment was imposed, where populations were displaced or reorganized, often resulting in the appropriation of private property. As Adam Michnik (1981: 70–1) states, after World War II 'a language was imposed' in Poland. This language blocked out and reorganized the daily habits of

entire populations for the sake of a utopian ideal. The failed communist experiment is perhaps the most recent example, and the one most
likely to bring a nod that acknowledges the problem, but the practice
is evident to different degrees in other sites of repression, occupation
or past imperialism. An act of political self-sacrifice speaks without
words, yet is louder than words, against a background in which silence
has been imposed on a population.

If the common problem is one of humiliation, the common goal is a
restoration of dignity. The restoration of dignity goes hand in hand with
the reconstitution of the community. The agent of political self-sacrifice,
often referred to as a martyr, becomes the embodiment of the suffering
nation. If Hobbes' *Leviathan* (1968 [1651]) is the symbol of the authoritarian sovereign, who embodies the people, the martyr is the embodiment of the nation, which seeks to transcend its humiliation through
a restoration of dignity and sovereignty. The two images, Leviathan
and the martyr, are not mutually exclusive in a situation of this kind
but are, rather, the site of contestation and a struggle for recognition.[14]
Sovereignty is not a static phenomenon but has to be reproduced continuously. The same basic principle holds true in the cases examined
here. The sovereignty of a people is constrained and becomes a site of
political contestation. The subordinate population seeks to reconstruct
the nation, which involves taking back its memory, its identity and its
practices. What distinguishes the various cases is the role of violence or
non-violence in the political self-sacrifice, as well as the culturally
specific memories, religious traditions and beliefs by which the act is
saturated with meaning and emotion.

## Conclusion

This chapter has drawn on several themes from the anthropological
literature on sacrifice to identify the distinct nature of more contemporary forms of political self sacrifice, as well as the 'family resemblances'
that link contemporary expressions to earlier practices. Political

---

[14] It was Georg Hegel who originally articulated the notion of a struggle for
recognition. Axel Honneth (1995: xv) has elaborated on the idea, referring to
the violence experienced by individuals or collectives resulting from the moral
injustice of an absence of respect that becomes a source of social conflict. By
their very nature, subjects 'struggle for the mutual recognition of the self-
understandings [that they] bring with themselves into every interaction'
(Honneth 1995: 165).

self-sacrifice was located at the intersection of pre-modern practices of sacrifice, a context defined by resistance to the modern state, and spectacularization via a globalizing media. In examining a notion of substitution, I argued that Girard's claim that the modern legal system has replaced the need for sacrifice as a way of dealing with vengeance does not adequately explain more contemporary forms of political self-sacrifice. Political self-sacrifice does not involve the substitution of a marginalized victim, as part of reinforcing existing power structures; rather, it communicates a political message on behalf of a marginalized community, which potentially contributes to its regeneration. The identification of the martyr with a larger social world reinforces the ritual elements of the sacrifice, highlighting its formality, its traditionalism, its invariance, its rule governance, its appeals to the supernatural and its spectacularization as a theatrical performance, all of which are mobilized in resistance to established claims to power. The political contestation evokes the dialectical tension between the 'bad' and the 'good' death. The audience decides whether death has been inflicted on a martyr or arises from the suicide of the isolated individual. Individuals are invested with sacrificial meaning, within a social and ritualized process. The ritual is located within a conflict between dominant structures of power and the anti-structure of a rudimentary *communitas*, which is part of a liminal transition that carries the potential for separation from old structures of community and the creation of new forms of governance.

In the next chapter I examine the dynamics of a conflict between a dominant structure of power and a rudimentary anti-structure in a context defined by an asymmetrical relationship between a repressive regime and agents of resistance. In the liminal state, the agents 'act as if' they are political subjects rather than criminals. A further objective is to conceptualize *self*-sacrifice in a modern context in which survival is understood to be the ultimate rational end.

# 2 | *Agency*

The last chapter explored a concept of self-sacrifice through the lens of the anthropological literature on sacrifice. I argued that elements of this pre-modern practice are evident in more contemporary forms. This chapter shifts attention to a more modern preoccupation with self, rationality and agency. From this perspective, the central question is how an act that is likely to lead to suffering or even a loss of life can be considered rational. A concept of *self*-sacrifice suggests, on some level, an individual who exercises agency in bringing about his or her own destruction. While the rational choice literature has been able to account for acts of altruism that take others into account, it is unable to deal with the ultimate loss of value – that is, of the self.

Rationality does have a role in decisions involving self-sacrifice, although of a different kind from in the rational choice literature. Making sense of political self-sacrifice requires a rethinking of the self and agency, shifting away from the individual ontology that underpins the rational choice literature towards a social ontology. A social ontology highlights how the social rules underlying the game constitute the materiality of objects and bodies. The central objective is to conceptualize agency in a situation in which sovereignty is lacking. The language of games is not meant to trivialize but provides a useful metaphor for thinking about the embeddedness of individuals and their actions in a social space. What follows deepens the notion of a game, shifting from a focus on the abstract interaction of disembodied rational actors towards the embodied agent who inhabits a world of contestation, interconnectedness and multiple frameworks of possible action. The last chapter developed the idea that contemporary self-sacrifice is an 'act of speech' in that the injured or dying body 'speaks' to a variety of audiences. An anthropological literature was the point of departure for examining a 'family resemblance' – yet clear difference – between pre-modern practices of sacrifice and contemporary forms of self-sacrifice. This chapter builds on the tradition within international relations of using a language of games to approach the strategic dynamics of interaction. Whereas game theory examines the strategic interaction between discrete actors, I examine the interaction between structure and anti-structure, and how this relates to agency.

The first section explores the limits of the rational choice model for understanding an act of political self-sacrifice. I argue that an analysis of rationality has to begin with the system of meaning within which an act has 'sense'. The second section moves to the question of agency and structure. If the dynamic of political self-sacrifice is defined by a relationship between structure and anti-structure, as discussed in the last chapter, agency must be situated within the latter, as it involves action in opposition to a dominant structure that demands conformity. Agency may thus result in a loss of life rather than survival. The loss of life has sense in a context in which sovereignty, and thus one's choices, are severely constrained. It has strategic sense in the context of a *communitas* that will potentially flourish as a result. The agency of anti-structure represents 'acting as if' a new game is in place. In this new game, the agent is constituted as a political subject rather than a criminal. In the third section I examine the warden's dilemma, which potentially arises from the prisoner's refusal to conform to the dominant rules – a confrontation that brings a liminal phase into being. Two distinct games are juxtaposed as conformity with the rules of existing structures of authority is withdrawn.

## Self-interest and self-sacrifice

The idea that every agent is motivated by self-interest has been a mainstay not only of economics but of political science and international relations as well. Scholars have become increasingly sceptical, however, that self-interest can account for the numerous forms of action that do not appear to be purely selfish (see Mansbridge 1990). One of the earliest critiques of this kind came from Amartya Sen, who in his famous essay 'Rational fools', first published in 1977 (see Sen 1990 [1977]), identifies problems that arise from a conception of humans as self-seeking egoists. In this conception a person's interests are defined such that that he or she can be seen to be furthering his or her own interest in every act of choice, regardless of what he or she does. If you have chosen X, then you have revealed a preference for X over Y. Your personal utility thus assigns a higher utility to this 'preference' than to an alternative. Within this framework, it is difficult to avoid maximizing one's own utility except through inconsistency. As Sen (1990 [1977]: 29) states:

[I]f you are consistent, then no matter whether you are a single-minded egoist or a raving altruist or a class-conscious militant, you will appear to be maximizing your own utility in this enchanted world of definitions... The rationale of this approach seems to be based on the idea that the only way of understanding a person's real preference is to examine his actual choices, and there is no choice independent way of understanding someone's attitude towards alternatives.

Economists and others have subsequently raised questions about the falsifiability of this type of claim, but falsifiability is not Sen's central concern. He instead focuses on the purely individual nature of the choice given that the individual's 'consumption bundle' is the only one over which he or she has direct control in his or her acts of choice. A departure from the self-seeking individual requires consideration of two concepts: first, sympathy, whereby concern for others directly affects your own welfare; and, second, commitment, whereby the experience of another does not make you feel personally worse off but you think it is wrong and are ready to do something to stop it. Sympathy relates to an 'externality', such as feeling sympathy for someone else (e.g. someone who is being tortured), which is ruled out by many rational choice models. Commitment does involve a choice, which may be counter to your first preference, such as acting on behalf of someone or something else (e.g. who is being tortured). This requires abandoning the assumption that a choice must be better than (or at least as good as) the alternatives for the person who chooses it (Sen 1990 [1977]: 33). Commitment is closely associated with morals. While much traditional rational choice theory identifies personal choice and personal welfare as synonymous, commitment drives a wedge between them. As Sen states, the purely economic man comes close to being a social moron, a 'rational fool', with one all-purpose preference ordering (37).

Although a notion of commitment points in the direction of self-sacrifice, Sen does not venture down this path. He presents a concept of meta-ranking, in which personal interests, personal welfare and moral concerns may form a complex structure of decision-making. He does not, however, explain how the balance between the three could or would shift so far towards the more social concerns that the individual, far from being better off, would knowingly make a choice that could lead to a loss of life. While altruism involves acting for the benefit of others, potentially to the disadvantage of the self, disadvantage is qualitatively different from the total loss of self.[1] Mark Carl Overvold (1980: 105) examines the rational choice literature in relation to the specific problem of self-sacrifice. He argues that the identification of an agent's self-interest, individual utility or personal welfare with what the agent most wants to do, all things considered, makes it possible to include more altruistic desires as a form of self-interest.

If altruistic behaviour is considered to be a form of self-interest, however, then it is impossible for an action to satisfy Overvold's first two criteria for self-sacrifice simultaneously (the loss is anticipated and voluntary) as well as the third (another choice would be more in one's self-interest) (Overvold 1980: 109–15). In all cases in which the agent has a realistic assessment of his or her alternatives, the act he or she actually chooses to perform will be the same as the act that he or she most wants to perform, and thus cannot be contrary to his or her self-interest. Overvold argues, by contrast, that if anything deserves to be called self-sacrifice, it would be those cases in which the agent knows full well what he or she is giving up, but still chooses to perform the act (116). From this it follows that, if self-interest is identified with what the agent most wants to do, it becomes logically impossible for there ever to be a genuine case of self-sacrifice. We therefore have to abandon the concept. This move ignores the fact, however, that self-sacrifice, or a willingness to sacrifice one's own welfare for the sake of others, is often what is considered most admirable and praiseworthy in moral life. Overvold does, in a footnote, state that the third criterion, of voluntarily passing up a more self-interested alternative, in order to perform an act in the knowledge that it will bring great personal loss, can be explained by a desire for the welfare of others and to see justice done. As he points out, 'desires' of

---

[1] Durkheim uses a concept of 'altruistic suicide', which has been adopted in discussing suicide missions. This concept grows out of a distinction between people who kill themselves for individual reasons and those who do so because of a higher value that transcends them (see Biggs 2006b and Gambetta 2006b). As suggested in Chapter 1, a category of suicide that consists of sacrifice for a greater cause contains a conceptual confusion.

this kind don't figure in the determination of an agent's self-interest, and, in their absence, it is entirely possible that he or she would have made another choice. In knowingly and voluntarily passing up his or her interest, the agent performs an act of self-sacrifice.

Sen and Overvold both move the rational choice literature towards a view of humans as social and moral. Sen raises the question of why one would sacrifice one's own happiness for that of another; he does not, however, pose the question in terms of actual loss of life. He presents a more suitable framework that goes beyond the rationalist emphasis on consequences, act evaluation and individual interest. He emphasizes the importance of exercising 'reason' as distinct from self-interest, of examining actions on the basis of commitment and of considering the value of rules. In place of the traditional dichotomy between egoism and universalized moral systems (such as utilitarianism), Sen (1990 [1977]: 43) argues that there are other groups, such as class and community, that provide the focus of many actions involving commitment. Self-sacrifice arises from an entirely different grounding of the self, in a social world of others in which welfare of the self cannot be separated from that of the community as a whole – a point of departure that is much more comprehensible within a religious framework. The literature on suicide terrorism raises a question about the rational interest of individuals, which is not irrelevant, given the potential cost to individual bodies. This question rests on an individual ontology, however, that separates individual rationality from social and moral structures of meaning that may embed the individual in a larger community, either earthly or divine.

There are several layers of rules that constitute a context of self-sacrifice.[2] The first is the structure of rules by which the self is constituted as meaningful. The notion of individuals as self-seeking egoists is a modern construct that is in conflict with most religious constructs of the self. The sacrificial choice has a much different meaning within a religious or cultural framework in which the loss of self in sacrifice may be articulated as the highest form of good. The major religious traditions emphasize the value of giving up one's self

---

[2] The distinction between constitutive and regulative rules and the extent to which they can be separated have given rise to an important debate in constructivist international relations (see, for instance, Kratochwil 1991; Onuf 1994; Fierke 2009a). The idea that rules are contested has been a feature of the literature on norms, and particularly the work of Antje Wiener (2008).

for others or God. This universal is less the universalism of utilitarianism than a universalism defined by socially situated actors who draw on different religious traditions to justify and provide a reason for action of one kind or another. Each of the case studies begins with an analysis of the embedded self of sacrifice as it relates to a religious or cultural tradition.

The second set of rules regards the meaning of the selfless act, including its relation to moral questions of right and wrong. Social scientists have tended to focus on the intention of the agent and whether an act was rational, which presents a problem of getting 'inside the head' of individuals (Hollis and Smith 1990; Adler 1997). Wittgenstein (1958: para. 337), by contrast, argues that intentions relate to customs and institutions, which shifts the focus away from what is going on inside any one individual's mind to questions of social meaning.[3] Here it is worth returning to the dialectical tension surrounding the act of self-sacrifice, and its meaning as a suicide or martyrdom. Key to this dialectic is the tension between suicide as a selfish act as opposed to martyrdom as selfless. Suicide has an individual ontology, while martyrdom embeds agency in a social ontology of community.

The third level of rules points more to the relationship between structure and anti-structure. Structure refers to the dominant rules of the game, which subordinates are expected to follow. Anti-structure takes the rudimentary form of agents 'acting as if' a different game is in place. In the contest between the two, self-sacrifice is, first and foremost, a by-product of refusing to conform to the dominant rules. A thicker notion of a game, and of multiple games, makes it possible to understand how two distinct social and political structures of meaning interact to produce a logic, with regulative as well as constitutive dimensions.

## Moves in a game

A game is a useful metaphor for thinking about the dependence of individual rationality, agency and choice on a structure of interconnected social rules. From this perspective, the question of why individuals

---

[3] For instance, he states (para. 337): '[A]n intention is embedded in its situation, in human customs and institutions. If the technique of the game of chess did not exist, I could not intend to play a game of chess. In so far as I do intend the construction of a sentence in advance, that is made possible by the fact that I can speak the language in question.'

choose to engage in acts of political self-sacrifice needs to be reframed in socio-political terms. Why have practices of voluntary suffering and death become so widespread in particular historical and political contexts? Emphasis on the latter suggests that the crucial insights are to be found not in the individual mind but within a social world in which a form of agency has meaning. To use game-like terms, the problem is less one of why the chess player decides to move the knight rather than the castle but of looking at how the movements of the knight make sense and have meaning only within a structure of rules belonging to chess.

There is a need in this case to create some distance from the idea that rationality is a property of individuals per se and, instead, to make the rules of the game the prior and necessary condition for understanding the rationality of acts. An individual makes a decision to play a particular game, but the rationality or 'sense' of any move is ultimately dependent on and constrained by the moves available to someone who is playing, for instance, chess. Chess players in Moscow and New York, would, if faced with the same strategic configuration in a game of chess, face the same possible choices, although, insofar as this is part of an evolving process, the outcome would not necessarily be the same. We may ask a question about the individual's intention in making a particular choice, but understanding the range of available strategic choices – that is, the social foundations of any decision, or the rationality of a move – is more a function of the rules of the game, or one's position within it, rather than individual interpretation per se. In this respect, the rules are prior to any one actor. In playing checkers, we may move within a very similar context as chess, namely a board divided into squares, but the pieces of wood have a different identity and move in different ways, guided by distinct rules of what constitutes good play or cheating. To move a checker in the way one moves a knight in chess would constitute cheating. Insofar as many games, from Diplomacy to Monopoly, abstract from the dynamics of real-life contexts, a thicker analysis might explore the social, historical or cultural dimensions of these structuring rules.[4]

It is not just the rationality of moves but also the materiality of objects that has meaning within a context of rules. I may have a

---

[4] For instance, Diplomacy takes place in the context of pre-World-War-I Europe, and its moves abstract from and simulate the balance-of-power logic that structured interstate communication at the time – a logic that is quite different from that of the balance of power during the Cold War.

number of wooden objects with which I play a game. The wood is the raw material, but the material object becomes a checker or a knight only by virtue of its constitution as one or the other in checkers or chess, respectively. How one moves and the rationality of doing so is thus fundamentally dependent on some mastery of the rules of either game. An audience that observes is also dependent on knowledge of the rules for understanding what it is observing. Each game could begin with the same material objects but interaction within the game is a function of the meaning attached to these objects. In this sense, while the flesh-and-blood body is the raw material of political self-sacrifice, the actions of the body, and the meaning attached to it, will be contextually specific.

Goffman (1961a) argues that human encounters are everywhere but the challenge is to understand how they work. Like any other element of social life, an encounter exhibits sanctioned orderliness arising from obligations and expectations. Actors define a situation, and this shapes its structure (Goffman 1961a: 19). Games place a 'frame' around a set of events and interactions, determining the type of 'sense' to be accorded to everything within the frame (20). This definition establishes rules that are less about the materiality of the situation than 'how one goes on'. As he states (19–20):

Whether checkers are played with bottle tops on a piece of squared lino-leum, with gold figurines on inlaid marble...the pairs of players can start with the 'same' positions, employ the same sequences of strategic moves and countermoves, and generate the same contour of excitement.

For the duration of the game, participants ignore any elements that are defined outside the rules of relevance, such as the monetary value of the objects or the aesthetics of the board. The rules of play constitute what can and what cannot be done. For instance, the rules of irrelevance in the traditional game of Diplomacy, or the neo-realist conception of IR as a game of billiards, block out anything other than state action, from terrorism to non-state action to culture (Waltz 1979), and highlight the actions of states in a condition of anarchy.

The character of an encounter is based in part on rules regarding the properties of the situation that should be considered outside the frame and therefore irrelevant. To adhere to these rules is to play fair (Goffman 1961a: 25). Therefore, for example, it is only in baseball that the event 'grounding out to third' can occur or that we find the position of third baseman. A matrix of possible events and the rules through which events are enacted together constitute a field of action, 'an engine of meaning, a world in itself, different from all other worlds except the ones generated when the same game is played at other times' (27).

Many practices of everyday life can also be understood to be game-like, in that they make sense only when embedded in a context of meaning that frames the activity, and define the rules of irrelevance. For instance, when we step into a Christian church to observe a marriage, a whole set of shared understandings are already in place. These shared understandings underpin the actions of the main participants and make it possible for observers to grasp what is happening, to understand themselves as participants in a wedding rather than, for instance, a baseball game. According to these rules, the main subjects are a man, a woman, a priest or minister and witnesses. The subjects make a number of moves in managing the transition from two unmarried individuals to the constitution of a marriage. This includes speech acts, such as 'I do', that bring the marriage into being (Austin 1962), and the expression of emotions of love by each for the other.

These shared understandings are, obviously, not uniform across cultural contexts. The act of stamping on a piece of glass is, for instance, central to the constitution of marriage in a Jewish ceremony. The rules may also be contested. Churches have struggled with the question, for example, of whether marriage by definition revolves around a man and a woman, or whether two people of the same sex can be allowed to marry. In this respect, the rules are flexible rather than law-like. In acting, we often follow rules blindly (this is simply what we do when getting married), but the rules may also be the object of contestation.[5]

The marriage example is multidimensional. The 'game' has an objective, namely to bring something into being that did not previously exist: the marriage itself. Emotion is, in many cultural contexts, fundamental to the rationality of the act rather than divorced from it. While there may be rational reasons to marry someone who is not loved, such as to get a visa to stay in a foreign country, these are likely to represent forms of cheating. The use of language (saying 'I do') is a performance

---

[5] Arranged marriages would represent a different category of action, with regard to emotion, as they do not involve the same level of individual choice.

that brings the marriage into being. Through this performance, the subjects become embodied as individuals of a different type – that is, as a married couple. Individuals make a choice to marry but the agency of becoming married is embedded within the rules of a social, cultural and legal context. This notion of a game is also useful for thinking about the meanings that surround an act of political self-sacrifice.

### Interacting games

The first section discussed the importance of embedding rationality within a social system of rules. The rules of a game constitute a set of acts and practices, which include an objective, the meaning of bodies, particular expressions of emotion, etc. What is relevant to one game may be outside the rules of relevance of another. The latter presumes the possible coexistence of multiple game structures, while raising a question about how they potentially intersect. Goffman (1961a) suggests that a social encounter may involve more than just one game, which he associates with a 'focused gathering'. Individuals can be parcelled out into different encounters – a 'multi-focused gathering' – and persons who appear to be engaged in one encounter can at the same time be involved in an additional 'subordinated' one. The 'subordinated encounter' is sustained through covert expressions or by a different framing such that the second encounter does not intrude on the dominant game (18). Thus, for instance, the emphasis on human rights that has developed in international law since World War II might be understood as a subordinate game that coexists with the dominant game of sovereignty. Within the former, agents 'act as if' human rights and dignity matter. A further position arises when an excluded or 'irrelevant' domain intrudes upon and disturbs the dominant game, which may lead to a process of scapegoating that both consolidates the identity of the participants in the dominant game and marginalizes the intruders – a position that might be analogous to the position occupied by rogue states in the international system or 'terrorists'. When actors come into a gathering who are not members of the existing one, and especially if they are strangers, then the group formation that is fostered by the encounter will be in conflict with the dominant group (14).

Goffman is talking about face-to-face interactions that are more or less relevant here. The point, however, is to shift focus to some notion of replicable patterns, rules or normative structures, in which case the face-to-face interaction is arguably less central than one's position in relation to a dominant game. The problem can be reformulated by focusing less on the face-to-face encounter and more on the intersection of multiple games. The question is: what happens when an action that has meaning within a subordinate game passes through the boundary of the dominant game, in which it has a different meaning? This question suggests the possibility that, while non-state players may have been socialized into the dominant rules of authority, there are subordinate games, relating more specifically to their historical position and cultural structures of meaning, that coexist and possibly conflict with the official structure.

Human interactions are more complex than a board game, of course, but Goffman's use of the game metaphor assists in making a theoretical point. An act of political self-sacrifice involves a material subject, a flesh-and-blood human being. In one game the move that destroys the body may be given the name 'suicide'. In another game it may be given the name 'martyrdom'. The contestation suggests that the attribution of meaning is not merely the application of an objective label to the subject/object. We have already established that the materiality of the object is the same in both cases, but its embodiment as one or the other has consequences for what follows. Equally significant is the constitution of this subject in relation to others within a social space; in other words, we know the interrelationship between different subjects and objects only by virtue of the rules through which they are attributed with meaning. Each is an example of world-making in which the same material object/subject is constituted differently within two worlds.

The coexistence of two worlds of meaning raises a question about which game is being played, a question that, as Joseph Nye (2005) notes, is crucial in an age of soft power and public diplomacy. This makes the role of the audience crucial. While the rationality of the act is one feature of either 'world', the audience is the ultimate referee, determining which game is being played and thus the legitimacy or illegitimacy of an act – a subject that will be a focus of Chapter 3. Which framework of meaning will shape the meaning of an act is a function of the social capital that becomes attached to the injured or dying body. The question of which game is being played has less a purely descriptive or individual function than a social one that is performative and constitutes the identity of the subject. The naming of a 'terrorist' or a 'criminal' delimits the social space surrounding the agent as he or she is placed outside the structures of the state, situated as a deviant in need of isolation or elimination. The naming of a 'martyr' within anti-structure expands the social space, however, making a connection to other historical and contemporary martyrs, as the 'body politic' becomes one in its identification with the martyr's body.

## The warden's dilemma

What I refer to as the warden's dilemma is a model for approaching a popular game, the prisoner's dilemma, from a different angle, in order to illustrate the relationship between self-interest and self-sacrifice. The model provides a useful first step away from the single game to the contestation between multiple games. The latter highlights the theoretical point that self-interest, insofar as it is a factor, cannot be detached from a particular type of context of both structural power and meaning. The warden's dilemma illustrates the strategic dynamics of the relationship between structure and anti-structure. As suggested in the introduction, Pape and Feldman (2010) refer to, but do not develop, the related concept of an 'occupier's dilemma'. Adler (2010) develops a 'damned if you do, damned if you don't dilemma', which focuses on non-state terrorists and their state supporters. The warden's dilemma is more concerned with the strategic dynamics of both the violent and the non-violent forms of political self-sacrifice used by those who play with a weak hand, and how this choice alters the options available to the 'warden'.

The creation of a choice structure for both the warden and the agents of resistance does not on the surface appear to go beyond the individual ontology of rational choice. It is important to clarify that it is not so much specific individuals who are the carriers of choice as the context itself and the possible moves available to agents given an existing structural position and resistance to it. The empirical chapters illustrate the role of cultural, religious and national symbols in constituting the parameters of these contesting games, which existed prior to the agency of individual actors within them. The discussion of self-interest and self-sacrifice highlighted the rational agent as an embedded and embodied self, whose act cannot be separated from social, cultural or religious frameworks of meaning. It is also important to highlight another aspect of these contexts: their hierarchical nature and the lack of autonomy, not only for the community but for individuals within it. The context, which is defined by a lack of sovereignty for the prisoners, limits the expression of agency or autonomy to a refusal to conform to the rules of the dominant game.[6]

## Power

Conformity or nonconformity in an asymmetrical context rests on a power relationship. Based on a definition of power as the ability of A to make B do what he or she otherwise would not do (Dahl 1957; Baldwin 1980), the relationship is straightforward: the warden has power over the prisoners, relating both to the capacity to use force and to legitimacy in doing so. Michael Barnett and Raymond Duvall (2005) refer to this form of power as compulsory power. In their conception, compulsory power is neither the central nor exclusive form of power but part of a taxonomy of power, which includes four potential expressions. This taxonomy is useful for specifying the forms of power that are potentially operating in the contest of intersecting games.

Barnett and Duvall (2005: 39) define power as 'the production, in and through social relations, of effects that shape the capacities of actors to determine their circumstances and fate'. This definition entails two analytic dimensions. The first focuses on the kinds of social relationship through which power works. They distinguish interactions, which are more direct, and social relations of constitution, which produce effects on the identities of occupants of different social positions. The second regards the degree of specificity – that is, how specific, direct, diffuse or indirect these social relations are.

---

[6] This differs from the approach to agency and structure in the extensive literature on the subject within IR, which has been criticized for being unable to get beyond the question of either structure or agency (Bieler and Morton 2001) and for its focus on the autonomous individual as agent (Doty 1997). The approach here shares an emphasis on the potential for action that conflicts with dominant structure. This makes the interaction between the two different structures the focal point of the contest rather than the individuals who follow either set of rules. On agency and structure, see Wendt (1987, 1992, 1999); Dessler (1989); Hollis and Smith (1991); Jabri and Chan (1996); Doty (1997).

From this distinction, they examine four concepts of power: compulsory, institutional, structural and productive.

It is useful to think about how these four forms of power might be expressed in the hierarchical relationship between the warden and the prisoners. The element of compulsory power has already been mentioned: the warden has power *over* the prisoners. Power is a property he or she possesses, and this has effects on the behaviour of the objects of power. Compulsory power, or the direct control of one actor over the conditions of existence, identity and practices of another, is, in the context of a prison, inseparable from institutional and structural power. Institutional power defines the social categories of warden and prisoner within an institution that mediates between A and B. The ability of the warden to exercise compulsory power is made possible by and is a function of the rules and procedures that define the prison as an institution, and the powers of the warden within it. Structural power is more diffuse, generating unequal social privileges and differential capacities. It constitutes both actors – that is, the prison authorities and the prisoners – shaping their self-understanding and interests. This taxonomy highlights the inseparability of individual power or action from a social context, which empowers or disempowers depending on one's position.

The key site of contestation in the warden's dilemma model is at the level of structural power and a fourth category, productive power. Both of these forms of power involve social processes that are not in themselves controlled by specific actors, but may be effected by their meaningful practices (Barnett and Duvall 2005: 55). Structural power, at its most basic, is produced and reproduced by the internally related positions of domination and subordination occupied by the actors. In this respect, the conformity of the prisoner has a role in reproducing the structural power of the prison. Productive power, by contrast, involves more generalized and diffuse social processes, and represents less a structure per se than systems of signification and meaning. Productive power relates to discourse, social process and the systems of knowledge through which meaning is 'produced, fixed, lived, experienced and transformed' (55). It is within this 'microfield' that processes of contestation over identity categories and practices of agency take place. The alternative 'game' at one and the same time presents a challenge to the productive power of the structure, involving acts of nonconformity, while bringing into being an alternative set of identities and practices by 'acting as if' a new game is in place. In this case, as Stefano Guzzini (2005: 495) notes, power 'has the effect of "politicizing" and moving actions into the scrutiny of a public realm where justifications are needed'.

The goal here is to examine the dynamics of contestation, including its constitutive properties and transformation over time. The players in a hierarchy of this kind are each playing a different game with different rules, as already suggested. The objective of the weaker party is to change the underlying rules of the dominant game such that they are constituted as subjects capable of engaging in dialogue over the conditions in which they live. The purpose of this more abstract model – or, more accurately, the metaphor of the prison – is to illustrate the central problem posed by the cases: the relationship between sovereignty and self-sacrifice in a hierarchical relationship, in which one party, the warden, is the keeper of the rules, and the other is expected to conform to the rules. The refusal of the prisoner to conform results in contestation over the constitutive rules that govern interactions within this structure.

The prisoner's dilemma is a popular framework for thinking about the problem of self-interest. The objective of the game is to maximize individual value. The suboptimal choice, which brings partial punishment, is considered most rational because it avoids the most risky, and thus potentially costly, penalty (see Hollis and Smith 1990: 124–5). Political self-sacrifice, by contrast, potentially involves loss of the ultimate value – that is, one's life. A religious framework may facilitate an understanding of the self as embedded in a larger community, and willing to sacrifice for it, but it is not primarily religion that ties these cases together, and others that have inspired political self-sacrifice, but, rather, a limitation on the sovereignty of the community, and thus of individuals within it, in a situation involving an experience of occupation or outside intervention. To the extent that agency requires some degree of sovereignty, the space for agency is constrained. IR models, including the prisoner's dilemma, emphasize the constraints imposed on sovereignty by the structure of anarchy, given the primacy of maintaining sovereignty; but a prison is a location populated by entities whose sovereignty is not only constrained but has been taken away, if temporarily, and a moral order that assumes some form of 'correction'. The prison metaphor in this case provides a structure for thinking about the problem faced by peoples whose political sovereignty has been taken away, when populations to various degrees have been constituted as subordinates, no longer able to define the rules by which they live. The assumption is thus that they are political prisoners rather than ordinary criminals.

Prisoners are generally expected to cooperate with the rules established by the prison regime and are not sovereign in making decisions. In this situation, there are three choices. The first is to accept one's status as a criminal and conform to the rules, in the hope of an early release for good behaviour, which is an abdication of one's sovereignty, at least temporarily. Given the political underpinnings of the conviction, one could say that the prisoner is accepting his or her status as victim and just wants a quiet, if less than fulfilling, life. The second is to respond with violence, such as a prison riot, as a way of demanding better conditions for those who have been imprisoned for political reasons. This choice is likely to justify a harsh clampdown and reinforce the image of the prisoner as dangerous criminal. The third is to refuse to conform to the rules, for example by refusing to wear the prison uniform, which is a symbol of criminal status, but to accept the punishment of the guards without hitting back.

The latter two choices both involve a defection – to use the language of game theory – that is doubled in the case of violent action, and thus would seem to signal a credible threat. In the case of the prison riot, the double defection involves both a refusal to cooperate with the rules and a violent reaction by the prisoner to attempts to enforce compliance. As Marek Kohn (2008: 25) argues, a signal whose effect is to advertise an individual's strength and size should be strong and sustained in the way that only a strong or large individual can produce. The prisoner in this situation does not possess strength of this kind, but is pitted against an institution that is backed by the power of the law and physical force. Continuing the double defection over several plays, in an attempt to establish the credibility of the prisoner's demands, will result only in defeat and an increasingly harsh penalty, which in the end reinforces the prisoner's status as dangerous criminal. The prisoner is unable to overpower the prison system physically. His or her use of violence only strengthens the legitimacy of that system.

It is this legitimacy that must be drawn into question for there to be a change of games. The third choice involves a refusal to conform to the rules but a decision to accept any resulting punishment without retaliation. The decision thus potentially results in harm to the self rather than the maximization of self-interest. Physical strength is not the only way to signal credibility, and indeed may not be the best way to do so, particularly in this type of hierarchy. A costly signal in this context may therefore also rely on a different kind of move. As in the first scenario, the prisoner refuses to conform to the rules of the prison and has a reason for doing so, namely that he or she feels his or her non-cooperation with an unjust rule or law to be justified (e.g. political prisoners should not be forced to wear the uniform of the criminal). As above, the warden reciprocates with punishment, but this time the prisoner continues to refuse to conform but also suffers the consequences of his or her non-cooperation, for example, clothing him- or herself only in blankets. This interaction progresses through repeated rounds. The prisoner refuses to conform; the prison warden punishes the prisoner; and the prisoner, rather than retaliating, accepts his or her worsening condition while still refusing to conform, again and again. When this repeated interaction reaches its culmination, such that the only further form of non-cooperation available is the refusal to take food, the costs of non-cooperation, and the reliability of the demand attached to it, have reached their ultimate expression. The cost of one's life is presented as of less value than the ultimate goal of changing the rules of the game, which would replace the prisoner's conformity with an open-ended negotiation over the conditions in which he or she lives.

At this point, the warden is faced with a dilemma. The prisoner is clearly not acting within a prisoner's dilemma game, in which realizing his or her self-interest in the shortest sentence possible is the ultimate objective. A consistent pattern of non-cooperation has led to a point at which the prisoner's life is at stake and he or she has already decided that he or she is more prepared to give up his or her life than to conform to the rules of the dominant structure, which he or she sees as unjust. The warden, having punished the prisoner repeatedly, must now decide whether his or her self-interest in appearing to run a humane prison is maximized by continuing the punishment, recognizing that the prisoner may die and become a martyr, or by engaging with him or her as a political agent. The emphasis on appearance suggests that the interaction is not purely internal to the prison and that the choice is part of the management of public perceptions and image, which are part of the larger network of structural and productive power. Even though the relationship to the prisoners may not be valued in its own right, the reputational effects of allowing a prisoner to die in this way provides an incentive to think carefully about the choice, since the warden does value the relationship to others, both inside and outside the prison, who might react negatively. The legitimacy of the structure would be called into question if it appeared that the warden was humiliating and abusing political prisoners who were acting non-violently.

The act of self-sacrifice communicates to each member of an audience the humiliation and injustice that is experienced by the social group that the agent embodies. Conformity would be more conducive to satisfying the self-interest of the individual in this context, for instance by biding one's time in the hope of an early release. Self-sacrifice in this situation cannot be viewed in terms of individual self-interest, as the result is greater suffering, and perhaps even the death of the individual. The self-sacrifice is part of a contestation in which the agent seeks to change the rules of the game such that the community he or she identifies with *can* act as sovereign agents, negotiating over the conditions in which they live. They thus seek to move out of the category of criminals, who lack agency, to be recognized as political subjects who act on behalf of a body politic.

The agent's response to the experience of humiliation is the core of this dynamic. In his research into 'total' institutions, such as asylums and prisons, Goffman (1961b) highlights the extent to which the curtailment of the 'self' is part of the socialization of prisoners through procedures of debasement, degradation and humiliation, often involving an 'obedience test' that involves immediate and visible punishment that increases until the inmate 'cries uncle' and humbles him- or herself. The obligation to request permission for minor activities that one would undertake on their own outside the prison puts the individual in a submissive role that is 'unnatural' for an adult. Those aspects by which a person has control over his or her world – that is, self-determination, autonomy and freedom of action – are denied.

As Avishai Margalit (1996) points out, however, the relationship between the humiliator and the humiliated is paradoxical. The humiliating act is intended to lower the value of the object, but, in order for the humiliation to be effective, the humiliated has to retain sufficient agency to recognize and acknowledge that he or she has been humiliated. It is this acknowledgement that substantiates the power of the prison regime (whether actual or metaphorical). The acknowledgement doubles the voice of the authorities, insofar as their power is reinforced by the conformity of those who consent. The act of political self-sacrifice reverses the relationship. This reversal was captured by Padraig O'Malley (1990: 22–3) in his depiction of the non-cooperation of the 'blanket men' in Long Kesh Prison in Northern Ireland. He said that, for every hardship inflicted on them,

> they were prepared to inflict a hardship of at least equal severity on themselves, thus devaluing the system's power to intimidate them. Their willingness to deprive themselves undermined the authority of the regime to do so. Whatever debasement or humiliation the regime might impose on them in the form of punishment was nothing compared to what they were prepared to impose on themselves in the form of protest.

The logic of political self-sacrifice is one of accepting harm to the body as punishment for refusing to cooperate with the rules of the dominant game. This requires a form of agency, in that it clearly goes against the grain of the dominant structure, and ultimately risks death. This form of agency is distinct from the other two choices presented in the warden's dilemma model: conformity with the dominant game, which reproduces the structural power of the regime; or violent retaliation, which may, given this hierarchy, reinforce one's status as a criminal who is outside the political community and lacks political subjectivity. The three choices are illustrated in Figure 2.1.

One can point to historical examples that reflect the three different choices. There are innumerable cases of populations living under dictatorial or repressive regimes that for one reason or another conform rather than resist. There are also numerous cases of violent resistance to colonial structures in the period following World War II. The latter can be situated in the context of a traditional prisoner's dilemma game, in which the optimal choice – continuing to arm with the hope of overpowering the adversary – risks the worst outcome of

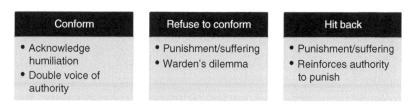

**Figure 2.1** The prisoner's choice structure

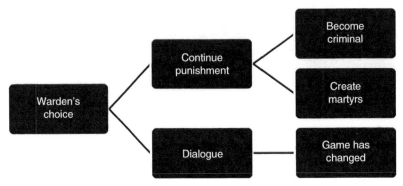

**Figure 2.2** The warden's dilemma

reinforcing the legitimacy of the powers that be, if sufficient strength cannot be mobilized. My focus is on the warden's dilemma that arises out of the middle category of action, in which self-sacrifice is an important element of the contestation between the powers that be and those who would resist, and who, to use the metaphor, accept the punishment of the guards without hitting back.

Figure 2.2 depicts the choices that arise out of the dilemma posed to the warden by the continuing refusal of the prisoners to conform after repeated attempts to punish them, based on the contrast between a case that was purely non-violent and one in which the self-sacrifice was non-violent but associated with a violent campaign outside the prison. In both cases, the martyrdom resulted in questions about the criminal nature of the government. For instance, in the Polish case, following the 'martyrdom' of Fr Jerzy Popiełuszko, there was no other choice for the government but to engage in dialogue with Solidarity. In the Northern Irish case, the death of the hunger strikers was followed by a stalemate, in which the Thatcher government remained inflexible and the IRA outside the prison escalated its violent campaign. Both examples are examined in greater depth in the chapters that follow. The key distinction, I would argue, regards the clarity surrounding the assignment of culpability for the deaths, the significance of which will become clearer from the cases.

The legitimacy to rule is at the crux of the warden's dilemma. The prison is a correctional institution for deviant behaviour, supported by a legitimate monopoly on the use of force. Its legitimacy rests on a clear distinction between the moral authority of the state and the criminal nature of the deviants. The warden faces a dilemma when the force required to discipline inmates, to enforce conformity with the dominant rules, appears disproportionate to a larger audience in light of the unwillingness of the agent to hit back. In this case, the category of criminal is destabilized, opening a discussion of whether the criminal label more accurately applies to the warden rather than those who refuse to conform. The game thus shifts from a focus on the identity of the agent of political self-sacrifice to contestation over the criminality of the regime. The dilemma for the warden is then whether to continue the punishment, realizing that this may lead to a further loss of legitimacy, with the creation of martyrs, and growing unease about the criminal nature of the regime, or to enter into dialogue with the subordinate party, at which point the game has changed. The prisoner is then no longer a criminal outside politics but a subject with whom there is an obligation to engage.

## Conclusion

This chapter began with a discussion of the difficulty of making sense of self-sacrifice within a rational choice framework. A case was made for a more social ontology, in which rationality was dependent on the underlying rules of a social game. I then examined the potential for multiple intersecting games, and, drawing on Goffman, provided a framework for thinking about how a subordinate game might intrude on a dominant one. This provided a foundation for examining an interaction between structure and anti-structure, as discussed in Chapter 1. Agency was situated as part of the latter, as a form of 'acting as if' a new game was in place against the backdrop of dominant power, whereby the refusal to conform was likely to result in punishment and possibly death. The warden's dilemma model illustrated the dynamics that emerge out of this conflict between structure and agency.

As a metaphor, the prison denotes a situation resting on an institutional hierarchy in which the movement of inmates is monitored and conformity is expected. The prison provides an order. As a 'correctional' facility, this is a moral order populated by deviants, organized around the disciplining of these deviants and their rehabilitation. The warden's dilemma is a metaphor for the problem faced by the authorities when confronted with resistance by those who wish to redefine their status as political prisoners and who, along with the communities they represent, have experienced an history of injustice. The metaphor most directly mirrors one of the cases explored here – the prison hunger strike – but is intended first and foremost to be an introductory exploration into the contrast between actions based on self-sacrifice, as distinct from self-interest, within a hierarchical relationship, and the spectrum of violent and non-violent choices within it. It is an exploration of the power inherent in a refusal to conform to the dominant rules while beginning to 'act as if' one is free.

The social nature of the rules opens a space for understanding the attachment of social capital to either game, and thus the expansion of one body politic rather than another; these rules can also be learned and reproduced by others in different social spaces. Any one player of chess or checkers may be more or less skilful in a strategic sense. Although this is partially dependent on the aptitude of the player, the major factor is the extent to which he or she possesses knowledge of the game and can effectively put this knowledge into practice in distinct contexts of interaction. This provides a basis for thinking about practices of imitation, which are explored in the next chapter.

While a 'dilemma' presumes a dilemma for someone, and thus an agent who must decide, the individual nature of both the dilemma for the warden or the decision of the agent has to be problematized. As the Polish example demonstrates, it has not to this day been established that responsibility for the kidnapping and murder of Popiełuszko, which led to his constitution as a martyr, went all the way to the top. Indeed, many have claimed that it was an effort by extreme elements within the government to destabilize President Jaruzelski. Whoever made the actual choice, Popiełuszko's martyrdom *became* a dilemma for the Polish communist state as a whole, given questions by various audiences, both national and international, regarding its culpability, which constituted a threat to the legitimacy of the state and the need to redefine the terms by which it interacted with Polish society. Strictly speaking, the choice to engage in dialogue with Solidarity came only after a martyr had been created who was unequivocally a product of violence inflicted by members of the secret service, if not the regime itself (see Litka 2010).

This chapter has provided a framework for analysing a range of different cases belonging to a 'family' of acts involving political self-sacrifice. The warden's dilemma is a metaphor just as the prisoner's dilemma is a metaphor. George Lakoff and Mark Johnson (1980) argue that metaphor relies on entailments of familiar, often everyday, experience to make sense of more complex phenomena. Much as the role of metaphor is denied for being unscientific, most theories of international relations rely on metaphors of some kind, from the prisoner's dilemma to billiard balls, or layer cakes or the state as a person. Metaphors are a useful tool for simplifying and making sense of otherwise complex phenomena. The power of the metaphor is its ability to reveal the logic of a particular type of context and thus to simplify and understand its structural dynamics.

# 3 | Body and emotion

A prison is an invisible space, away from the glare of cameras or public judgement. It may be a literal prison, like the Maze Prison in Northern Ireland, or a physical edifice, such as the wall that separates Israel from the Palestinian territories, or the Berlin Wall during the Cold War, which separated East from West. The prison walls may also be a system of political control that is so all-pervasive, like Foucault's (1979 [1975]) Panopticon,[1] that it is less physical structures that contain than awareness of the omnipresent eye of social surveillance. The prison is, in this respect, psychological. It draws a wall of fear around the individual mind that is reinforced by the barricades of external identity, of identification as the abject Other who should not be heard and therefore must not speak. The act of self-sacrifice potentially blows a hole in the internal barrier of fear and the barricade of external identity. The materialization and visualization of the suffering body creates an opening for the reconfiguration of social and political space. Observers are thrown off balance by the unexpected, the refusal to forgo the locus of decision-making in the self, the freedom to act without fear. This act may then have a cascading effect that circulates through further layers of the wall, as others abandon their fear.

Chapter 1 explored contemporary self-sacrifice through the lens of the anthropological literature on sacrifice, pointing both to a family resemblance and to several important differences. Self-sacrifice, it was argued, is an 'act of speech' and a performance that communicates to an audience, giving rise to contestation over the identity of the body as a criminal or martyr. The last chapter explored the agency of self-sacrifice in relation to modern notions of rational choice, situating the act in a thicker conception of a game, underpinned by inter-subjective rules, and a contestation between structure and anti-structure. The context presented a choice to the prisoner of participating in the reproduction

---

[1] The idea of the Panopticon did, in fact, originate with Jeremy Bentham.

of the prison rules, through his or her conformity, or acting as if a different game were in place by refusing to conform. This contestation would potentially result in a warden's dilemma, in which the warden risked appearing to be the criminal, through the creation of martyrs, or engaged with the prisoners in dialogue over the conditions in which they lived, at which point the game had changed.

The purpose of this chapter is to deepen the analysis further, to look more closely at the dynamics of liminality attached to acts of self-sacrifice in a breaking down of the prison walls and a transformation of the boundaries that separate the prison from the larger world. This shifts the focus to the materiality of the dying body, the emotions this evokes and the 'stickiness' of these emotions in relation to various audiences, both local and global. It thereby involves a more postmodern exploration of how emotions circulate and shape the boundaries of a body politic, which highlights notions of performativity, multiplicity and imitation on a global stage. I argue that community identity is neither fixed nor static; rather, communities of recognition are constituted and reconstituted through the movement and the circulation of emotion, evoked by the bodily self-sacrifice, and given resonance and power through memory. The self-sacrifice of the individual body becomes an expression of the loss of collective sovereignty, which materializes the injustice experienced by the community and thereby creates the conditions for its restoration. The cases in later chapters explore how this process is shaped by the use or non-use of violence by the agent.

Acts of political self-sacrifice become a site of contestation. The location of the contestation in *language* is important for the transfer of meaning from the individual body of sacrifice to the suffering 'body politic' and others who witness the act. The visualization of 'bare life' in images of the body is a central element of the emotional impact. The main issue is one of how the dying body is *embodied* with emotional meaning, which then becomes 'stuck to' the nascent community as the walls of the prison are dismantled and a social world is restored. *Emotion* is central to the process by which the meaning inscribed on the body of the individual agent moves to and impresses on the surface of the body politic. Emotion comes from the Latin *emovere*, which means 'to move' or 'to move out'. In this respect, as Sarah Ahmed (2004) argues, emotions are not only about movements but also about attachments and what connects us to this or that.

Meaning in this case is neither purely inside the individual mind nor outside in the social world. While penetrating both, the relationship is more temporal in nature. The stickiness of the emotions is a function of the connection to past social experience and norms. In this respect, *memories* of the past are an important part of the movement in the present and towards the future. Memories of past martyrdom are the source of emotional resonance to a more local audience. The audience, in its identification with the sacrifice, abandons its fear and is transformed, engaging in acts that *imitate* or express support for the cause to varying degrees.

The first section of this chapter examines a question of how the material body becomes the embodiment of meaning. The second explores how this meaning, which is laden with emotion, moves out towards a larger audience. The third section makes a further link to memory as a reservoir of meaningful emotions and its 'stickiness' vis-à-vis different audiences. The final section examines how these acts, as forms of public diplomacy from below, impact on a larger environment, setting the stage for possible imitation by others.

## The body politic

There is a long tradition of thinking about the political community as a 'body politic', or the individual body as a metaphor for the collective (Harvey 2007). The famous cover of *Leviathan*, for instance, shows the head of a monarch and a body that is composed of the peoples he protects. In Jean-Jacques Rousseau's thinking, the body chooses the head. An authoritarian ruler whose power rests on outside support does not fit with any notion of social contract, particularly if the sovereign becomes a threat to the individuals he or she is meant to protect. If the 'body politic' has historically been a metaphor of the flesh-and-blood body of the individual, the act of self-sacrifice represents a reversal, in which the death of the individual becomes a metaphor for the death of community and its potential regeneration. In this shift, we replace the Leviathan on the cover of Hobbes' famous book, a large body of power enclosing a people, with the body of the martyr, who suffers on behalf of a community.

This inversion requires a rethinking of the theoretical and methodological assumptions by which 'bodies' have been understood in international relations. First, the focus is not on the security of *states* but on the political contestation arising from the insecurity produced for subordinate communities by the security practices of dominant states. Second, it thus highlights the central fear that marks the study and practice of international relations – that is, the fear of sovereignty lost. The focus is on a context in which sovereignty has *already* been lost, however, and a question of the different ways in which communities fight their way out of a position in which they play with a losing hand, which necessarily involves abandoning the fear of brutalization that is likely to arise from the attempt to speak as self-determining agents. Third, the focus shifts from the fixed body of the state and state survival to the transformative potential of political self-sacrifice.

The study of international relations has often rested on a theoretical assumption that we can treat states as if they are the 'persons' of international relations (Ringmar 1996; Neumann 2004), and as individual rational actors whose bodies are represented as billiard balls, the insides of which are out of view (see, for instance, Waltz 1979; Jackson 2004). Constructivists have more recently imbued these bodies with emotions (Wendt 1999; Mitzen 2006; Steele 2008). Alexander Wendt (1999, 2004), for instance, explores 'how states are constituted as the "people" of international society'. In contrast to the assumption of much IR theory that we can treat states 'as if' they are, or as being like, persons, he argues that states are real actors to which we can legitimately attribute anthropomorphic qualities such as desires, beliefs and intentionality. He sets out to give the state a 'body' by showing that it is an actor that cannot be reduced to its parts, to demonstrate how state–society complexes affect state behaviour in interactions, and to give the model of the state 'life' by identifying its intrinsic motivational dispositions or 'national interests' (1999. 197).

The tension in this argument is between the individual and the state as actors, and how the transition and location of practice from one to the other takes place, thereby producing one culture of anarchy over another. Wendt outlines a relationship between individual and social bodies, emotions and institutions, and suggests that a transformation of one level may influence the shape of anarchy (1999, 2003). This is useful inasmuch as it opens a space for thinking about the relationship between individual, state and international culture, as well as their potential for transformation. Conceptualizing the state as a person has the consequence of fixing the boundary between inside and outside, however, which makes it difficult to understand how this works.

Wendt's claim that we can bracket struggles for recognition within states (2003: 516) locates interaction in the relationship between state persons. As Seth (2011: 179) notes, however, the terms that we use to refer to the bonds that hold collectivities together, such as cultures, civilizations, peoples, do not neatly 'map onto' the nation states of the world, which makes it highly problematic to treat states as if they are individuals, even by analogy. If sovereignty is often a site of political contestation,[2] and the martyred nation may, through acts of political self-sacrifice, reconstitute itself, then the theoretical focus necessarily shifts away from a focus on static sovereign bodies to the processes and practices by which the boundaries and identity of the sovereign body are contested and potentially transformed.

The problem of political self-sacrifice pushes at the boundaries of the constructivist debate regarding the question of agency and interaction, which has tended to focus on the state. The rationalist and constructivist models, as applied to international relations, both have a top-down structure, and they both assume that the state can be treated 'as if' it were an individual or a real person. Wendt's concept of multiple realizability suggests that there is some space for more individual-level practices within a culture to shake up corporate identity and, subsequently, the logic of anarchy. His struggle for recognition and evolution towards a world state rests on recognition between states, however, and brackets processes inside the state – a distinction that has the effect of fixing an inside and an outside. The concern here is the struggle for recognition by marginalized or oppressed communities, which may cross state boundaries or be contained within states or occupied territories. Patrick Thaddeus Jackson's (2004) concept of 'personation', originally articulated by Hobbes, seems more directly relevant to the present exercise in that it raises a question about how individuals or states are *constituted* as persons, with the potential for intentionality as well as external definition. 'Personation' does not, however, account for the dialectic of political self-sacrifice, in which the destruction of the material body – a metaphor for the absence of collective recognition – produces the conditions for the latter's regeneration. In what follows I approach the problem from a different

---

[2] Seth (2011: 182) further notes that Hobbes discussed sovereignty in terms of the ability to impose and stabilize meaning. In this respect, '[i]t is always a function of strategies and tactics, struggles and conflicts and, to that degree, is contingent and variable'.

angle, providing a theoretical framework for thinking about how the surface and fixity of subjects or objects, or of the inside and outside, are constituted.

## Matter

The last chapter explored the contestation surrounding acts of political self-sacrifice, nudging the focus away from the individual ontology of state interaction, which has characterized the IR literature, to the interaction between structure and anti-structure and a contestation that, in its resolution, defines the identity of the body and the meaning of its moves. This chapter has begun by developing a more explicit link between these 'language games' and bodily materiality or matter.[3] The game metaphor, as discussed in the last chapter, highlights the extent to which material objects have an identity and interests only within a game-like structure of rules. The knight, in the absence of the rules of the chess game, is a mere piece of wood or metal. Likewise, we cannot make sense of the sight of an injured or dying body without situating it within a world of meaning. The dead body in Gaza may be alternatively scripted as a terrorist, who presented a security threat; as a victim, who should have been the subject of humanitarian rescue; or as a martyr, who has died in the process of resistance. The 'intention' of the agent may be in conflict with any of the external characterizations of identity, but is no less dependent on 'customs, uses and institutions' (Wittgenstein, 1958: para. 199). That there may be a difference between the intention of the agent and the ascription of meaning by different audiences lies at the heart of the potential contestation surrounding the body. As discussed in Chapter 1, the 'act of speech' is a perlocutionary act. In this case it is a non-verbal performance that, in the act of communicating, produces consequential effects upon the feelings, thoughts or actions of an audience (Austin 1962: 103–4). Most crucial, however, is the potential change in the audience's perspective on the body – that is, whether members are convinced or persuaded, or develop distinct feelings, about the act they have witnessed. Several claims have already been made about this act. First, as a visualization of 'bare life', the act is so spectacular and

---

[3] Matter is alternatively defined as: (1) substance of a stated type, (2) physical substance, (3) to be important (Procter 1995: 874).

so outside the everyday that it disrupts or causes a rupture in the fabric of the everyday. Second, the destruction of the individual body is a metaphor for the humiliation or destruction that has been experienced by the community. Third, the act of speech is an inversion of the speech act. The marginalized are silenced and unable to speak for themselves. The sacrifice speaks louder than words, without using words, through the suffering of the body.

The metaphoric inversions of the flesh-and-blood body and the body politic, and of the speech act and the act of speech, are reflected in a further inversion related to power. Discussions of material power in international relations tend to focus on capabilities and the relative ability of sovereigns to exercise power over others – that is, to wield economic or military power. The power of capabilities grows out of the magnification of individual strength through the extension of forms of social organization and the multiplication of the implements of violence (Arendt 1986 [1970]). The body of the individual stands in stark contrast. The individual stripped of both of these – with the exception of the suicide bomber, whose body becomes an implement of violence – would seem to be the antithesis of power and an expression of what Agamben (1998) refers to as 'bare life'. As the cases to varying degrees demonstrate, though, the sacrifice of the individual body can become a site of power in another sense of the term. Hannah Arendt (1986 [1970]: 64–5, 71) argues that, although power often is underpinned by violence, the two are, strictly speaking, opposites, in that power depends first and foremost on the ability of humans to act in concert. The power of political self-sacrifice – as distinct from coercion – does not lie in the ability to harm another, which, as the discussion of suicide terrorism in Chapter 8 argues, may circumscribe soft power. On the contrary, it rests on accepting harm to the self, which, as an act that appears to defy self-interest, opens a space for contestation regarding the identity of the agent and the meaning of the act; in other words, it raises a question as to which game is being played. Insofar as the act beckons to an audience rather than the self, it can result in both imitation of the act and/or expansion of the community of trust upon which power rests. The power of the sacrifice arises from its performative aspect. While the game emphasizes the importance of rules, action and meaning, the performance metaphor shifts attention to the spectacle of the social drama and its visualization to an audience. The dying body at one and the same time becomes the embodiment of the death of community and the condition for its restoration – that is, the act that destroys life in order to create new life. The conceptualization of the injured body as a performance differs from that of a construction.

Judith Butler (1993: 4) argues that construction assumes some prior agent who does the constructing, and, in so doing, acts upon nature, which is a passive surface that is both outside the social and its counterpart. 'To construct' is a verb, which suggests an agent who enacts or performs the construction. Butler's argument, however, is that, if a category such as gender – which is her focus – is constructed, it does not follow that there is or could be an 'I' or 'we' who is prior who has not him- or herself been subjected to gendering. The 'I' emerges only 'within and as a part of the matrix of gender relations themselves'. Her claim that the subject is 'produced' does not do away with the subject but, rather, switches attention to the conditions of its emergence and generation. The matrix of gender relations is prior to the emergence of the 'human'. For instance, the very humanness of abject beings, who are not properly gendered (e.g. 'the queer'), is called into question, and in this respect the construction of gender 'operates through *exclusionary* means, such that the human is not only produced over and against the inhuman, but through a set of foreclosures, radical erasures, that are, strictly speaking, refused the possibility of cultural articulation' (1993: 8). Thus it is not only that human subjects are produced but, in the process, the less 'human', the inhuman and the humanly unthinkable are as well. These exclusions come to be bound to 'the human as the boundary by which they are constituted, and which always face the possibility of disruption and rearticulation' (8).

In place of construction, Butler (9) proposes to return to a notion of matter, not as a site or surface to be imposed on but as a 'process of materialization that stabilizes over time to produce the effect of boundary, fixity and surface that we call matter'. The idea of performativity focuses on the discursive practices that enact or produce that which it names (Austin 1962), and is therefore compatible with the performative in speech act theory (Butler 1993: 13). The agency of performativity is contrary to any notion of a voluntarist subject who exists apart from the regulatory norms he or she opposes. Rather than a voluntarist subject, we see that the subject who resists these norms is him- or herself enabled, if not produced, by them.

Therefore the constitutive constraint, far from foreclosing the possibility of agency, locates it in a reiterative and rearticulatory practice,
which is surrounded by power rather than in external opposition to
power. It is the abjected or delegitimated bodies that fail to count as
'bodies'. The materiality of a practice, which in her exploration is sex,
is demarcated in discourse and produces a domain of excluded and
delegitimated 'sex'. As such, it is as important to think not only about
how and to what end bodies are constructed but also about how and
to what end bodies are not constructed – and, further, to ask how the
bodies that fail to materialize provide the necessary 'outside' and
support for the bodies that, in materializing the norm, qualify as
bodies that 'matter' (Butler 1993: 15). She asks (16):

How does materialization of the norm in bodily formation produce a
domain of abjected bodies, a field of deformation, which, in failing to
qualify as the fully human, fortifies those regulatory norms? What challenge
does that excluded and abjected realm produce to a symbolic hegemony that
might force a radical rearticulation of what qualifies as bodies that matter,
ways of living that count as 'life', lives worth protecting, lives worth saving,
lives worth grieving?

Gender is one of many hierarchies that constitute the subjectivity of
the human in relation to a boundary that distinguishes abject Others.
Butler's (2004) later work expands the materiality of the body to the
Western self in relation to abject non-Western Others, who are less
than human and whose bodies do not matter. Given this co-production,
the self-sacrifice of the abject Other would, it follows logically, also
destabilize the subjectivity of the subject, as it destroys the boundary
by which this subject has been defined and thus reiterated as a distinct
material and political body. In this light, an act of self-sacrifice by
abject Others raises a further question about the latter's status as
an agent. If the non-subjectivity of the less than human abject Other,
of the body that does not 'matter', is continuously reiterated along
with the political subjectivity of the human subject, how does the
performance of the abject Other as agent become possible? Butler
states that it emerges from the regulatory norms and in response to
them. It remains difficult to see, however, how the non-subject can be
reiterated by the norm while also challenging the norm, which is the
necessary condition for becoming human and thus a political subject.
The discussion of the dialectic of humiliation in the last chapter

offered a partial clue. If, in Margalit's argument, the non-subject/
object of humiliation must retain sufficient agency to acknowledge
his or her humiliation, and thus the power of the humiliator over him
or her, and if, as in Butler's argument, this is a condition for maintaining the dominant human self, then withholding recognition of authority and refusing to conform are acts that constitute the abject Other as
an agent with a body that matters. Here lies the source of the dialectical tension, reminiscent of more ancient practices of sacrifice,
between the victim who it is criminal to kill but who potentially,
through the killing, becomes sacred.

## Injustice embodied

The power of nonconformity is closely linked to the materiality of the
body of the abject Other, who suffers injury as a result of the refusal.
Scarry's (1985) classic work *The Body in Pain* is a useful stepping
stone for understanding this link. Her focus is the relationship
between the material body and power as they relate to war and
torture. Her argument provides a point of departure for thinking
about political self-sacrifice as a performance of resistance. Scarry
presents traditional war as a contest that involves mutual injury and
the consent of individuals within affected populations to give their
physical bodies. The outcome, although arising from mutual injury,
leaves the victor with more agency to impose his or her own meaning
(or what she refers to as 'self-description') on what has transpired and
what is to come in the future, while the loser has less of this agency.

  In this respect, there is always an 'as if' function to the waging
of war (Scarry 1985: 108, 138). At least one side is fighting over a
construction that does not yet exist in material form. For instance, an
image of an Ireland or Serbia or Europe 'worth dying for' is necessi-
tated by the absence or potential loss of this construction in fact.
Traditionally, with the conclusion of war, a victor was able to realize
his or her self-description. In this respect, the injuring contest is about
determining which of two existing social constructs will be produced
as an outcome. Stated differently, war is a violent contest over which
set of meanings will come to structure material reality. While there is
no difference between the physical bodies of soldiers on either side –
the injured body of an Irish or a British soldier is simply an injured
body – there is also no inherent relationship between these bodies and

the ideas of either side. It is through the process of massive physical injury that the construct comes into being as a material reality – that is, that the disembodied idea is embodied. According to Scarry (125), it is through the process of war that 'the incontestable reality of the physical body to now become an attribute of an issue that at the moment has no independent reality of its own' becomes possible.

Normally we affirm the existence of objects through our direct experience of them, by seeing or touching them. In war, the observer sees and touches the hurt body of another person, which is juxtaposed to the disembodied idea, or issue, over which the war is being fought. The injury is thus not merely a means of deciding the contest. In the 'massive opening of human bodies', otherwise unanchored and disembodied beliefs are reconnected with the force and power of the material world (128). Insofar as war involves a contest over conflicting beliefs or constructs, the affirmation of one side's self-description contributes to the deconstruction of the competing construct. What collides in war is each population's right to generate its own forms of self-description.

The mutual injury that is central to the execution, process and outcome of war ultimately brings the experience down to the most individual of levels, given that pain is in and of itself an individual experience. Pain isolates. Scarry reveals how the pain of torture closes the suffering individual off from the civilized world, in a room with no windows, no ability to extend the self to others, and no voices except that of the torturer. Torture is different from war because it is a hierarchical relationship between two individuals, in which one causes pain to the other without his or her consent.

Torture, as Scarry argues, is, in many ways, the opposite of the social artefact. The social artefact allows for the extension of the self to the world in the service of particular functions. The chair, as a positive artefact, is a self-extension that increases the comfort of individuals and enables movement out of the boundaries of the body. In inflicting extreme pain, torture brings about a contraction and collapse of the consciousness of a larger world. It transforms the room, which is normally a structure providing safety and connection to a larger world, through its windows and doors, into a closed space, where all its objects become potential weapons. To the extent that pain is 'produced', it becomes an artefact in itself, whereby the bodily condition becomes an attribute of the torturing regime's power. War occupies the same ground as torture, in that it 'produces' physical distress and bodily injury, as distinct from the artefact that enhances comfort. War involves a contraction of social consciousness, insofar as the minds of those involved become filled with events related to dying and killing. It also separates the attributes of the hurt body from the body, projecting them onto other constructs (such as sovereignty, freedom, etc.). There is a critical difference between torture and war, however. In the one it is the body of the non-believer (the tortured) and in the other that of the believer (the population, soldiers) that is enlisted in the process of embodying power. The victim of torture does not consent to his or her treatment. Torture is a one-way relationship between the torturer and the tortured, in which injury is imposed on the victim, and in which the victim's voice, in confession, becomes a vehicle of self-betrayal, in the mock act of consent and participation. Consent is not given freely. It is part of the negotiation of pain, the primary purpose of which is to magnify the regime's power.

Scarry does not deal with the relationship between the materiality of political self-sacrifice and ideas of justice. Her contrast between war and torture does provide an interesting site for developing this connection, however. Like torture, an act of political self-sacrifice takes place within a hierarchical relationship, between a regime that is often bolstered by external power and a marginalized community that experiences a level of day-to-day humiliation. Unlike torture, but like war, an act of self-sacrifice involves a degree of agency in the refusal to conform to the dominant structure, as already argued. The agency of political self-sacrifice is situated within a social framework. In this respect, the bodily injury becomes a social artefact that enables the movement of emotions out from the individual body to the liminal community.

In torture, the victim, through an act of self-betrayal and mock consent, substantiates the power of the torturing regime. Self-sacrifice reverses the relationship. The crucial move that transforms the relationship from one of humiliation to one of political agency is the refusal to double the voice of the regime through acknowledgement of the humiliation, which, like the confession extracted through torture, would involve a self-betrayal. As is further elaborated below, if this acknowledgement is the condition for removal of the pain, then a withdrawal of consent would logically entail a continuation of the pain with the failure to acknowledge superior power. This may involve a refusal to cooperate in any way, even if this means death or, in the more extreme version, the choice to take one's own life. Far from the choiceless choice of the victim, who in an act of confession or mock consent reinforces the power of the regime, the refusal to conform, which potentially becomes an act of political self-sacrifice, is the only real choice left to the abject Other from a position of humiliation when sovereignty is otherwise absent.

The weapons of violence may be turned on the self, and harm innocent others, as in the case of suicide bombing, or the violence may be anticipated and absorbed by the self, as in an act of non-violent witness. The *political* weapon is injury to the body and its performance of a power of resistance, however, in which the body speaks against the background of its silencing. Like injury to the soldier's body in war, self-sacrifice speaks to a larger audience, rather than contracting and losing consciousness of the world, as with torture. It allows otherwise disembodied beliefs, in this case about justice, to be reconnected with the force and power of the material world. Like war, the contest is over competing ideas, but in this case the focal point of the competition is two different structures for giving meaning to the bodily injury. The act itself raises a question as to what could be so important that an individual would sacrifice his or her own life for its sake. For that portion of the audience that already identifies and knows what is important, namely dignity and autonomy, the death represents the overcoming of fear and a call to imitation. The interaction is not between two conflicting forces wielding violence but between the injured body and an audience that must determine the meaning to be attached to the body. The meaning of the act circulates vis-à-vis the emotions expressed through it.

## Circulating emotions

The role of emotion is relatively new terrain for international relations scholars,[4] but it has recently given rise to an expanding literature.[5]

---

[4] There is a significant literature on emotions in other fields, including sociology and anthropology (see, for instance, Harre 1989; Milton and Svasek 2005; Svasek 2006), as well as the body (see, for instance, Coakley 1997; Howson 2004; Fraser and Greco 2005; Turner 2008).

[5] Neta Crawford's (2000) seminal piece on emotion, published prior to 11 September 2001, played a significant role in starting this debate. Fear is an emotion that has been implicit in the realist paradigm all along (see Booth and

Janice Bially Mattern (2011) argues that many approaches to emotion within IR tend to become caught up in the 'levels of analysis problem'. Despite self-conscious attempts to avoid reductionism, there is a tendency to oversimplify and reduce emotion to one of its constitutive components. The challenge is to conceptualize the relationship between these components. For the purposes of this analysis, I emphasize four points about emotion.

First, emotion is a rational measure of value. This claim is counterintuitive, given the tendency to view rationality and emotion as opposites. Martha Nussbaum (2001: 4) calls this opposition into question, arguing that emotions are 'appraisals or value judgements which ascribe to things and persons outside the person's own control great importance for the person's own flourishing'.[6] In this respect, emotions are an expression of our vulnerability to people and events that we don't control. Rather than the opposite of rationality, emotions involve a form of evaluative judgement that she refers to as eudaimonistic judgement (EJ). EJ involves thought of an object combined with thought of the object's salience or importance to one's own survival and flourishing.[7] The emotion also has a history, and is thus related to memory, which includes traces of a range of other background emotions that give it specific content and cognitive specificity. In this argument, emotions express a relationship between feeling and value. Positive emotions, such as happiness or joy, relate to the presence of the valued subject or object and the ability to realize one's objectives and goals, while negative emotions, related to humiliation or betrayal, arise from a loss of dignity, value, safety or agency and a subsequent inability to flourish. One purpose of sacrifice, in its

---

Wheeler 2007). Trauma and emotion have begun to find a place in the literature of international relations since 9/11 (see Edkins 2003; Fierke 2004; Mercer 2005; Ross 2006; Bleiker and Hutchinson 2008; Leep 2010). Humiliation has also become a specific focus (Danchev 2006; Saurette 2006; Fontan 2006), and, increasingly, their counterparts of respect, trust and dignity (Fierke 2009c; Fattah and Fierke 2009; Wheeler 2009; Ruzicka and Wheeler 2010; Wolf 2011). Richard Ned Lebow (2008) has also emphasized the importance of honour.

[6] Jon Elster (1996) also explores the relationship between emotions and rationality, commenting on the failure of economists to recognize their main role as providers of pleasure, happiness, satisfaction or utility. He also examines their role in relation to social norms, which resonates with the second point.

[7] For instance, Nussbaum recounts the irretrievable sense of loss experienced at the sight of her mother's dead body, which was an expression of the value and importance she held in her life.

pre-modern expression, was to re-establish an equilibrium that had been upset. Emotion is one response to a loss of equilibrium or a loss of value. Emotions, far from being the opposite of rationality, can be understood as a rational measure of value or a response to feelings of lost value and the need to restore dignity (Fattah and Fierke 2009). Emotions are a response to things that matter.

Second, emotion, while most often experienced at the individual level, is inherently social and relational. Constructivists in the tradition of Wittgenstein have situated the self in a common world of language, in which expressions of pain or joy, or other expressions of our inner life, are radically dependent on customs, uses and institutions (Wittgenstein, 1958: para. 199). In this view, emotion finds expression only in a language and a culture, which is linked to a moral order and moral appraisal (Harre 1989). The emotions thus do not stand alone but are attached to further entailments by which various subjects, objects and acts have meaning. The experience of emotion may be individual, but, if it is expressed, it is expressed in relation to others, and in a language understandable to them, particularly if the experience is shared. In this respect, the appraisal or value judgements discussed by Nussbaum are not purely cognitive. Individuals within a culture make appraisals and value judgements that draw on cultural knowledge. When ongoing suffering or humiliation is the shared experience of a people, expressions of this pain may come to occupy a central place in the language and the practices of a culture (Fierke 2006) and thereby find expression in the world of political action.

To examine emotions as socio-cultural phenomena is to detach them from their association, in the West, with a Cartesian distinction between mind and material world. I instead approach emotions as socially meaningful expressions, which depend on shared customs, uses and institutions. The meaning of emotions cannot be separated from a relational world and a past. The central question is how experiences are given emotional meaning and how this meaning legitimizes certain forms of practice, and thereby shapes future interactions. The issue is less one of whether, for instance, the agent of humiliation intended to do harm than an analysis of meaning in use and its historical sedimentation over time. Emotions such as love, compassion, humiliation or betrayal are evident across cultures; they are given meaning in culturally specific forms, however, and in response to historically and contextually specific events.

The third characteristic of emotion builds on the latter, as well as Ahmed's claim that emotion involves movement. If emotion is ultimately a social phenomenon, it is neither purely inside the head nor purely in the social world. Our everyday language of emotion tends to assume interiority, such that individual feelings move out-ward towards objects and others (Ahmed 2004: 9). Sociologists such as Durkheim, who, by contrast, view emotion as a social form, reverse the direction, such that emotions come from without and penetrate the individual mind. Both assume the objectivity of the distinction between inside and outside, the individual and the social. Ahmed, building on Butler's work, argues that emotions create the very effect of the surfaces and boundaries that allow us to distinguish an inside and an outside in the first place. Emotions are not a property – that is, something that I or we have. Rather, the surfaces of bodies 'surface' as an effect of the impressions left by others. Emotions produce the very surfaces and boundaries by which specific kinds of objects can be delineated. In this respect, the objects of emotion 'circulate'. As they move through the circulation of objects, such objects become 'sticky' or saturated with effect, as sites of personal and social tension or contestation, as emotions are 'made'. Emotions are thus a form of world-making, which allow us to address the question of how subjects come to embody both meaning and belonging.

This brings us to the fourth point, highlighted by Bially Mattern (2011), who argues that emotion is a practice that is emergent from the complex interplay between four components – the material, social, structure and agency – such that the original components dissolve and become indistinct from each other (Bially Mattern 2011: 72). In this conception, emotions are understood as competent, socially meaningful bodily performances (76) that generate human being or human doing.

These general points about emotion relate to specific dimensions of the case studies that follow. As discussed in the last chapter, emotions related to an experience of humiliation can be a powerful impetus to resistance. The point of departure for understanding humiliation is a prior equilibrium. Within this equilibrium, all humans have identity and a degree of agency measured in self-respect, trust in their social world and thereby a sense of safety. This is an analytical assumption rather than a statement of fact, given that it is contrary to the notion that, in practice, some are constructed as less than human abject

Others. According to the Universal Declaration of Human Rights, all human beings 'are born free and equal in dignity and rights', which establishes a fundamental equivalence between them (United Nations 1948: article 1). While this category, like that of human rights, is often assumed to be a product of Western values, dignity has an important place in other cultures, and shares a family resemblance with the international meaning without being identical to it (Kamali 2002). Humiliation involves a lowering or a loss in relation to this equilibrium, and thus emotion is a rational response to a humiliating experience. Loss of sovereignty is a lowering of this kind.[8]

Emotions related to humiliation find expression in most cultures and, as the cases demonstrate, are prevalent in those where there has been an ongoing loss of value through the presence of an outside power. Having said this, the institutions, customs or uses by which these emotions are expressed are culturally specific across the cases and link to other, more positive emotions, related to respect, trust and human dignity and the possibility of their realization, while resting on different claims about the relationship between violence and non-violence in realizing human dignity and trust. Humiliation may be an important impetus to resistance, but this emotional experience is arguably displaced by the emotions that circulate around the injured or dead body, which highlight more positive emotions associated with martyrdom and the nation.

In a situation marked by past humiliation, there is a further dynamic related to the distinction between the individual emotional experience and the type of emotional expressions that are allowed by a society, which Peter Stearns and Carol Stearns (1985) call emotion and emotionology, respectively. The latter, the social element, refers generally to how the norms of different societies shape the expression of emotion and the locations in which this expression is appropriate. The emotionology of most cultural contexts arguably influences the individual experience of emotion through processes of socialization. In a society that is under the thumb of a repressive regime, however, the gap between the individual emotional experience and the range of

---

[8] As Paul Saurette (2005: 12) argues, humiliation takes place within a relationship when one party, who expects a higher status, is lowered in status and feels shame or a loss of self-respect. The association with being lowered in status or value may be one reason for the frequent association between humiliation and feminization (Dawson 1994).

emotions that are publically allowed may be far greater and the scope for the expression of emotion far more constrained. Thus, in a society, such as Communist Poland, where open criticism was repressed, economic shortages or frustrations of other kinds often erupted into an avalanche of emotion, followed by violent repression.

In a context dominated by fear, which silences and isolates, there is no public space for the expression of relevant emotions. Inner fear in this case becomes the counterpart of external conformity. Political self-sacrifice may constitute a breakthrough, in which fear is more widely abandoned as the walls that separate the private from the public begin to dissolve. The political self-sacrifice is symbolic of the transition from a world defined by fear and lacking a public space for emotion to one in which participants freely express emotions associated with autonomy, dignity and independence. Political self-sacrifice thus becomes the embodiment of overcoming fear and moving out towards new life, crossing over the ultimate fear of bodily death. The emotional dynamic circulating out from the sacrificed body is crucial to the larger societal process that may emerge in response, as the *communitas*, the anti-structure, becomes the staging ground for an alternative game. This alternative shapes the contours of a different emotionology, which moves from fear and humiliation to dignity and social dialogue. In this respect, the act of speech that flows from the dying body is a performance. The various inversions turn the everyday world upside down. The dead body communicates the possibility of new life. In speaking, it breaks through the silence and performs a rebirth of dignity.

## Memory

The power and resonance of memories of past martyrdom are reinforced in mourning the loss of the sacred subject. Memory thus provides an answer to the question, raised by Butler's analysis, of how the abject Other, defined as less than human and thus outside the dominant structure, is able to perform an act of agency. This agency is, on the one hand, defined in opposition to dominant structure, but it is performed within an alternative framework that relies on a matrix of meaning and emotion that draws on memories of past martyrs. The agent is thus involved in a repetition of an historically sedimented practice (Ahmed 2010: 247).

Suicide and martyrdom both involve harm to the body, but an act of martyrdom stirs a meaning that goes beyond the bodily violence or any kind of causal explanation to an elucidation of the symbolic meaning of the act and the emotions it evokes (Margalit 2002: 169). The stickiness of the emotions, and the meaning attached to them, are often strengthened by cultural memories of 'martyrs' or other symbols of self-sacrifice. Allen Young (1995: 221) refers to memory as 'the proof as well as the record of the self's existence, and the struggle over memory as the struggle over the self's most valued possessions'. Without a memory of the past, it is impossible to say who or what one is. The issue, particularly in politics, is rarely one of either individual or collective memory, however, but, rather, the relationship between them. As one of the early memory theorists, Halbwachs (1992 [1925]: 40) claims: 'One may say that the individual remembers by placing himself in the perspective of the group, but one may also affirm that the memory of the group realizes and manifests itself in individual memories.'

Many studies of memory assume a bounded space in which conflicting memories compete for life-and-death dominance in a zero-sum game, or a straight and fixed line between memory and identity, which excludes elements of alterity and forms of commonality with others. Michael Rothberg (2009), in a critique of these two tendencies, offers instead a concept of multidirectional memory in which memory is subject to ongoing negotiation, which involves cross-referencing and borrowing, and is productive. The past is happening in the present, and is a form of 'work, working through, labour or action' (Rothberg 2009: 3). As Alon Confino and Peter Fritzsche (2002: 5) note, 'Memory [is] a symbolic representation of the past embedded in social action'; it is a 'set of practices and interventions'. Rothberg (2009: 4) examines multidimensional memory as a series of interventions, focusing in particular on the intersection between Holocaust memory and decolonization, through which social actors bring multiple traumatic pasts into a heterogenous and changing post-World-War-II present. Rather than being a fixed competition or an articulation of established identities, memories involve a dialogical interaction with others in a malleable discursive space.

Memories, Rothberg (5) argues, are not owned by groups – nor are groups 'owned' by memories. Instead, the borders of memory and identity are 'jagged'. What appears at first to be a fixed property often turns out to have been borrowed or adapted from various histories. The anachronistic quality of memory arises from the joining together of disparate strands, which is the source of its powerful creativity and ability to build new worlds out of the material of older ones. Rothberg (5) states that 'the struggle for recognition is fundamentally unstable and subject to ongoing reversal'. Through a process of communication, shared memory integrates and calibrates the various perspectives of those who remember the past into a single version. This can be distinguished from conceptions of collective memory that are built on the aggregation of individual memory. The process of integration and negotiation is fundamental to the construction of *communitas* or anti-structure in resistance to a dominant structure. Memories that are shared are experienced by individuals, but are also mediated through networks of communication, institutions of the state or the social groupings of civil society. Multidimensional memory goes somewhat further than either collective or shared memory in recognizing the degree of displacement and contingency that marks all remembrance (15). As in the cases examined here, many decolonization struggles have revolved around a question of recognition, over whose history or culture will be recognized.[9]

Memory is not like a camera that captures or reflects reality 'as it is'. It is, rather, a product of the stories people tell about themselves and others, and therefore it involves an active process of giving meaning to the past. These stories, like narrative more generally, are populated by others who exist within a moral order of right and wrong; emotions emanate out from these stories, none of which are exclusively about the past but have implications for action in the present and future as well. In this respect, what matters are the ways in which actors produce the past through a dynamic engagement with the present (Collins 2004: 22) and produce the present through a dynamic engagement with the past. Telling stories offers insight into what Moore (2006: 187) refers to as 'the dialogue of encounter between the past and present'. Memory is a performance, and this production always takes place within a social world, and an already existing discursive universe, which necessarily shapes, limits and renders possible particular formulations as legitimate, to the exclusion of others. In the

---

[9] On the struggle for recognition, see Honneth (1995); Thompson (2006); Wolf (2011).

case of martyrdom, these stories are granted meaning in the performance. The ritual of the martyr is one performed by the agent and for those who survive after the death. A relationship is established between the *presence* of self, articulated in death, and an *absence* that remains in the memory of the living (Pitcher 1998: 28).

The official memories of the state often rely on historical narratives of the suffering 'body politic', and may invoke the agent of resistance as a past source of suffering, attaching his or her identity to 'terrorists'. Memories of resistance often act as a counter to this narrative. The martyrdom of the agent may raise questions about the official narrative, as the emotions surrounding the death circulate out from the body, reconstituting the boundaries of the 'body politic' or influencing the terms of its recognition, both within and outside, while inspiring others to muster the courage to imitate acts of resistance, potentially breaking down the boundary between outside and inside. What is competing in cases of political self-sacrifice, on the one hand, is the official memory of the state, which excludes the alternative memories of the abject Others it constructs, and, on the other hand, memories of martyrdom, which constitute the agency and political subjectivity of the 'martyr' and the community that he or she embodies.

## Audience and imitation

The terms 'audience' and 'community' have purposely been used in a somewhat fuzzy way to this point given that these boundaries become unfixed in the liminal state. There may be several different audiences, both domestic and international, to whom the injured body potentially 'speaks'. The *communitas* of the liminal state, while formed in opposition to more formalized dominant structures, has by definition a less formal identity, which fluctuates. The liminal 'body' is of a different kind from the reconstituted community that may emerge out of any process of transformation that follows. There is no necessary relationship between *communitas* and the eventual structures that may stabilize later. Indeed, one question underpinning the case studies is the extent to which the various forms of self-sacrifice are conducive to particular outcomes. *Communitas* is about resistance to a dominant structure and the construction of a liminal state rather than an expression of path-dependent process. As stated in the introduction, a 'community' that has lost its sovereignty lacks the structures by which communal identity is reproduced in a 'state'. There may be prohibitions on speaking a native language. Traditional institutions for communicating cultural or religious practices may have been suppressed, as well as forms of publicity and media. Historical archives containing memories of community may have been destroyed, along with geographical landmarks and other signposts of identity. It is less the case that someone in these circumstances lacks a sense of his or her own identity and more that the barrier of fear, which destroys social and political space, makes it both difficult and costly to express his or her identity and provides strong incentives to conform to the dominant structure. The issue is one of how members of the audience move out of the individualized and depoliticized acceptance of a status as abject Other into a social space of resistance. Individuals may be pulled between communal loyalties and the economic, political or security incentives to conform. Individuals, both inside the dominant structure and outside in the global realm, may potentially sympathize, but may also have accepted the dominant narrative without question, simply because its assumptions are part of the everyday language of the context in question. In this respect, notions of audience or community or, to use Turner's term, *communitas* are malleable rather than fixed.

Here Sen's (1990) concepts of sympathy and commitment are relevant, although in this case the concepts are less symptomatic of rational choice than the push from or pull towards a position as audience, either repulsed or sympathetic, and, in the latter case, towards identification with the *communitas* through acts that involve commitment. On the surface this appears to return to a question of the rational preference of individuals. The rational choice model cannot, however, account for the transition in three respects: first, because of its individual ontology, which Sen also questions; second, because of the importance of circulating emotions as they move out from the injured or dead body and impress on the surface of audience, thereby shaping notions of belonging; and, third, because the stickiness of emotions is dependent on social memory, which draws the audience into the performance, and constitutes the legitimacy and authority of an alternative set of rules. What is transformed in the process is the identity of individuals as they begin to participate in various ways in the alternative game, thereby substantiating the identity of *communitas*.

## A *public diplomacy of suffering*

Although the emergence of a global media culture has increased the ability of states to influence populations beyond their own border, it has also made it far more difficult to exclude alternative narratives. In this respect, the images and language games surrounding the body of sacrifice may be as important as any direct contact with its materiality. The audience does not necessarily touch the body but views the image through the medium of a third party – that is, the media – that provides an angle and narrative, attributes meaning and contributes to the expansion or contraction of the potential audience.

Lene Hansen (2011) points to several features of the image that distinguish it from the purely textual account. Images produce an immediate emotional response that is stronger than that of text. The resonance of the iconic image is all the more immediate because it links to a community's 'collective visual memory', which may evoke responses ranging from compassion to rejection (Brink 2000: 135, 138). The authenticity of the image gives it a privileged epistemic status, which both verifies that the act happened and brings the audience closer to it, perhaps including an emotionally charged iden- tification, which draws the spectator in. Reinforcing Ahmed's point that emotions circulate out from the body, Hansen notes the greater circulability of visuals over words, accentuating the significance and speed with which the former are distributed through modern media technologies, thereby reaching more audiences. Unlike the text, which speaks through a particular narrative frame, the visual images may be constituted through a larger intertext, such that different audiences, although 'seeing' the same image, may 'read' it in different ways.

While visuals may thus lend themselves to different political inter- pretations and open up a space for action, they do not make explicit policy demands (Hansen 2011: 58). The ambiguity may be all the greater for more international audiences that lack the specific cultural repertoire of the audience for which the image was produced. The image may evoke compassion or revulsion in the audience, given these different locations. As stated in Chapter 1, international audiences may have more difficulty grasping the ritual elements of the act, and therefore its meaning. This work raises a question about the extent to which different forms of political self-sacrifice are likely to evoke these contrasting reactions, given the greater cultural nuance for the domestic population, set against the larger global space, where the narrative attached to the image may be much more unsettled, yet decisive for how the contestation is resolved. As Hansen (61) states: '[T]o examine audience response is not only to look at whether there is a response but at what kind of register such responses are expected to be constituted through.'

In central and eastern Europe in 1989 and north Africa and the Middle East in 2011 a global audience witnessed the spread of revolutions from one country to another. The latter were triggered by an act of self-immolation in Tunisia, which was then repeated by individuals in other north African countries. The spread of acts of self-sacrifice, whether in the form of self-burning or as a result of official retaliation, raised a question about the nature of imitation.[10] The imitation of self-sacrifice, to whatever degree, cannot be accounted for in terms of the preferences of the individual, insofar as the desired end is less death than the independence of a community of which the individual is a part. It also cannot be understood in causal terms, insofar as the imitation represents a choice to join in the anti-structure of *communitas*, which may bring suffering. Imitation involves 'acting as if' a new game is in place. When conceptualized in this way, what is reproduced is the subordinate structure of meaning, as others in various locations also begin to engage in play. The rules are not fixed but rest on family resemblances.

Community has already been destroyed. Through the self-sacrifice, the individual body becomes the materialization of that loss. The observer is faced with 'bare life' (Agamben 1998) stripped of its social meaning, standing alone and facing his or her own mortality. The act is most powerful when the source of the bodily destruction is indisputable, arising not from the agent who refuses to conform but from the dominant power, which punishes in the hope of re-establishing its authority. The objective is to put an end to the contestation regarding the source of danger. It must be crystal clear to the audience that the horrific pain that has been visibly inflicted on the martyr is the same pain and from the same source as the pain that has been inflicted on the community in its loss of sovereignty.

---

[10] There has been very little literature on this question within the IR field. One exception, by Benjamin Goldsmith (2005), raises a question about the preferences of foreign policy actors and how they learn.

The 'act of speech' that flows from the injured or dying flesh-and-blood body communicates that 'I am sovereign, you have no power over me. You can kill me for my disobedience but you cannot take away my ability to act as a sovereign agent even if this means my death.' In saying 'I am sovereign, you have no power over me', the self and the community to which it belongs is, in one and the same movement, destroyed and reborn, the first as a martyr and the second in its connection to contemporary and past martyrs who suffered on behalf of the nation. The self-sacrifice becomes the performance by which sovereignty is enacted. Just as fear is a strong emotion in response to an existential threat, the agent, in a situation in which sovereignty has already been lost to some degree, overcomes the nation's fear, recognizing that there is no life outside a community in which he or she is a sovereign member, a participant in determining the rules by which the community lives.

## Conclusion

The process of reproducing bodies that matter is a performance insofar as it relies on a prior script, which in its repetition reproduces not only the human subject but abject Others 'outside' community, who are less than human. This raises a question as to how those who occupy the latter position might resist, given the continuous performance of dominant power, which has the effect of writing out any potential for the agency of bodies that do not 'matter'. Agency arises from a refusal to contribute to the dominant performance, which is the only autonomous act available to the non-sovereign being. The abject Other then becomes the object of bodily injury as punishment for this failure to conform, which, rather than doubling the voice of authority, potentially doubles the voice of the sacrificed body, as its materiality becomes attached to ideas of justice and a community. In the first instance, emotional power arises from an historical experience of humiliation or a lowering of value, but the sight of the injured or dying body evokes further emotions related to martyrdom and resistance that express the desire to recover dignity and sovereign value. The sight of the suffering body represents a confrontation with 'bare life' that is followed by a struggle to inscribe it with meaning, which is spectacularized by the visual nature of the performance. These emotions circulate out to an audience that must decide whether the injured or dead body is a 'martyr' or a 'criminal'. Each identity carries further entailments regarding the meaning of the death as a 'suicide' or a 'witness to injustice'. The stickiness of the emotions will be heavily influenced by memories of past martyrdom. In embracing the sacred subject, the audience may join in the liminal community and begin to act as if a new game is in place, which results in imitation, the expansion of resistance and the potential restoration of community. In the next chapter I begin the empirical exploration of these ideas, and those in the previous two theoretical chapters, by examining the 1980–1981 hunger strikes in Northern Ireland.

# PART II

# The Historical Cases

# 4 | *Hunger strikes in Northern Ireland, 1980–1981*

The last three chapters have laid the theoretical groundwork for the case studies. In Chapter 1 political self-sacrifice was presented an 'act of speech' that communicates a message of resistance to foreign interference or occupation. Chapter 2 analysed the agency of anti-structure, which involved 'acting as if' one was free in the context of a dominant structure that demands conformity. The various inversions explored in Chapter 3 translated the experience of humiliation and 'bare life' into a form of power in which the sacrificed body becomes the embodiment of community and its potential restoration, as emotions circulate out from the body to a liminal *communitas*.

Of the cases examined in the next four chapters, the Northern Irish hunger strikes of 1980–1981 most closely mirror the context of the warden's dilemma, explored in Chapter 2, given the location within a prison. The hunger strikes in the Long Kesh Prison in Belfast were the culmination of a prison protest by republican prisoners between 1976 and 1981. The protests were a response to the introduction of a policy that criminalized republican prisoners who claimed to be prisoners of war. What began as an extended campaign of non-cooperation evolved into the hunger strikes, which began in 1980 and ended in October 1981. The 'non-violent' hunger strikes involved paramilitary members who were imprisoned because they were alleged to be 'terrorists', but who gained unprecedented legitimacy for the nationalist cause through acts of self-sacrifice. While confronted with a dilemma, the British prime minister, Margaret Thatcher, refused to recognize the demands of the hunger strikers, arguing that this would represent an acknowledgement of Irish Republican Army violence outside the prison. The massive public support generated by the hunger strikes did, however, destroy the myth that the republicans had no political support.

The first section of this chapter examines the cultural meaning surrounding the hunger strike in Ireland and the political context from which the 1980–81 hunger strikes emerged. The second section explores the agency of the prisoners' campaign and the political contestation that arose from it. The third section examines the subsequent warden's dilemma faced by the Thatcher administration as the hunger strikers faced death. The conclusions analyse the implications of this episode for the peace process that developed a decade later.

## The culture of *cealachan*

Hunger strikes in Ireland can be traced back to a more ancient form of sacrifice expressed in the oral legal code of ancient Ireland, the Brehon Laws,[1] which were based on a method of 'self-help' in response to a perceived wrongdoing. As George Sweeney (1993b) notes, a grievance could either be addressed directly against a person who had caused offence (*athgabal cintaig*) or against a surrogate of the offender (*arthgabal inmeleguim*). The powerful, including tribal kings, chief druids and poets, could use either means for seeking redress. Since neither of these methods was available to the powerless of Celtic Ireland, the former (*athgabal cintaig*) was modified as fasting (*troscad*). The Brehon Laws provided a means for seeking a form of restorative justice, which included an element of sacrifice, as discussed in Chapter 1, in which the powerful could employ a substitute. For the less powerful, *self*-sacrifice was the only viable option for redressing a perceived injustice or recovering a debt from the powerful – an act that became a duty of the injured once all other avenues had been exhausted. If the faster starved to death, the wrongdoer was considered responsible and had to pay compensation to the victim's family. Given the taboos and fears of pollution surrounding death, however, which provided impetus for the powerful to settle quickly, the fast rarely ended in death (Sweeney 1993b).

In medieval Ireland, fasting had a place in the civil code, the *Senchus Mor*. *Troscad* was fasting on or against a person and *cealachan* was achieving justice by starvation. The code provided guidance for its appropriate use, either to recover a debt or to address an injustice, with the victim fasting on the doorstep of the offender. According to David Beresford (1994: 15), the moral force of fasting at this time

---

[1] The term is derived from the Gaelic *brithem*, meaning 'judge'.

arose out of the honour attached to hospitality, and thus the dishonour of someone starving outside one's house. Fasting in Ireland also had Christian roots, which began with the legends surrounding St Patrick, the patron saint of Ireland, who, according to the *Book of Armagh*,[2] ascended the Holy Mount to seek favours of God and was told by an angel that he was asking for too much. Patrick then went on a hunger and thirst strike, lasting forty-five days, after which God gave in (Beresford 1994: 15).

Starting in the twelfth century, with a wave of outside interventions, from the Norman invasions to the Plantation of Ulster, Catholicism began to fuse with nationalism. The Great Famine (1845–1852) cemented this connection. The crippling exploitation and gradual destruction of Irish culture and traditional values contributed to the cultivation of a cult of self-sacrifice, which was expressed in the interweaving of religious practice with nationalism and militant republicanism (Sweeney 1993b). In the late nineteenth and early twentieth centuries a literary revival, which encouraged learning the Irish language, traditional folklore and mythology, reinforced a sacrificial motif. The traditional folk hero was Cuchulain, whose bravery in the face of foreign invaders, as well as his self-sacrifice and death, became the subject of poems during this period. The literary themes inspired the patriotism of the 1916 Easter Rising, which led to the Anglo-Irish War and the eventual establishment of the Irish Republic. The sixteen leaders who were executed during the Easter Rising were transformed into secular saints. The self-sacrifice of the rebels became part of the collective memory of Irish Catholics, as their deaths came to be identified with the sacrifice of Christ, the ancient martyrs and heroes and the honoured dead from previous revolts (Sweeney 1993b).

Several elements from the long history of hunger strikes in Ireland formed the background against which the hunger strikes in 1980–1981 were given meaning. The Brehon Laws and *cealachan*, in particular, have been part of the mythology that surrounds the memory of the hunger strikes, but there is also some evidence that this ancient concept shaped how the hunger strikers understood

---

[2] This composite volume of great importance to the literary history of Ireland, and the life of St Patirck, is believed to have been written about AD 807 by a scribe named Ferdomnach.

their practice. A republican prisoner (quoted by Feldman 1991: 214) highlighted the connection between learning and speaking Gaelic within the prison:

With the Gaelic you began to get back in touch with the political and ideological concepts. For instance, *cealachan*, where in the Brehon laws to express a grievance against an injustice, a guy sat outside the wrongdoer's house and starved himself to death. Now *cealachan* had a whole moral import to it that it wasn't a hunger strike as a protest weapon; it was a legal assertion of your rights. The hunger strike was a legitimate and moral means for asserting those rights, and it had legal precedents dating back to antiquity.

The hunger strikes were a means of redressing an injustice. They were given meaning within an anti-structure that was expressed in the Gaelic language,[3] as distinct from the language of captivity that underpinned the institutions of penal enforcement (Feldman 1991: 216). 'Acting as if' was therefore an enactment of a more authentic Irish culture, drawing on elements of the ancient legal system associated with it.

The relationship to Christian symbolism was somewhat more complex. On the one hand, the hunger strikes did not fit easily with any notion of Christian martyrdom, or, for instance, the non-violence of Martin Luther King or Gandhi. While King is associated with a form of Christian self-sacrifice and Gandhi with hunger strikes,[4] both emphasized non-violence all the way down. By contrast, the hunger strikes were secular in orientation (Feldman 1991: 219) and grounded in the violent ideology of the IRA, which rested on a claim that 'force is by far the only means of removing the evil of the British presence in

---

[3] As McKeown (2001: 67–9) notes, speaking Irish had both a practical and a political objective. The use of a language that could not be understood by the prison authorities provided a 'secret' means of communication in very difficult circumstances, but it was also an expression of identity. It was thus both subversive and political.

[4] The Northern Irish republicans, like Gandhi, were acting in a context of British imperial power, with the objective of removing an occupying force, although employing very different means. Long before 'the Troubles', Gandhi (1951: 113) had commented negatively on the Irish campaign for independence: 'We can, if we will, refrain, in our impatience, from bending the wrong-doer to our will by physical force as Sinn Féiners are doing today, or from coercing our neighbours to follow our methods.' Both contexts also have traditions of fasting or hunger strikes (Gandhi 1951; O'Malley 1990).

Ireland' (as quoted by Coogan 1987: 685). The republican prisoners
saw their imprisonment as an extension of the war outside (McKeown
2001: 3). Precisely because of this association with violence, the stance
of the Catholic Church was equivocal at best, and the hunger strikers
criticized the Church for the lack of support. In contrast to the central
role played by John Paul II in Poland, discussed in the next chapter,
the Pope, who was asked to intervene on behalf of the prisoners,[5]
did not come to Northern Ireland.[6]

Christianity did, however, play a positive role in two respects. First,
as Bobby Sands (1981: 12) noted in his diary for 3 March 1981, 'The
boys are now saying the rosary twice every day', and some were
reading the Bible. Christianity was, in this respect, a source of spiritual
support for those who were undergoing tremendous suffering as a
result of their resistance. Second, Christian symbolism was important
for communicating the meaning of the sacrifice to a larger audience, as
reflected, for instance, in a Sinn Féin Christmas leaflet with a picture
of Christ on the cross, including the caption 'He too was a prisoner
of conscience' and an image of a blanket man next to it (English
2003: 210).[7] Popular support for the 1981 hunger strikes in both
Ireland and the larger international community was built on the
'pacificist' or 'religious' iconography that surrounded it (Feldman
1991: 220). The sacrificial deaths of the ten hunger strikers made
sense within this framework. The IRA's conclusion that the deaths
legitimized an escalation of violence did not.

The most explicit symbolic framework for giving meaning to the
hunger strikes came from the memory of IRA resistance within
the prisons going back almost a century. In the period surrounding
the 1916 Easter Rising the hunger strike began to be used as a political
weapon, with more than fifty hunger strikes in the period between
1913 and 1923 (Sweeney 1993b). Hunger strikes were undertaken by
prisoners with grievances directed against both the British government

---

[5] The invitation by Sam Millar from H-Block 5 in 1980 was written on toilet
paper and smuggled out of the prison (English 2003: 210).
[6] While he did visit the Republic of Ireland in 1979, and had planned a trip to
Armagh in Northern Ireland, it was cancelled because of the murder of Lord
Mountbatten a day beforehand, as well as the ambush resulting in the deaths of
eighteen soldiers in Warrenpoint, both of which the IRA was responsible for.
[7] Richard English (2003: 210) also refers to Bobby Sands' response to an effort by
Father Denis Faul to persuade him to stop his hunger strike, which invoked John
15:13: 'Greater love hath no man than that he lay down his life for his friends.'

from 1913 to 1922 and the Irish Free State after the Anglo-Irish War. One of the most notable uses was by the republican Thomas Ashe, who was imprisoned after the rising and who refused to work or wear prison clothing.[8] His death, as a result of force-feeding while on hunger strike (English 2006: 280), was immediately viewed as a martyrdom, and part of the heroic legacy of the 1916 rebels, whose executions transformed the political situation in Ireland (O'Malley 1990: 26). Ashe's funeral procession was attended by between 30,000 and 40,000 people and became the occasion for an outpouring of nationalist grief, which provided a rallying point for Sinn Féin (Beresford 1994: 17). In 1923 more than 8,000 political prisoners who were opposed to the 1921 Anglo-Irish Treaty went on hunger strike, and two prisoners died before the protest was called off (Sweeney 1993a). The hunger strike has been used by political prisoners in north and south on many occasions since then, with varying degrees of success, but most often as part of a strategy that was embedded in a campaign of political violence. The psychology of the hunger strike in the Irish context was summed up by Terence MacSwiney, the mayor of Cork, who starved himself to death in 1920: 'The contest is one...of endurance. It is not those who inflict the most but those who endure the most who will conquer. Those whose faith is strong will endure and in the end triumph' (Witherow 1981a). There was a tension, however, between the strategy of self-sacrifice and the more violent sentiment expressed by Frank Gallagher, another prisoner around the same time in Mountjoy Prison, Dublin, who stated: 'By smashing their prison system we become free to continue the smashing in Ireland of the Empire' (as cited by McKeown 2001: 238).

## The political context

The history of British oppression in Ireland goes back centuries. Henry II of England declared himself lord of Ireland in 1171, although English influence at the time concentrated around Dublin. Henry VIII took the title 'King of Ireland' in 1542. A century later a Catholic rebellion was brutally suppressed by Oliver Cromwell. In 1690 supporters of the deposed Catholic king James II were defeated by

---

[8] The first was in 1913 by James Connolly, whose fast ensured his quick release from prison (Witherow 1981a).

William III in the Battle of the Boyne. The seventeenth century also saw the confiscation of lands in the counties of Ulster by the English crown and their distribution to Protestant English and Scots settlers. During the eighteenth and nineteenth centuries revolutionary movements, such as Wolfe Tone's United Irishman (1796–98) and later Young Ireland (1848) and the Fenians (1866–67), fought for Irish freedom. Suffering in the Great Famine from 1845 to 1852, which was related to the exploitative policy of English landowners, reduced the population by over 2 million. The Easter Rising, an armed rebellion in 1916, was followed by the Anglo-Irish War, which ended with the partition of Ireland following the signing of a treaty in 1921. In the six northern counties, which remained a part of the United Kingdom, violent conflict between the majority Protestant and minority Roman Catholic communities broke out in 1969, which led to the establishment of a British army peacekeeping force.

The Northern Irish hunger strikes in the early 1980s took place in the context of 'the Troubles', or the increase in sectarian violence that followed the perceived failure of the civil rights movement in the late 1960s. Prior to the outbreak of the Troubles Northern Ireland had had a large degree of autonomy from the UK Westminster government, with its own parliament and government at Stormont, which was dominated by Protestants, who described themselves as 'loyalists' (committed to membership in the United Kingdom). Their majority status had been brought about with the partition of the island in 1921, leaving the Catholic population a minority in the six counties of the north. Protestant control of government was reinforced by a system of gerrymandering constituency boundaries, which ensured their dominance in the Stormont government, as well as widespread discrimination against Catholics, particularly in employment and housing. After civil rights marches began in 1968, followed by a Protestant backlash, British troops moved in, initially to protect the Catholic population, and direct rule was imposed. This coincided with the mobilization of paramilitaries on both sides of the sectarian divide, including the Ulster Defence Association and the Ulster Volunteer Force on the loyalist side, and the IRA on the republican side. Following a split within the IRA, the 'Provisional' IRA took over from the 'Officials', and the conflict turned into an ongoing confrontation between the Provisional IRA (the 'Provos') and the British government, which led to a massive deployment of manpower and resources to the province. *The Green Book,* which was an IRA manual written in the mid-1970s, claimed that the Provisional IRA were (as quoted by Coogan 1987: 679–80):

the direct representatives of the 1918 *Dail Eireann* parliament and that as such they are the legal and lawful government of the Irish people. The Irish Republican Army, as legal representatives of the Irish people, are morally justified in carrying out a campaign of resistance against foreign occupation forces and domestic collaborators.

The hunger strikes built on several developments that took place in 1972. The first was Bloody Sunday, in January 1972, when thirteen unarmed civil rights demonstrators died after being shot by British paratroopers.[9] In June 2010 David Cameron, the then British prime minister, finally acknowledged that British soldiers fired on unarmed civilians, in circumstances in which there was no serious threat to the soldiers' lives. While this is consistent with accounts given in the immediate aftermath of events on the day, the Widgery Report, produced eleven weeks later, claimed that British soldiers were shot at before they fired the shots that resulted in casualties. As English (2003: 153) notes, the Widgery Report shattered any confidence among northern Catholics that the state would treat them fairly or that UK law and authority would or could protect them. He further states that 'if people marching to protest against government policy could be killed by the state, when no serious threat to soldiers' lives existed, then (yet again in Irish history) the violence of the state forces provided a powerful argument for popular disaffection from the state itself' (151). English emphasizes that, while Bloody Sunday was a turning point, it was the culmination of a series of events in an unfolding drama, rather than decisive in and of itself. It did, however, like other examples of British violence in Ireland, generate extensive Irish nationalist sympathy, not only in Ireland but among Irish American opinion, leading to extensive financial support for Noraid.[10] After Bloody Sunday the number of people ready to support the IRA increased (Bean and Hayes 2001: 41).

---

[9] A fourteenth died several months later.

[10] Noraid, also known as the Irish Northern Aid Community, was an Irish American fundraising organization that was established in 1969 after the start of the Troubles. Often claimed to be a front organization for the IRA, the organization's mission statement claimed to support the establishment by peaceful means of a democratic thirty-two-county Ireland.

Second, Lord Diplock released a report of a commission he chaired in response to 'the escalation of terrorist activities since 1969', as well as the huge increase in the prison population in the intervening period from fewer than 500 to nearly 3,000. One cause of this increase was the policy of internment without trial, which had been introduced in August 1971, resulting in large numbers of Catholics being rounded up on suspicion of IRA involvement. In 1972 a review committee headed by Lord Diplock was set up to examine 'what arrangements for the administration of justice in Northern Ireland could be made in order to deal more effectively with terrorist organizations...otherwise than by internment by the Executive' (Diplock 1972: para. 1). Among other things, the committee recommended extending army and police power to stop and question, search and seize, arrest and detain, as well as relaxing the law on the admissibility of confessions, which made it possible to convict on the basis of confession alone. Most of the Diplock Commission's proposals were enacted by parliament in the Emergency Provisions Act 1973. Section 2(1) of the act stated that 'a trial on indictment of a scheduled offence shall be conducted by the court without a jury' (McEvoy 2001: 221–2).[11]

The third development was the hunger strike for prisoner of war status by Billy McKee, and others, in the Crumlin Jail. After thirty-seven days of fasting, and prior to any deaths, the British government granted 'special category status' to all those convicted of 'scheduled offences'.[12] In addition to granting privileges to prisoners, such as wearing their own clothing, associating with fellow prisoners, and being relieved of prison work, the officer in command (OC), as representative of the prisoners, was recognized by the prison administration and negotiated directly with the authorities (McKittrick 1980a).

[11] 'Scheduled offences' referred to a list of offences including murder, manslaughter, serious offences against the person, arson, malicious damage, riot, offences under the Firearms Act (NI) 1969 and the Explosive Substances Act 1883, robbery and aggravated burglary, intimidation, membership of proscribed organizations and collecting information that would potentially be of use to terrorists. These were activities that were usually associated with the activities of paramilitary organizations for which jury trial would be suspended (Hogan and Walker 1989).

[12] 'Special category' status was viewed by republicans as political status in all but name. As Beresford notes, whether the hunger strike actually influenced the government's decision is debatable, given that the concession was at least in part to secure a ceasefire that was being negotiated with the IRA at the time (Beresford 1994: 22).

Soon afterwards prisoners were moved to Long Kesh Prison, also known as 'the Maze', which was run like a prisoner of war camp, with inmates, whether republican or loyalist, living in dormitories in Nissen huts, and segregated according to paramilitary allegiance.

In 1976 the British government introduced a three-pronged policy of 'Ulsterization' (the scaling-down of British troop numbers in the north), normalization (granting the Royal Ulster Constabulary primacy in security matters) and criminalization. The latter meant that all prisoners convicted after 1 March 1976 would be denied special category status, and would be housed in the H-blocks in Long Kesh Prison.[13] They would be treated like normal criminals, wearing prison clothing and doing prison work. Kieran Nugent was the first republican to be imprisoned under the new rules, and the first to go 'on the blanket'. He was quickly joined by other republican prisoners, who refused to wear prison uniforms or to do prison work on the grounds that they were political prisoners rather than criminals.

The blanket protest paved the way for the 'dirty protest', and an extensive campaign of non-cooperation. Because the men were refusing to wear the prison uniform, they either had to wear their towel or go naked when going to the toilets or to wash. A request was made for a second towel, since the first towel was needed to cover them after washing. This request was refused. In protest, the men refused to leave their cells to wash, as they would be naked, which they considered 'a gross humiliation'.[14] The warden also refused a compromise offer to provide buckets for the men to 'slop out' (empty their chamber pots). As a result, the prisoners emptied the contents of their chamber pots out of their windows into the exercise yard, because they were overflowing into their cells. The prison guards responded by using high-powered hoses to flood the cells and then shovelled the human waste back into the cells in the early hours of the morning while the men were sleeping. The men then decided to smear the excreta on their cell walls to prevent the guards using it as a 'weapon' and to empty their urine into the corridor as a protest against the continued hosing. The prison guards then removed all furniture from the cells, leaving only a

[13] After the introduction of the criminalization policy Long Kesh was divided into two prisons, with the special category prisoners, convicted prior to the change in 1976, still in the Nissen huts, and a new complex for the 'criminalized' prisoners, referred to as the 'H-blocks' (Beresford 1994: 24).
[14] National Smash H-Block Committee (no date), AMNI.

foam mattress and three blankets for each man. The hunger strike was the weapon of last resort after a campaign of non-cooperation lasting more than four years, and culminating in the ultimate self-sacrifice of death, which was presented as proof that the hungers strikers were motivated by the strength of their convictions rather than self-interest. These convictions related not only to the conditions of their own imprisonment but the imprisonment of Irish Catholics in a system that turned them into second-class citizens.

## Agency and contestation

The location of the hunger strikes was a prison, and therefore very similar to the framework explored in Chapter 2. The anti-structure of non-cooperation within the prison was linked to the violent campaign of the IRA outside the prison. Anti-structure came into being as the inmates 'acted as if' they were 'prisoners of war' rather than criminals, as they were defined within the prison structure. 'Acting as if' involved a refusal to conform to the rules of the prison, which included a refusal to wear prison clothing, which was symbolic of 'criminal' status. As discussed in the first section, it also involved learning and speaking in Gaelic.

The campaign of non-cooperation was a battle over the designation of the prisoners.[15] From the perspective of the British government, the prisoners were 'criminals' like any other.[16] In the words of the then prime minister, Thatcher, there was 'no such thing as political murder, political bombing or political violence. There is only criminal murder, criminal bombing and criminal violence.'[17] All prisoners were expected to follow the same rules within the prison, accept prison discipline and conform to the prison regime,[18] and any privileges would be in reward

[15] The following narrative is based on a discourse analysis of a body of texts, from government, media and republican sources, from 1980 to 1981. The examples cited in the footnotes are representative of the larger body of texts that were drawn on in undertaking the analysis. Notes from the 1980s are listed under archival sources for Northern Ireland following the general bibliography.

[16] Holland (1980); O Duill (1981); Malone (1981); Arnlis (1981a).

[17] Iqbal (2008).

[18] Northern Ireland Office (1980); Ryder (1980); Cowley (1980); Northern Ireland Information Service (1981). In republican discourse, the administration's emphasis on conformity with the rules was replaced by 'conformity with the status of criminal'. See, for example, Republican prisoners of war (1976).

for this conformity. The position of the Thatcher government was one of an unwillingness to make concessions or bend,[19] with depiction of its position ranging from inflexible, in the more mainstream press, to intransigent, in the republican.[20] The government argued that the prison provided humane conditions, but that the prisoners willingly inflicted suffering on themselves[21] and, by their own decision, lived in conditions 'which must be offensive to all civilized people'.[22]

To the republican prisoners, and increasingly to the outside world, the apparent inflexibility of the Thatcher government rested not on a consistency of policy – as suggested by their 'principled' stand – but a basic contradiction. First, the policy hadn't been consistent, given that special category status had, at an earlier point in time, been granted. Second, although the Thatcher government claimed that the republican prisoners were criminals and should be treated like any other criminal, they had not from the beginning been convicted on the basis of legal procedures used for ordinary criminals. On the one hand, they were products of the Diplock courts, and often imprisoned on the basis of 'confessions' obtained under extreme duress,[23] resulting in the arrest and imprisonment of many who in normal times would never find themselves in jail.[24] On the other hand, they lived in the same building with prisoners who had been arrested prior to the change of policy and who still enjoyed special category status. These contradictions magnified their claims to be POWs, who should have some control over their own lives within the prison and some role in negotiations regarding the rules governing them, as well as representation in these negotiations by the OC.[25]

---

[19] Northern Ireland Office (1980); McCartan (1980); Thomas (1981); *An Phoblacht/Republican News* (1981a); Cowley (1981).

[20] Holland (1980); Hunger strike (1981); Ryder (1980); Cowley (1980); Arnlis (1981a); Thomas (1981); McKittrick (1980a). The European Commission of Human Rights also labelled the government's position 'inflexible'.

[21] McCartan (1980).      [22] Northern Ireland Office (1980).

[23] Malone (1981). As Kieran McEvoy notes, the courtroom became a site of struggle between the authorities and prisoners. The harsh interrogation methods were products of the Diplock system and became 'a powerful point of symbolic reference in asserting the political nature of the process that incarcerated them' (McEvoy 2001: 221).

[24] National H-Block/Armagh Committee (1981).

[25] McKittrick (1980b). The possibility of managing their own affairs is in opposition to government claims that it 'will not surrender control'; Cowley (1981).

The struggle was not only about the prison and the refusal to conform to specific practices within it. The day-to-day practice of wearing prison clothing and the regulation of bodily functions were symbolic of consent to the authority and rules of what was claimed to be an illegitimate occupying power.[26] The unwillingness to consent was also a response to inhumane treatment, including constant and unprovoked beatings, the restriction of food, hosing down, humiliating mirror searches, and practices that were often referred to as 'torture'.[27] In this respect, the discourse of political war and the right to be treated as POWs[28] merged into a more extreme structure of meaning, in which the prison became a 'concentration camp'.[29] An earlier letter (1976), from the republican POWS from H-blocks 3, 4 and 5,[30] included this formulation, stating that the inhumanity of the H-block was

comparable only with that perpetrated on the Jews at such hells as Dachau, Treblinka, Belsen and so on… Our only crime and the crime of the oppressed nationalist people is that we uphold the deeply rooted desire for national independence. Our crime in the H-block is that we refuse to be depoliticized or forsake our political conscious for that of a common criminal.[31]

The logical extension of the concentration camp analogy – and the allegations of torture – was that the British government was committing a crime against humanity in its treatment of the prisoners. Here a close identification is made between the criminalization of the prisoners and the criminalization of the nationalist population.[32] The

[26] Moloney (1980: 27). The notion of an occupying power links to claims of imperialism. See, for example, Hunger strike (1980).
[27] The torture claim was backed up by the European Commission of Human Rights; see Fallon (1981). See also Devlin (no date); O Duill (1981); Malone (1981); Arnlis (1981a). There are also references to 'evidence of torture' in Commonwealth of Massachusetts (1981).
[28] National Smash H-Block Committee (no date); address to Charter 80 (no date); Moloney (1980).
[29] National H-Block/Armagh Committee (1981).
[30] Republican prisoners of war (1976).
[31] The language of prison camp was more prominent in later and more public documents. The depiction in Steve McQueen's film, and the various accounts of prison life, primarily based on correspondence from the prisoners (see, for instance, Beresford 1994; O'Rawe 2005; Walker 2006), suggest that the violence directed at the prisoners was brutal.
[32] See, for instance, Whale (1980); Malone (1981).

prisoners were a symbol of Northern Ireland's imprisonment, and their non-cooperation with the prison regime was inseparable from the struggle for Irish national self-determination.[33] Some have asked why the prisoners would put their lives on the line for something as insignificant as the clothes they wore in prison. The answer is that the meaning of the demand was far greater than the clothing or the prison – it was about the identity and autonomy of the political subject, which is inseparable from the political sub-jectivity of the people of Northern Ireland. Sands captured this connection:

I am a political prisoner, a freedom fighter. Like the lark, I, too, have fought for my freedom, not only in captivity, where I now languish, but also on the outside, where my country is held captive.[34]

The 'blanket men' were re-enacting the experience of domination that characterized Britain's historical relation with Ireland (Feldman 1991: 227), while reconstructing the Irish language and culture. The site of struggle was the body, from the no wash protest, to the dirty protest, to the hunger strike, and down to the inspection of prisoners' orifices.[35] The prison is a site for the regulation of bodies, not for political engagement. The prison separates deviant elements from society for their rehabilitation. The authorities wanted the prisoners to conform to the prison rules, and rewards and punishments were extended in response to compliance or non-compliance. As the pris-oners refused to cooperate they were faced with a progressive increase in the suffering and vulnerability to which the body was exposed, from the absence of clothing, to being surrounded by their own excrement, to the ultimate sacrifice of last resort: their lives. After four and a half years of the dirty protest, with the blanket men living in increasingly degrading and inhumane conditions, a number of prisoners decided in October 1980 to begin a hunger strike.

The meaning of the hunger strikes became a subject of political contestation, as the naked starving bodies of the prisoners were politi-cized. The Roman Catholic bishops in Northern Ireland referred to the hunger strike as a 'peculiarly deliberate form of suicide', and

---

[33] *An Phoblacht/Republican News* (1981c, 1981f).    [34] Witherow (1981a).

[35] Feldman (1991). The latter was a response to the practice of smuggling messages written on cigarette paper, referred to as 'comms', out of the prison in bodily orifices.

consequently 'gravely wrong in all circumstances'[36]; at the same time, there was some acknowledgement, from Catholic bishop Edward Daly, that they were fuelled by a memory of past injustice.[37] On the one hand, opponents highlighted the fact that the hunger strikes were closely linked to the 'cruel and inhuman campaign of violence by the Provos' and 'stage-managed' as part of the IRA 'propaganda machine'.[38] On the other hand, the hunger strikes gave rise to large street demonstrations, reminiscent of the civil rights campaign in the early 1970s.[39] The willingness to lay down their lives was presented as proof of the strength of their political convictions and the selflessness and justness of their cause,[40] and as the latest phase in the 800-year struggle by the Irish people to rid their country of imperialism, exploitation and oppression,[41] which, along with the 'loud voice of the Irish people and world opinion, would bring the British government to their senses'.[42]

The first hunger strike was called off shortly before one of the hunger strikers was to die and just before Christmas, based on an agreement with the British government, which, the prisoners believed, included a promise that they would be allowed to wear their own civilian clothes. Instead, they were given prison-issue civilian clothing, a move that was interpreted as 'reneging' on the promises of the December agreement,[43] and a further betrayal by the Thatcher government. This was followed by a decision, led by the officer in command, Sands, to initiate another hunger strike, which began on 1 March 1981, the anniversary of the 1972 hunger strike that had led to the granting of special category status.[44] A press release from the protesting prisoners, to the National H-Block Committee office in Dublin,[45] outlined the rationale:

We genuinely and sincerely attempted to end the deadlock in the H-blocks and though we realised very early after the ending of the last hunger strike

---

[36] Whale (1980). See also Parry (1981).  [37] Whale (1980).
[38] Whale (1980); Beake (1980).
[39] Holland (1980); Department of Social Studies (1980).
[40] *An Phoblacht/Republican News* (1981a); *An Phoblacht/Republican News* (1981b); Arnlis (1981a).
[41] Malone (1981).  [42] *An Phoblacht/Republican News* (1981a).
[43] O Duill (1981 ); Zimbabwe H-Block/Armagh Committee (1981).
[44] Hunger strike (1981).
[45] As cited in Zimbabwe H-Block/Armagh Committee (1981).

that the British were reneging, we felt duty-bound to explore all avenues in attempting to find peace in prison. All our efforts were ruined by British intransigence and it is because we have no other choice that we again state that the hunger strike in the H-blocks will go ahead on Sunday as planned and that it will be launched initially be Republican P.O.W. Bobby Sands.

Despite opposition from republicans 'outside', the second hunger strike went ahead. The real breakthrough came with the sudden death of Frank McGuire, the MP for Fermanagh and South Tyrone, a heavily Catholic constituency. The strategy of putting Sands forward for this seat was recognized as risky, and the consequences of defeat great (McCrory 2006). Defeat would only reinforce Thatcher's argument that the IRA was a bunch of murderous thugs who had no support.[46] The nomination of Sands went ahead but, despite this initial show of support, it could by no means be assumed that Sands would be elected (*Irish Times* 2001). First, the abhorrence of the Catholic community for violence after ten years of the Troubles raised a question as to whether they would be willing to cross over sectarian lines to vote for the loyalist candidate rather than an IRA candidate.[47] The issue became less one of party policies or personality than of political violence, with a vote for Sands presented as a vote for terror and chaos, according to the loyalists, and a vote for the loyalist as a vote for institutional violence, according to Sands.[48] Second, the nationalist SDLP (Social Democratic and Labour Party) encouraged the Catholic electorate to abstain from voting because it was angry that it had been landed with a member of the Provisional IRA, to which the party was vehemently opposed.[49] Third, while Sands was not prohibited from standing as a prisoner, due to an earlier precedent, his election was confronted with all kinds of obstacles.[50] Despite these obstacles, the turnout for the elections was a massive 86.8 per cent. Sands was

---

[46] *Irish Times* (2001).     [47] Beresford (1981a).
[48] Beresford (1981a).     [49] Beresford (1981a).
[50] These ranged from the refusal of access of press, radio and television journalists to Sands, to the lack of support from the SDLP, the main nationalist party, the harassment of Sands' campaign workers by the Royal Ulster Constabulary, the Ulster Defence Regiment and the British army, and intimidating suggestions by unionist politicians (which were taken up by the media) that Catholics seen voting by their Protestant neighbours would be marked down as IRA supporters, thus escalating their vulnerability to loyalist paramilitaries. Arnlis (1981b, 1981c); *An Phoblacht/Republican News* (1981e).

elected with 30,492 votes, almost 10,000 more than Thatcher had received from her constituency when she was elected in 1979.

The media claimed that the election was a propaganda victory for the republicans. They also acknowledged that the elections demonstrated massive support and sympathy on the part of the nationalist population, which destroyed the core mythology of the government's propaganda campaign, that the republicans had no support. The *Irish Independent* claimed that the victory gave the 'Provos something denied them throughout the last decade: an electoral mandate'. *The Guardian* stated that the vote destroyed the myth that 'the IRA in its violent phases represents only a tiny minority of the population'. *The Times* said that it could no longer be assumed that the demand for political status, 'and the means they [the IRA] choose for enforcing it, do not engage the emotions of the greater part of the nationalist community in Ulster'.[51] This message was reiterated by the republicans themselves, who in their Easter statement, on 28 March 1981, which linked the hunger strikes to the Easter Rising in 1916,[52] claimed that the election of Sands had shown the British government that the people supported the prisoners.[53]

The election of a POW MP by a massive vote in a peaceful and democratic election became the basis for an IRA argument that violence works. In the general election of 1918, following the Easter Rising, the British government had shown that it was not prepared to recognize the will of the people, 'even when that will is expressed peacefully and democratically'. From this it followed that armed struggle was the only other option, an option that was 'tried and trusted in Ireland' and by other peoples throughout the world. The Easter statement claimed: 'Only through armed struggle will we be listened to.'[54] Given the efforts to prevent Sands from taking up his

---

[51] The various newspapers are quoted by Sean Delaney (1981).

[52] This symbolically powerful link between the two dates is recurring. Martin McGuinness, for instance, speaking on 17 May 1987 (published in *An Phoblacht* on 28 May) said: 'Not since the declaration of arms in the Irish Republic on the steps of Dublin's GPO in 1916 has any event in modern Irish history stirred the minds and hearts of the Irish people to such an extent as the hunger strike of 1981.' Jim McVeigh, the chairman of the commemoration committee for the hunger strikes, also said that, for many republicans, the 1981 hungers strikes were 'our 1916' (Morrison 2006).

[53] *An Phoblacht/Republican News* (1981d).

[54] *An Phoblacht/Republican News* (1981d); Arnlis (1981d).

seat, there may have been some logic to this argument, and indeed it was taken seriously by the authorities, such as the Secretary of State for Northern Ireland, Humphrey Atkins, who warned that the IRA was ready to launch a terror offensive if Sands died, and warned the population of savage reprisals.[55] The close connection between the struggle of the prisoners and the armed struggle of the IRA was there all along, even though the hunger strikes did not always have the strong support of the IRA leadership, and this connection linked to earlier memories.

One can question, however, whether the 'Irish people' were voting for renewed violence or expressing sympathy for men who were prepared to lay down their lives for the sake of a united Ireland. As English (2006: 378) notes, many of those who voted for Sands didn't support IRA violence, but they did support the demand of the prisoners to be recognized as political agents rather than criminals. The prisoners' campaign of non-cooperation, and the intransigence of the British government exposed by it, had given rise to a 'rekindling of the burning sense of injustice that sparked the civil rights movement' and threatened to 'arouse post-internment and post-Bloody Sunday sentiments of grief, sorrow and anger, if the will of the Irish people on the prison is ignored'.[56] The Irish MEP Neil Blaney further warned of the potential 'detriment to the British image abroad, particularly now that Sands was an MP, if this man is allowed to die'.[57] By contrast, protestants in Northern Ireland tended to view Sands as nothing more than a convicted terrorist who, 'unlike many victims of the IRA attacks, had a choice of life and death'.[58]

## The warden's dilemma

Following the elections, the hunger strikes became worldwide news. Sands had become an elected MP with undeniable backing. Thatcher was suddenly under pressure to compromise, but instead her government set out to change the law to stop prisoners standing for parliament. Sands appealed to people of influence 'with a conscience' to recognize that it was not he who was the problem, but Britain's failed

[55] Breig, Erskine and Scott (1981); Campbell (1981). See also Witherow (1981a).
[56] *An Phoblacht/Republican News* (1981g).
[57] *An Phoblacht/Republican News* (1981g).   [58] Witherow (1981a).

policy of branding Irish political prisoners as criminals that left the government 'scurrying for legal principles to unseat a dying man', which would 'shame' the government in the eyes of the world.[59] The Massachusetts House of Representatives passed a resolution that was sent to US president Ronald Reagan, urging him to request that the British government recognize the POW MP, referring to Sands as a 'political dissident' who had been sentenced to prison by a juryless court within a system that encouraged inhumane treatment in an 'occupied Ireland'.[60] The logic of this expression of support was not one of justifying armed struggle but, rather, that the electorate of Fermanagh and South Tyrone was 'entitled to representation of its legitimate interests rather than martyrdom of its chosen man of conscience'. The resolution further stated that, in embracing Sands, the nationalist movement had subscribed to the democratic process, as everyone urged it to do, and demonstrated that a considerable portion of the population supported its demand.

The Massachusetts House criticized the British House of Commons for trying to expel Sands, in order to place him, once again, outside politics. At the same time, Sinn Féin/IRA held to a politics of abstentionism, refusing to acknowledge the political structures of an occupying power, and using the hunger strikes as an argument for a reinvigorated armed struggle. Neither side could fully grasp the potential or the significance of this landslide democratic victory, nor see it as a path forward to a more peaceful future. Instead, each accused the other of being engaged in a propaganda war.

Sands died in May 1981 after sixty-six days without food. When the House of Commons was told by George Thomas 'I regret to inform you of the death of Robert Sands, esquire, the member for Fermanagh and South Tyrone', the ripples spread around the world. There were protest marches across the United States and Europe. The US Longshoremen's Union boycotted British ships and the queen was snubbed in Norway. The Indian parliament in New Delhi observed a minute's silence. Some 100,000 mourners turned up for his funeral.

The death of Bobby Sands and other hunger strikers communicated a powerful message to a larger audience, both in Ireland and abroad.[61]

---

[59] Arnlis (1981c); Beresford (1981b).     [60] Howe (1981).
[61] Gerry Adams (1996) said that the death of Bobby Sands had a greater international impact than any other event in Ireland in his lifetime.

While Thatcher was cheered by some, particularly loyalists at home, for having held fast and praised for her fortitude in the face of the hunger strikers, she was also widely damned for her intransigence and inflexibility, for appearing hard and unfeeling, starkly illuminating the government's 'moral bankruptcy and the colossal and criminal incompetence of Conservative governments of all times in their dealings with Ireland'.[62] Most of the world's papers carried leading articles on Sands and the Irish question.[63] Worldwide judgements on the death of Sands also questioned whether he was a criminal or a martyr.[64] In many places he was revered as a martyr. As Danny Morrison (2006: 17) notes, Sands' name was raised by people as diverse as a prisoner facing death in the Philippines, a Palestine Liberation Organization teenager on the streets of west Beirut and a Russian at the grave of Ezra Pound in Venice. African National Congress prisoners on Robben Island, when planning a hunger strike, used the expression of 'doing a Sands'. In Iran a street near the British embassy was named Bobby Sands Street.[65] In Ireland each local hunger striker was 'immortalized on the lips of old and young alike, and a fierce pride in the memory of each man and the detail of each man's life is passed down through the generations'.[66] Thatcher, on the other hand, became a hate figure 'of Cromwellian proportions' after the hunger strikes ended – a hate figure who had inadvertently injected life into the Irish republican struggle (English 2003: 207). Figure 4.1 summarizes this shift in meaning.

After the election an attempt was made to prevent Sands from occupying the seat, and there was a continuing unwillingness to acknowledge any kind of concessions to the prisoners. After Sands' death, the British government was shamed worldwide for its policies in Northern Ireland, appearing heartless in allowing a Westminster MP to die in prison. There were significant questions in the domestic and international press about who the criminal was at this point, and whether the United Kingdom was breaking its own laws in Northern Ireland.[67] The problem remained the same as it had been from the beginning, however: any concession to the political status of the

---

[62] *Times* (1981). See also Fallon (1981).     [63] Thomas and Witherow (1981).
[64] Thomas and Witherow (1981); Fallon (1981).
[65] Ellsworth-Jones and Ryder (1981).
[66] In addition to Sands, nine others died in the 1981 hunger strikes.
[67] *Times* (1981); Fallon (1981).

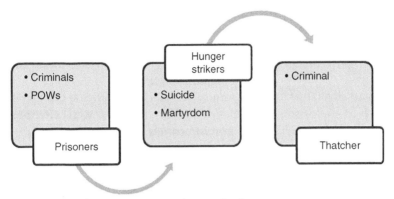

**Figure 4.1** Shifting games in Northern Ireland

prisoners constituted an acknowledgement of IRA violence. As Thatcher said, the government could never concede political status because it would be a licence to kill innocent men, women and children.[68] In this respect, precisely because the hunger strikers were connected to the violent campaign of the IRA, the government was constrained in how it could respond to them, even following their deaths, and not least because of the outrage that could be predicted from the Protestant majority in Northern Ireland.[69]

The strategy of non-cooperation within the prison was at odds with the IRA's strategy of violence outside, although consistent with republican tradition. This tension was at the heart of the dilemma faced by the Thatcher administration. Though constrained by the violent reputation of the IRA, it also failed, in this challenge to its authority, to leave itself and the other party some room for man oeuvre.[70] The perception that it was not dispensing justice with an even hand, or tempering the values of laws with understanding,

---

[68] *Times* (1981).

[69] Documents obtained by *The Sunday Times* under the Freedom of Information Act revealed that in July 1981, after four men had died, and a fifth was about to die, Thatcher did enter into secret negotiations with the IRA, offering concessions to end the hunger strike. The government said prisoners would be allowed to 'wear their own clothes…provided these clothes were approved by the prison authorities'. Although the opening for negotiations was a conciliatory statement from two IRA men in the prison, the IRA Council rejected it, after which five more men died (Clark 2009).

[70] Witherow (1981b).

sympathy or mercy for the humanity of the strikers, placed it in a position of appearing to many to be the criminal.

## Self-sacrifice and violence

The narrative above was constructed around the changing categories by which the prisoners' bodies, and their demands, were inscribed with meaning. The Thatcher government claimed that the republican prisoners were murderous thugs and criminals, who had no support within the nationalist community and who, like any other criminal, had to conform to prison rules and accept their criminal status. The republican prisoners claimed they were POWs engaged in a legitimate war against an occupying power, which was attempting to criminalize not only them but the nationalist population as well. The experience of the nationalist community historically, like that of the prisoners, was one of humiliation. The prison campaign sought to expose the attempt to criminalize, normalize and rehabilitate the political prisoner as a system of degradation and abuse. As Allen Feldman (1991: 236) states, 'The performance of the hunger strike would stage the abuse and violence of the Other in the eviscerated flesh of the dying protester.' While the starving body absorbed the power of the state, its sacralization with death transferred this power from the state to the republican community.

The prisoners sought to be recognized as political subjects capable of negotiation over the conditions in which they lived. As the hunger strikes progressed, and with the deaths of Sands and others, the discourse shifted. Questions were raised about whether the Thatcher administration was criminal. For many, the hunger strikers were transformed into martyrs whose acts of self-sacrifice were proof that they were acting not out of self-interest but political conviction for a just cause, and with undeniable support, both at home and abroad.

Inside the prison, the 'POWs' engaged in a strategy of non-cooperation; outside, the IRA escalated its violent strategy following the hunger strikes, despite the unprecedented political momentum that had developed behind the republican cause as a result. As David McKittrick (1981) notes:

There is, of course, a paradox at the centre of all this success for the Provisionals. It is this: the gains they have won have not come through their traditional method, violence. They have come through an election won by the very opposite of a Provo campaign, a campaign based on an appeal to save life; and they have come through the self-sacrifice of one of their men. They have achieved more with these methods than they did by blowing up Mountbatten. Because this is so, the question is whether a resort to the gun would reverse some of the gains they have made.

The bombing of the Grand Hotel in Brighton in 1984 was referred to by Danny Morrison as 'the hunger strike coming home to roost for Mrs Thatcher' (*Times* 2001). Patrick Magee, one of the bombers, has suggested that this was a turning point, at which Thatcher realized that 'these guys aren't going to go away', which thereby opened a space for talks (English 2003: 248). Whatever the case, it took several years of bitter violence on both sides before there was another opening. The hunger strikes had mobilized unprecedented support and political momentum within the Catholic community. The people of Fermanagh and South Tyrone had entrusted their political representation to a POW MP. Thus, while the prisoners demanded, but did not receive, political recognition from the government, the hunger strikes did result in political recognition of a kind. First, the hunger strikes destroyed the myth that the republicans didn't have any support and highlighted the political nature of their cause, calling into question the categorization of the hunger strikers as 'criminals'. As one Provisional IRA prisoner stated (quoted by Feldman 1991: 258):

What are they dying for? The Brits have been telling people for years that we were political maniacs, that we had no political understanding and that we were not going anywhere. People were beginning to say, 'They can't be criminals; criminals don't die on hunger strike. Criminals don't live five years on protest.'

Second, the tremendous success in the elections also made it difficult for the strict abstentionists within the IRA to argue against the development of a political strand within the movement.[71] The existence of Sinn Féin as a distinct body, in theory if not always in practice, was a

---

[71] The position of the IRA had been that it would have no involvement in constitutional politics outside a thirty-two-county sovereign and democratic Ireland. After the hunger strikes, on 31 October 1981, Danny Morrison, speaking at the party convention in Dublin, reassured people that Sinn Féin's involvement in electoral politics wouldn't dilute the republican commitment to the use of force, at which point he famously coined the 'Armalite and ballot box' strategy (English 2003: 224–5).

necessary precondition for the later push, precipitated by the war weariness of all sides, to find a peaceful path forward.

## Conclusion

Northern Ireland is the by-product of the partition of Ireland in 1921, which followed on a war of independence from Britain and a civil war over the status of the north of the island. Even though most Britons and unionists in Northern Ireland would not consider the province to be 'occupied', nationalists and republicans were more likely to refer to 'the occupied six counties' or 'the North', and the end goal for the latter is a united Ireland. The Catholics in Northern Ireland, like other subjects in this book, represent the other side of international relations – that is, those peoples who have been the victims of balance-of-power politics and imperialism or otherwise 'fallen through the cracks'.

The hunger strikers in the 'occupied' north of Ireland 'acted as if' they were POWs within a structure that defined them as criminals and terrorists. Agency was expressed in a refusal to cooperate with the dominant rules of the game, and acting as if a different game was in place. This agency brought punishment from the authorities, which led to greater suffering for the prisoners. The crucial act that transformed the relationship from humiliation to political agency was the refusal to double the voice of the regime. If acknowledgement is the condition for the removal of pain, along with acknowledgement that humiliation has taken place, the withdrawal of consent logically entails an acceptance of continuing pain and an unwillingness to acknowledge the superior power. The willingness of the agents to accept suffering without hitting back increased the perception that the official inflexibility was disproportionate. The prisoners refused to conform even to death.

At stake was the question of whose voice would be heard: whether the humiliated, through an act of acknowledgement, substantiate the voice of the powerful or whether they assert their own voice through an act of resistance, which is potentially doubled if it is understood as a martyrdom. The act of resistance is part of a struggle over the meaning to be inscribed on the subject's body – that is, whether they are deviants, who are depoliticized and delegitimized, or political agents engaged in legitimate resistance. It is the meaning attached to the martyred body that is significant and the extent to which it 'speaks' to the injustice of the community, not the self-interest of the agent. The meaning of the strikes went beyond the demands of the prisoners. The hunger strikers viewed the individual as a symbol of the collective condition of the Irish nation. As Feldman (1991: 241) notes, the hunger striker 'would sacrifice his individuality at the same time that he committed the most individual of acts'. Sands and the other hunger strikers in Northern Ireland made the decision to undertake a hunger strike, a strategy that would culminate in death if not reversed, and that resulted in questions about whether the hunger strikers were committing suicide, an immoral act in Catholicism, or were martyrs who had sacrificed their life on behalf of a united Ireland.[72] The 'stickiness' of the emotions was a function of the meanings this act evoked, based on memories of martyrdom within Ireland. With their deaths, the contestation shifted from the identity of the agent of political self-sacrifice to a question about the criminality of the Thatcher regime.

The powers that be first granted concessions, then reneged on the agreement, which was followed by a clampdown. This pattern is also evident in the Polish case that follows. Punishment was inflicted and resulted in greater suffering for the agents, which culminated in the death of 'martyrs'. At this point the contestation over the meaning of the dead and dying bodies expanded into a global space, and the warden was confronted with a dilemma as to whether to continue with the status quo, and lose further legitimacy, or to engage in dialogue, which would represent an acknowledgement of the political subjectivity of the opposition. Although the Thatcher administration faced a dilemma, its room for manoeuvre was shaped by the degree to which either party came to be identified as the principle agent of violence. The extent to which the deaths of 'martyrs' could be attributed to the regime, as opposed to the hunger strikers themselves, was crucial. The violent strategy of the IRA outside the prison, and the prisoners' decision to abstain from food, both contributed to contestation over the death as 'suicide' or 'martyrdom', and ongoing contestation regarding the designation of the criminal.

As Sands and other hunger strikers began to die, and were named as martyrs, Thatcher was accused by many of being a criminal, breaking the United Kingdom's own laws in Northern Ireland. She said that she

---

[72] The fact that the hunger strikers did, in the end, receive a Christian burial, and became a central theme in the mythology of republicanism, suggests how this tension was resolved within the Catholic community of Northern Ireland.

couldn't make concessions to the hunger strikers because this would condone republican violence outside the prison. There was a clear tension between the logic of self-sacrifice, as expressed by Terence MacSwiney – that is, those who endure the most, rather than inflict the most, will conquer – and the IRA claim that independence would come only through violence, but the two were nonetheless linked in historical memory. The authorities assumed the deaths would lead to renewed IRA violence, and the IRA used the inflexibility of Thatcher towards the hunger strikers as an argument for an escalation of violence. The huge political momentum generated by the hunger strikes did, however, give rise to discussions about the need to expand the political and electoral role of Sinn Féin, without abandoning the violence – that is, the Armalite and ballot box strategy – which established a foundation for the political dialogue that emerged a decade later, when the context was ripe for a change with the end of the Cold War.

The hunger strikes constituted not only the political identity of the hunger strikers but the possibility of political subjectivity for the larger republican movement through Sinn Féin, which provided a crucial foundation for the peace process. The key question is why we should think of this context as in any way constitutive of 'international' relations. First, the problem is an expression of the underside of international relations – that is, of a people who understood their second-class status to be a function of an occupying power, arising out of an historical experience of imperialism. Second, the audience was not purely domestic, as reverberations were felt across the globe, from Irish Americans in the United States to resistance fighters and populations in other post-colonial societies. Third, the 'terrorists' were embedded in a broader international network. These later became links between 'partners in peace', as, with the end of the Cold War, agents from Belfast to the Middle East to South Africa imitated the superpower dialogue that had contributed to ending the global logic that had defined these more local conflicts. Finally, the Anglo-Irish Agreement of 1985,[73]

---

[73] The agreement set up an intergovernmental conference through which London and Dublin would address a wide range of matters in relation to the north, and thereby gave the Republic of Ireland an ongoing, consultative role in the affairs of Northern Ireland.

which came in the aftermath of the hunger strikes, was the first step in building cross-national institutions between the United Kingdom and Ireland, and provided the foundation for further framework documents and eventually the Belfast Agreement. In short, while the 'north' of Ireland remains formally within the United Kingdom, the hunger strikes planted a seed that eventually contributed to the possibility of moving beyond conflict.

# 5 | *Martyrdom in Poland, 1984*

On 19 October 1984 Father Jerzy Popiełuszko, 'Solidarity's priest', was kidnapped. His gagged body was dredged from the river Vistula reservoir near Włocławek eleven days later. His funeral, on 3 November 1984, was attended by hundreds of thousands of people and he was declared a martyr worldwide. Following his death four agents of the secret service were subjected to what was, in the communist Eastern bloc, an unprecedented public trial. They were convicted in February 1985 but later acquitted after controversial sentence revisions. At the time, the official line of the regime headed by General Wojciech Jaruzelski was that the kidnapping and death were a political provocation by communist hardliners who were opposed to its conciliatory policies after the lifting of martial law (Luxmoore 2010). To this day it is not clear how high up the orders went or what exactly happened between Popiełuszko's abduction and the recovery of his body.[1] The purpose of this chapter is to situate the martyrdom of Father Popiełuszko in the context of Solidarity's non-violent resistance to the Polish regime. I examine the cultural and religious framework that informed the resistance, the dilemma faced by the Polish regime as Popiełuszko, gaining all the time in popular support, continued to speak freely in the context of martial law, and the impact of his death.

One of the biggest challenges to sustaining a non-violent campaign is persuading large numbers of people to remain non-violent even in the face of government retaliation. The moment of violence, or the aftermath of bitterness, can involve an emotional, even traumatic, element that can start and/or reproduce a cycle of vengeance. The Northern Irish experience after Bloody Sunday in 1972 is a case in point. After peaceful protesters were shot down by government forces, the civil rights movement collapsed and support for the IRA

---

[1] For a recent account of the continuing controversy surrounding Popiełuszko's death, see Litka (2010).

increased. This raises an important question as to how Polish Solidarity's campaign in the early 1980s managed to remain non-violent.

One obvious answer, given Poland's position on the front line of the Cold War, would be that the threat of intervention by the Soviet Union had a disciplining influence.[2] Indeed, the fear of a Soviet military invasion had been one of the impediments to building resistance. Memories of Budapest in 1956 and Prague in 1968 left many people believing that Soviet leaders would not allow any kind of change. As Michnik (1985) argues, however, the issue was more complicated. While the threat of Soviet intervention was real, neither the Soviets nor the Polish leadership nor the democratic opposition had an interest in this outcome. The Soviets did consider invasion, even in the absence of violent resistance by the Poles, but were advised against it.[3] The problem of whether the Soviets would potentially invade is a somewhat different issue, however, from how the resistance, once it had developed, maintained a non-violent stance over several years in the face of government brutality.

The Northern Irish case revolved around a tension between a non-violent strategy of hunger strikes within the prison and the violent campaign of the IRA outside. The primary contrast within Poland in the late 1970s was between a history of violent resistance to occupation and the central role of 'talk' in translating the symbols of this past into non-violent action and struggle. Talk was the primary means by which calm and discipline were maintained. The compatibility and convergence of various types of talk were crucial to overcoming previous divisions between intellectuals, workers and the Church, providing the foundations for solidarity and dialogue in a broader sense. The various forms of 'talk', which I explore in what follows, were informed by historical memories of resistance and martyrdom. Christian metaphors already had a deep emotional resonance and provided a structure of meaning for a particular kind of agency. This

---

[2] Jaruzelski used the threat of Soviet invasion to justify the imposition of martial law in Poland on 13 December 1981.

[3] Stanisław Kania, Jaruzelski's predecessor as prime minister, argued it wasn't necessary, and, given that the Soviet plan, detailed by Colonel Kukliński, would have included summary court martial and liquidation of the Solidarity leadership, the Poles wouldn't have tolerated what would have been interpreted as a second Katyń massacre. The stronger reaction of the United States to the 1979 Soviet invasion of Afghanistan also suggested that an invasion of Poland could have greater consequences than the Soviet invasion of Czechoslovakia had had (Wiegel 2005: 405).

agency involved 'acting as if' it was possible to live with dignity (Beyer 2007: 210) in a context in which the foundations of everyday life were built on lies and humiliation (Tischner 1984: 24; Davies 2001: 62).

The first section explores the meaning of resistance and martyrdom in Catholic Poland and the political and symbolic context from which Solidarity emerged. The second examines the conflict between structure and anti-structure and the political contestation that arose from Solidarity's agency and the government crackdown with martial law. The third section examines the warden's dilemma faced by the government headed by General Wojciech Jaruzelski after the murder of Popiełuszko and the role of the latter's martyrdom in the construction of an independent Polish *communitas*, which provided the foundation for independence and Soviet withdrawal by the end of the decade.

## Culture of resistance and martyrdom

The meaning of martyrdom in the Polish context was shaped by a long history of foreign intervention and violent attempts to resist it. The nineteenth century's balance-of-power politics in Europe, which often left Poland victim to its neighbours Germany, Austria and Russia, was also the age of insurrection in Poland, which further corresponded with the heyday of Polish Romanticism (Davies 2001: 148).[4] Polish Romanticism emerged from a fascination with folklore, historical tradition, medieval legend, the supernatural and the cult of freedom, like other forms of European Romanticism, but added a specifically Polish notion of Catholic piety (Davies 2001: 148).

Polish Romanticism rested on a number of key ideas. First, history was understood to have a spiritual core. Second, Poland's political collapse was due to the deterioration of its traditional national virtues. Third, re-establishing Polish independence required recovering those virtues as the foundation of a new Polish state (Wiegel 2005: 33). Perhaps the purest expression of Romanticism grew out of centuries of

---

[4] Interestingly, the three towering figures of Polish Romanticism, Adam Mickiewicz (1798–1855), Julian Słowacki (1809–1849) and Zygmunt Krasinki (1812–1859) – all came from what is today Lithuania, and were familiar with Western versions of Romanticism, and Lord Byron in particular (since they all travelled to Paris, one of the main destinations of the so-called Wielka Emigracja, or Polish Great Emigration, of the nineteenth century; the main trigger of the emigration was the failure of the November Uprising in 1830).

living a double existence, which combined a minimal degree of political conformity, in order to stay out of prison, with secret Polishness. As expressed by Norman Davies (2001: 172): 'Their bodies were captive, but their spirits were free. Poland was a prisoner, but its soul was unbound.' Adam Mickiewicz provided the guidebook to this spiritual journey with his *Books of the Polish Nation and Pilgrimage* (1833), in which he states:

[T]he Polish nation alone did not bow down... And Poland said, 'Whosoever will come to me shall be free and equal for I am FREEDOM.' But the Kings, when they heard it, were frightened in their hearts, and they crucified the Polish nation, and laid it in its grave, crying out, 'We have slain and buried Freedom.' But they cried out foolishly... For the Polish Nation did not die. Its Body lieth in the grave; but its spirit has descended into the abyss, that is into the private lives of people who suffer slavery in their own country... For on the Third Day, the Soul shall return again to the Body; and the Nation shall arise, and free all the people of Europe from slavery.

The poetry of Michiewicz was learned by every Polish school child. For him, the passion for Polish independence was expressed in the tension between the rationalist pride of the Enlightenment and the humility required by faith (Wiegel 2005: 33). As George Wiegel (1992: 140) notes, John Paul II returned frequently to this literary tradition for allusions, references and images, but, in the process, married Polish Romanticism to non-violence as the only morally acceptable form of resistance. The message was rechannelled such that, in refusing to be victims, Poles also refused to be executioners. Polish Romanticism acknowledged Catholicism as the yeast that had given rise to Poland's distinctive national character (Wiegel 2005: 33), and the symbolism of martyrdom was central to this.

## Talking non-violence

A refusal to ingest food was the action that directly led to the martyrdom of Sands and others in the context of the Northern Irish hunger strikes. While death may not have been the desired end, it was a predictable one. Although talk, no less than eating, is a basic human activity, its link to the potential for injury or death is less direct, and more a by-product of resistance. The issue in post-World-War-II Poland was the coexistence of two types of talk, the one relying on memories of the Polish nation, Church and martyrdom, and the other based on Marxism-Leninism, which had been imposed on Polish society. In the 1980s Michnik (1981: 70–1) asked:

What do I mean when I say that the Poles allowed themselves to have a language imposed upon them after 1945? One example is the attitude toward the German question. The role of Stalin in the annexation of territories and in the victory over the Germans was only mentioned positively. To do so was to accept a language that was compromised. One was free to say many things of Stalin – whether it was true or false was irrelevant – as long as the rhetoric was positive. To be sure, those who played this game (journalists, for example) understood full well that it was a game with rules. Their readers, however, were not always so well informed. Due to the long habit of covering Stalin's real face with a mask, the mask seemed more real than reality.

The idea that the Poles allowed themselves to have a language imposed, suggests that their own language was pushed to the background. It is not that they were forced to speak Russian instead of Polish but, rather, that the boundaries of what could and couldn't be said were redrawn, and, in the process, narratives of Polish history, memory and other cultural markers were situated outside these boundaries. Michnik's point is that these language games did not necessarily involve lies, although they might; rather, playing the game involved knowing the rules and what could and could not be said in relation to any particular subject. While the distinction between truth and lies had a central place in the discourse of Polish Solidarity, the relationship was more complex.[5]

Everyday notions of lying presume a distinction between what an individual is thinking or knows to be true and what he or she is saying. The distinction between truth and lies in this case is not purely individual, however. In suggesting that a language was 'imposed', Michnik points to the possibility of two different language games giving meaning to the same phenomenon. To refer to these as games suggests a system of meaning within which one could manoeuvre in a variety of ways and, as he says, which imposed boundaries on what

---

[5] Wittgenstein (1958: para. 249) claims that lying is a language game like any other. To lie effectively involves following rules. For instance, the lie may have to be repeated in future contexts so that one's deception is not exposed, and, in this respect, must be replicable. The effective lie also invokes a range of shared meanings that will appear truthful even though they are not.

could and could not be said within its rules. The language of Marxism-Leninism, imposed after 1945, established one set of manoeuvres and boundaries, within which certain types of truth claims could be made but which was often at odds with a different game, which had a much deeper historical resonance in Poland.

These two language games relied on distinct conceptions of the 'self', which were elaborated by Józef Tischner (1984, 1987), Solidarity's chaplain and philosopher. In the conception of self that was imposed by the regime, human beings were primarily material and their value was linked to the process of socio-economic production. This conception was marked by a struggle of opposites, which led to suspicion and division. The crucial problem of life thus became truth and falsehood and the need to pretend. Everyone was constantly hiding and afraid, and unable to leave his or her hiding place. The result was isolation, which made resistance and rebellion impossible while making exploitation and humiliation possible. A lie is a sickness of speech just as exploitation is a sickness of work.

In the Christian conception, by contrast, the core is a human essence, with a spiritual element that makes ethics possible. Life and work are, for Tischner, a conversation and a dialogue in which humans through exchange, whether with words or raw materials, construct meaningful relationships or objects, respectively. Living in truth and speaking in truth require authenticity and social trust. Dialogue requires coming out of the hiding place and recognizing that the other is always to some extent right and that truth can never be known in isolation, only by engaging with the other. One had to convince the adversary rather than coerce him or her, and dialogue was to be the central objective – even with those who had been a source of betrayal. Dialogue held out the hope that the latter would look at themselves in the mirror, see themselves as they were and undergo a transformation.

While there is a clear 'othering' in the distinction between truth and lies, the other was defined less in terms of a particular identity than by the willingness to engage in a particular kind of human practice. The philosophy of Tischner was not an abstract body of work. The central concepts of authenticity, truth-telling, fidelity, dialogue and sacrifice were part of the daily language of Solidarity activists. For many, heroism was one of the key ingredients of the Polish ethic of solidarity, which in extremis could demand martyrdom, but more often rested on a willingness to fight for justice in the various arenas of society, from the workplace to the political sphere, even at the expense of one's self-interest (Beyer 2007: 210).

The communist regime attempted to create a new set of habits, which were imposed on most activities of daily life. After thirty-five years of communist rule, and a second post-war generation, some of these new language games would have become more or less habitual. The unspoken subtext, which sustained an otherwise vacuous discourse, was the threat of Soviet intervention (Kołakowski 1971: 46). The other language game, informed by the thousand-year history of the Polish nation, and the central role of the Church within this, revolved around the spiritual essence of the human being (Tischner 1987). This alternative gave meaning to the resistance and suffering of Poles under communism, drawing on historical symbols of martyrdom and biblical metaphors. Convincing people of the need to remain non-violent meant persuading them to accept suffering as a part of resistance without hitting back in response to government brutality.

The potential of this situation was articulated by the Czech playwright Václav Havel (1985 [1978]: 27–8), in his story of the greengrocer. For years the greengrocer, without thinking, had hung a sign in his window that stated 'Workers of the world, unite!', a familiar communist slogan. The hanging of the sign had become a habit, and he did not stop to think about whether he believed the slogan or not. At the point at which he did think about it, however, he would become dangerous. In questioning the necessity of reproducing this slogan, he was recognizing it as a game with rules that could be broken. This feature of 'talk' was the core of the non-violent campaign that emerged after the visit of the Pope in 1979. As one Catholic priest stated, Solidarity's campaign was about 'giving people back their memory', such that an older language of the Polish Church and nation could come to the foreground, as Poles began to 'act as if' an alternative game were possible.[6]

Given that 'divide and rule' is a common strategy of governments, dialogue had to begin at home in order to give a stronger opponent an incentive to engage. What distinguished the Solidarity movement from past efforts to bring about reform was the joining together of forces

---

[6] As stated by Father Jancarz of Kolbe church, Nowa Huta, as cited by Wiegel (1992: 151).

within society that had previously been divided. The construction of Solidarity between intellectuals, workers and the Church was essential to any kind of underlying solidarity in confronting the regime.[7] A distinction between truth and lies was at the heart of Solidarity's philosophy and self-understanding. To lie was to reproduce the imposed language, while to live in truth was to 'act as if' Poland were free.

## The political context

There are at least two types of analysis, coming from very different quarters in the late 1970s, that defined the terrain upon which Solidarity's non-violent battle was fought later. The first came from intellectuals who looked back at past reform efforts and concluded that any real change had to come from civil society, rather than elites, given their propensity for either co-optation or removal from power. Michnik (1985: 136) argued that the earlier Revisionists and Neo-Positivists had sought change from above, from an evolution in the Polish United Workers' Party (PUWP; Polish: Oświadczenia KC PZPR). Although these movements had failed to bring change at that level, they had played a role, on the positive side, in developing a basis for independent participation in society. According to Michnik, the choice between reform and revolution, the dilemma of nineteenth-century leftist movements, wasn't the issue for Poland. The opposition instead needed an evolutionary path that sought to expand civil liberties and human rights from below, demonstrating that real concessions could be won only by applying steady public pressure on the government. Jacek Kuroń (1979: 12–13), leader of the Workers' Defence Committee (KOR), the first countrywide, grassroots civic self-help organization in Poland to unite intellectuals, students and workers, spoke more directly to the threat of an explosion of popular anger, 'larger than the combined force of June 1956,[8]

[7] In his famous and controversial essay, published in 1977, Adam Michnik reviewed the history of opposition in Poland and argued that its weakness had been a function of the division between the Church and Marxist intellectuals who fought for democratic socialism in the 1950s and 1960s (Ascherson 1981: 141).

[8] In Poznań in 1956 workers went on strike over wage, food and working conditions and marched on Stalin Square. The demonstrators turned violent, after being stonewalled by bureaucrats. They attacked a nearby prison, released the prisoners and commandeered firearms. The authorities responded with tanks. In what followed, hundreds were injured and as many as seventy were killed. The authorities managed to suppress the rebellion but their authority was badly shaken.

December 1970,[9] June 1976,[10] and March 1968',[11] arising out of economic crisis and a continuing assault by the government on the country's standard of living, which was at the time evoking sharp opposition within society. He proposed a programme for social self-organization – that is, for the organization of Polish society into independent social movements with institutions, such as the Committee of Peasant Self-Defence, free trade unions, and student committees of solidarity, as the only way to realize the aims of the opposition and the aspirations of people. In order to limit the potential for an explosion, self-organization had to be constructed far more slowly than the growth in social anger.

For social self-organization to be effective, people, on the one hand, had to overcome their fear of involvement; on the other hand, once involved, destructive emotions had to be kept at bay. In this respect, the role of the Catholic Church was crucial (Michnik 1985: 145), starting with the visit of the Polish Pope, John Paul II, to Poland in 1979. By that year it was clear that Poland was in a deep and permanent economic crisis, with widespread shortages of basic food-stuffs and progressive rationing. The work of KOR and other groups was a seed from which a large-scale organized opposition grew. John Paul II's visit to Poland provided this potential with 'an impulse,

---

[9] In 1970 a growing economic crisis provoked price increases in food just before Christmas, and workers in the Lenin Shipyards in Gdańsk declared a strike. The next day, Bloody Tuesday, the unrest escalated and culminated in the burning of the city's PUWP headquarters and the spread of strikes to Gdynia and Szczecin, The result was a state of siege throughout the country and the resignation of Władysław Gomułka, the party leader. The events resulted in forty-five deaths and 1,165 injuries.

[10] In 1976, following food price increases of around 60 per cent, a wave of sit-down strikes swept across the country, particularly in the Ursus truck plant, outside Warsaw, and Radom, the site of a major armaments plant, where the party headquarters was torched. There were fewer casualties than in 1956 or 1970.

[11] In January 1968 the Warsaw authorities closed down a production of Mickiewicz's play *Dziady*, which led to student demonstrations and the arrest of Michnik, which was followed by further demonstrations at the University of Warsaw in protest at the arrest. Police were brought in to quell the disturbances, which led to eight hours of unrest. Student protests spread throughout Poland. Six Jewish professors were dismissed from their jobs at the University of Warsaw, which was followed by demonstrations demanding their reinstatement. The university responded by closing eight departments and announcing that their 1,300 students would have to apply for readmission.

a focus, a unifying symbol, and a language to articulate the accumulating disaffections and aspirations' (Ornatowski 2009: 110). The Pope chose to deliver his sermons in places of great historical significance, often invoking the names of important religious and historical figures (Zagacki 2001: 691). The talk of the Pope shaped the context, or the structure of meaning within which Polish Solidarity formulated its own actions and responses to the regime, with the organization's emergence a year later. As Kenneth Zagacki (2001: 690) notes, the sermons were significant in three ways. First, as already mentioned, the sermons translated the Polish romantic tradition into a message of non-violence. Second, the Pope gave meaning to the day-to-day suffering of Poles and the suffering or death that arose from resistance. In the process, he constructed a link between the past suffering of the Polish nation and present actions. Through the use of Christ and past martyrs as symbols, the Pope clarified the sacrifices that would be necessary for non-violent protest (Zagacki 2001: 702). Third, he transformed the fear of the Polish people into courage and hope. The scriptural theme for the 1979 visit was the words of Christ, 'Do not be afraid', and the leitmotif was renewal, expressed in the Pope's call 'Let your spirit descend and renew this land' (John Paul II 1979: 30), which became the most famous quote of the visit, and galvanized the demoralized nation. These three features were framed in terms of a distinction between a secular sphere, characterized as unjust and temporary, and a permanent Christian tradition, which spanned a thousand years of Polish history.

The day after John Paul II was installed as Pope he indicated a desire to go back to Poland for the 900th anniversary of St Stanisław (Wiegel 1992: 96). St Stanisław, who was martyred in 1079 at the hands of King Bolesław, was the symbolic embodiment of the idea – so central to Polish identity – that resistance to government oppression is the essence of the Church (Wiegel 1992: 99). His name is also associated with the birth of the Polish nation out of this resistance. The Pope's decision to visit on this anniversary, and the way in which he drew on the memory of St Stanisław, marked out the distinction between two communities. On the one hand, the Polish nation had survived for a thousand years, much of it marked by partition and other forms of outside interference. On the other hand, the brief history of an occupying power, whose presence is more inferred than directly mentioned, was contrasted with the much longer history of the Polish nation (John Paul II 1979).

The symbol of martyrdom extending back to St Stanisław provided the framework for articulating the suffering of Poles, both at the time of the visit and historically. Far from a defeat, Pope John Paul II named death through martyrdom to be a living victory, like that of Christ. In his homily at Auschwitz in 1979, he juxtaposed the experience of Auschwitz with the experience of Poland, which lost some 6 million lives during World War II. The lack of independence and the violation of human rights in Poland, past and present, like Auschwitz, was presented as a 'painful reckoning with the conscience of mankind' (John Paul II 1979: 126). These themes of martyrdom, victory over death, and crucifixion were brought together in a further biblical metaphor, of the seed that has to die in order to bear mature fruit, containing a logic in which the suffering of Poles, far from being a defeat, would bring not only the resurrection of an independent nation but would have redemptive value for the entire world (Wiegel 1992: 99). In his homily at Victory Square, John Paul II (1979) presented Stanisław as the first mature fruit of the millennium of Poland's baptism, while linking the seed to many other martyrs, from the soldier who shed blood on the battlefield to the sacrifice of martyrdom in concentration camps or prisons, or the daily toll in the fields, mines or factories. The suffering of the nation in all its historical forms was presented as the suffering of Christ. The body of the Polish nation was bound up in the body of Christ, and the martyrs who imitated him. The Polish nation was 'crucified', like Christ. According to Wiegel (1992: 130), the nine days in June 1979 that John Paul II spent in Poland, delivering some thirty-two sermons,[12] were the beginning of the end of the Yalta system,[12] the source of a moral and spiritual earthquake in which Poles were able to confront the 'fear and acquiescence' that kept society in the grip of power. It was at this point that millions of Poles decided it was time to live 'as if' they were free (Wiegel 1992: 134). Father Tischner, Solidarity's chaplain, said of the social compact that formed in Poland in June 1979 that 'people said to themselves and to each other

[12] The 'Yalta system' refers to the post-war reorganization of Europe discussed at the conference held at Yalta between 4 and 11 February 1945 by US president Franklin Roosevelt, UK prime minister Winston Churchill and Soviet premier Joseph Stalin. Although the discussions focused on the re-establishment of European nations, after the war they came to be seen as the basis for the division of Europe during the Cold War.

"Let's stop lying"'. This 'we' and 'they' were further clarified: 'we' would try to 'live in truth'; 'they' would continue to live within the lie (as cited by Wiegel 1992: 136). As Jan Kubik (1994: 146) notes, 'The society was offered a possibility to rehearse an alternative social order founded on a set of values different from those propagated by the party.' The Pope 'redefined the rules of the social game in the country' (Kubik 1994: 135).

The Pope was not speaking in a vacuum. The groundwork had been laid a decade earlier by Cardinal Stefan Wyszyński, who, in 1966, the year of the Great Novena, the 1,000th anniversary of the Polish nation,[13] had brought the painting of the Black Madonna of Częstochowa, seen as the protector of Polish sovereignty,[14] to villages and households across the country. In a context in which the socialist state had for decades tried to inculcate the spirit of socialist humanism and marginalize the Church, Wyszyński's Novena was like lighting a candle in the dark.[15] As a result, the Pope's words fell on ground that had been well prepared, and this

---

[13] The Novena was a programme that spread over nine years, which was unprecedented in the history of modern Christianity. Every year from 1957 to 1966 was devoted to one great theme that corresponded with the general goal of the Novena, which was national and religious renewal (Kubik 1994: 111).

[14] According to myth, the painting had throughout history been moved from place to place according to the shrinking or expanding boundaries of the state. On one occasion the Madonna appeared to the Polish king in a dream, in which he was ordered to place the icon on Jasna Góra (Bright Mountain) in the town of Częstochowa in Silesia (1382), where a Pauline monastery was built later. The monastery was attacked by Hussites in 1430, during which the painting was struck twice with a sable, after which the perpetrator immediately died. As others tried to run away with the painting on a mule cart, the mule refused to move beyond the monastery grounds, and a freshwater spring appeared at the place where it was found. The scars on the Madonna's face remained after the damaged painting was restored as a symbol of persecution and suffering and came to represent survival and ultimate victory over invaders. There are numerous myths about other miracles associated with the painting that mark the most traumatic periods when the state was under siege (Jakubowska 1990: 11–12). The Black Madonna pin, which has a black stripe across it, represents mourning, and became a symbol of resistance against communist rule, worn by people in Warsaw. Wałęsa wears the Black Madonna pin (without the black strip across it) to this day.

[15] Wyszyński was likened to the interrex of Poland, between 1572 and 1795, when Roman Catholic primates became acting heads of state between the death of a Polish king and the election of his successor by the Polish nobility. He acted as a substitute for the absent authority of the country's political rulers between 1948 and 1978 (Wiegel 1992: 107).

subsequently influenced the non-violent stance taken by Solidarity a year later. The presence of the Church during Solidarity's campaign was pervasive. Masses were held daily at the shipyards and other places of work.

## Agency and contestation

In December 1979, some six months after the Pope's visit, a group in Gdańsk called the Free Trade Union of the Coast organized a rally to commemorate the 1970 strikes. The strikes had involved several thousand workers outside the Lenin Shipyards, many of whom were arrested. At the Elektromontaż Works about twenty-five workers who had taken part were fired, and a commission, including the electrician Lech Wałęsa, was set up to fight for their reinstatement. The tensions between government and opposition groups continued to heat up in early 1980, and escalated after July, when the government introduced a new price system for meat and meat products. There were no demonstrations or riots; rather, work began to stop spontaneously in major plants across the country, establishing a pattern that would be followed for the next six weeks. Workers left their machines, and a strike committee was formed to press for a wage rise to compensate. The government, hoping to avoid a repetition of 1970 and 1976, ordered factory managers to concede (Ascherson 1981: 130). By the end of the month stoppages had affected every region of Poland, with the exception of the Silesian coal basin.

With official news of the stoppages suppressed initially, KOR set itself up as an information exchange, and by early August it had also become an active contact bureau linking the factories, thus providing the foundation for a coordinated movement. At dawn on 14 August 1980 the morning shift at the Lenin Shipyards refused to start work, after which Wałęsa was hoisted over the steel fence and took charge. The entire shipyard declared an occupation strike and presented a first list of demands. On 15 August workers at the Gdańsk and Gdynia shipyards joined the strike. On 31 August, after weeks of negotiations, the Gdańsk Agreement was signed, which, among its twenty-one points, included the need for new unions 'which would be an authentic representation of the working class' (Ascherson 1981: 173).

The government reneged on the agreement and in December 1981 imposed martial law,[16] at which point Solidarity's leaders were criminalized and either arrested or driven underground. In the run-up to the declaration of martial law, the language of criminalization was pervasive in newspaper accounts throughout the Eastern bloc, securitizing Solidarity as an existential threat to Poland. For instance, in the months prior to the imposition of martial law, the Communist Party of the Soviet Union (CPSU 1981) wrote the following:

The enemies of socialist Poland are making no special effort to hide their intentions; they are waging a struggle for power, and are already seizing it. One position after another is falling under their control. The counterrevolution is using the extremist wing of Solidarity as its strike force, employing deception to draw the workers who have joined this trade union association into a criminal conspiracy against the people's power... The extremely serious danger that hangs over socialism in Poland is also a threat to the very existence of the independent state.

Similar language was used in a PUWP Central Committee (1981) resolution, which stated that 'implementation of the party and government's policy is still being disrupted by forces hostile to socialism. They are conducting political campaigns that threaten the stabilization of the state, its security and sovereignty. The goal of these forces is to seize power and overthrow socialism.'

Despite the imposition of martial law, Solidarity vowed to continue its struggle, although there were significant debates about strategy under these changed conditions and significant problems of organization (see Kuroń, Bujak and Kulerski 1982), given the criminal status of the organizers and restrictions on movement and communication.[17]

---

[16] Although the government did enter into an agreement with Solidarity, and was obsessed with the appearance of legality and juridical process, it used legal manoeuvres and obfuscations to try to derail the movement. When Wałęsa returned to the Warsaw Provincial Court on 24 October, the judge, Zdzisław Kościelniak, announced that Solidarity was legally registered but he had inserted a clause into the agreement that recognized the PUWP's leading role in society, the socialist system and Poland's international alliances. The 8 million members of Solidarity were angered by this manoeuvre and Wałęsa denounced the insertions, saying the movement would never accept changes that had been arbitrarily imposed on statutes that had been adopted through a democratic process (Wiegel 2005: 404).

[17] The criminalization of Solidarity activists by the Polish regime was reinforced by metaphors of war or terrorism, even though Solidarity activists never resorted to arms. Solidarity also relied on metaphors of war to refer to its own

At this point, the choice would appear to be to do nothing or to engage in violent underground resistance, as happened in Poland during World War II. The response of Polish Solidarity was neither of these. It was, rather, to continue under martial law to 'be what you want to become'. The framework was not one of resistance or active opposition in the form of protests or other forms of direct action – and, indeed, this had arguably never been the case when Solidarity was above ground. 'Acting as if' was about the reconstruction of 'civil society' through culture as a means of economic and political change. As Wiegel (2005: 529) notes, information was a key to this resistance, which gave the Church an important role as a 'sanctuary of truth telling in a world dominated by lies'. Solidarity was, first and foremost, trying to organize an independent trade union in the context of a workers' state on the principle that 'if you want to have free speech, speak freely; if you want to have a trade union, found a trade union' (Weschler 1982: 56).

This particular form of 'acting as if' – that is, organizing an independent trade union – was constrained under martial law. 'Acting as if' relates to every aspect of daily life, however, and it continued in others, and not least within the Church. The Church was the only institution in Polish society that had an independent status that was recognized by the Polish state. Historically, the Church had engaged in negotiations with the authorities. The archbishop following Wyszyński, Cardinal Józef Glemp, was keen to maximize this dialogue and minimize the perception that the Church was actively opposing the regime. However, at the parish level many priests were much more outspoken.

The priest who came to be perceived by the regime as the greatest threat was Father Jerzy Popiełuszko of St Stanisław church in Warsaw, who was later murdered by the secret services. At the time of his murder, in 1984, the international press presented him as an outspoken champion of Solidarity and a political activist, as well as a 'martyr'.[18] Father Popiełuszko, while still alive, presented his own acts within

actions, which were juxtaposed with the actual use of the weapons of war by the regime, such as the following. 'Solidarity's weapons are calm, dignity and good organization, its strength is the solidarity of all working people in Poland and a general strike is our response to this act of violence' (*Labour Focus on Eastern Europe* 1982). 'Leaders in hiding were considering a national warning strike. Solidarity must fight for democracy' (Bujak 1982). 'All Poles fight for dignity. The Polish nation demonstrated abilities of self defence. Architects of the state of war are enemies of our freedom and sovereignty' (Solidarity 1982).

[18] See, for example, Pick (1984b); *Newsweek* (1984).

a very different framework, which is more consistent with references by his parishioners to his quiet, almost monotone, style of communicating and the calming effect of his words.[19] Popiełuszko claimed that he was not a political activist but a priest tending to his 'flock' in extraordinary circumstances.[20] Many of his flock were imprisoned for activities in support of Solidarity, or had lost loved ones at the hands of the state or suffered the daily humiliation of life under martial law. What made Popiełuszko more dangerous than other, more firebrand, priests was the large number of people he attracted to his monthly Mass for the fatherland at St Stanisław church in Warsaw (Murphy 1985),[21] with crowds numbering in the tens of thousands and fanning out across the surrounding churchyard and park. These sermons became the primary venue, not only for keeping the spirit of Solidarity alive but for expanding social solidarity under martial law.

The Masses for the fatherland also provided a framework for under-standing how to go on with life under martial law, and the daily choices faced by Poles in these restricted and dangerous circumstances. While preaching a Christian sermon is not usually a political act, in the context of communist Poland carrying out the normal duties of a priest *became* political by virtue of the challenge it presented to the prevailing moral order of socialist humanism. The sermons were significant not just because they kept the message of solidarity alive; they were also significant for framing the response of parishioners to their painful and humiliating circumstances. Letters from parishioners to Father Popiełuszko repeatedly speak of coming to St Stanisław church filled with hatred and a desire for revenge, and the calming effect of his words.[22] Much as the Pope had, earlier, translated the more violent history of Polish Romanticism into a Christian message of non-violence, Popiełuszko's sermons, and the Masses for the fatherland as a whole, had the effect of transforming people's hatred and desire for vengeance into a non-violent framework for understanding the suffering and humiliation they experienced.

As the volume of sermons is rather substantial, spanning several years, I highlight just a few of the structuring elements that cut across

---

[19] See Popiełuszko (2004).     [20] Popiełuszko (1984).

[21] An anonymous secret service person in Bydgoszcz said that he was dangerous because the crowds listened to him and because he was intelligent and calm. He said further that they weren't afraid of the priests, who were playing up because they were hardly heard by anyone (Herold 2004).

[22] Popiełuszko (2004): 1982: 591; 592; 593–4; 594; see also Bogucki (1984b).

the sermons, linking these back to themes raised by the Pope. The first, which is also evident in the context of the Northern Irish hunger strikes, points to the widespread experience of humiliation and the desire to restore dignity.[23] Restoring dignity is associated with keeping the Polish nation alive by Poles 'acting as if' they were free.

A second related move was to frame the experience of humiliation or death not as a defeat but as a victory,[24] by juxtaposing it with the suffering and sacrifice of past Polish martyrs. These past memories of martyrdom, going back to General Romuald Traugutt during the 1863 insurrection,[25] the time of partition from 1795 to 1918,[26] Maximilian Kolbe in Auschwitz and the 1944 Warsaw Uprising[27] to Poznań in 1956, Gdańsk and Gdynia in 1970[28] and Ursus and Radom in 1976,[29] form the deep roots of the martyred Polish nation,[30] which extend back a thousand years.[31] During this thousand-year period the 'crucified nation' had the protection of Mary[32] – a reference to the Black Madonna of Częstochowa, which evokes an image of Poland the nation as the child being held and protected by the Madonna.

These references to martyrdom and protection were important for giving meaning to the suffering and/or death of those who were at the time imprisoned or murdered at the hands of the state, and also for giving meaning to everyday actions, when any individual could be faced with a choice of how to act or how to respond under conditions of martial law. Here the conflict between two structures of meaning becomes crucial: between conforming to the language games of the regime, and thereby 'living a lie', or acting as if one lived in a free Poland, namely 'living in truth', and potentially suffering the consequences of efforts by the state apparatus to impose conformity.[33] The 'cost' or 'price' of the sacrifice that often accompanies freedom and 'living in truth' was contrasted with the price of betrayal of one's

---

[23]  Popiełuszko (1986): November 1983; January 1984; March 1984.
[24]  Popiełuszko (1986): November 1983.
[25]  Popiełuszko (1986): January 1984.
[26]  Popiełuszko (1986): November 1983.
[27]  Popiełuszko (1986): November 1983.
[28]  Popiełuszko (1986): November 1983; August 1984.
[29]  Popiełuszko (1986): November 1983.
[30]  Popiełuszko (1986): August 1984.
[31]  Popiełuszko (1986): November 1983; May 1984; June 1984.
[32]  Popiełuszko (1986): August 1984.
[33]  Popiełuszko (1986): September 1983; December 1983; May 1984.

dignity or truth.[34] This represented a call to make a choice for dignity over slavery, recognizing the costs of either choice. Freedom and dignity are an inner condition, while slavery is external. The distinction between dignity and slavery thus becomes one between the choice to be an agent, despite the costs, as distinct from being constrained by official expectations, and therefore a slave to the system.[35]

One further message of significance is the metaphor of the seed that falls into the ground and has to die before it bears fruit,[36] which appears repeatedly in the sermons of both the Pope and Father Popiełuszko. It is a metaphor that connects to the symbol of the crucifixion, in which death is not the end but is followed by the 'resurrection' of genuine freedom, justice and peace.[37] Resurrection also became a central metaphor of Popiełuszko's death. As his Masses for the fatherland attracted larger and larger crowds, he become more of a thorn in the side of the regime, and secret service agents would also frequent the Masses, waiting outside and looking for any hint of evidence that Popiełuszko was whipping the crowds into a political frenzy. Although the sermons in fact had the opposite effect, the official Soviet press, in the years following martial law, depicted the more outspoken Catholic priests in a manner similar to the earlier depiction of Solidarity activists.[38] In the case of Popiełuszko, the Polish authorities went further, planting actual weapons and subversive literature in his apartment and then arresting him.[39]

---

[34] Popiełuszko (1986): November 1983; January 1984; March 1984.
[35] Popiełuszko (1986): January 1984.
[36] Popiełuszko (1986): March 1984; May 1984.
[37] Popiełuszko (1986): March 1984.
[38] On 26 August 1984 the Soviet newspaper *Izvestia* demanded that Popiełuszko be silenced (Fox 1985: 18), on 9 September Popiełuszko was mentioned by name and condemned for his sermons and his hatred of socialism (Boyes and Moody 1986: 127) and on 12 September the paper accused Popiełuszko of close collaboration with 'counter-revolutionaries' (Fox 1985: 18). The depiction of priests included serving up 'poison and slander', 'displaying a defiant contempt of the legal order in People's Poland' and the use of military metaphors such as 'expanding sphere of influence', 'interfering in foreign policy', 'taking the offensive', 'spoiling for a fight', 'engaging in psychological warfare', 'operating under camouflage', 'conducting undercover operations', 'subversive activity' and 'veiled methods of combat' – all of which present the Church as an existential threat to the state. See, for instance, Yermolovich (1984a, 1984b).
[39] Popiełuszko's sermon during the Mass directly following his arrest (December 1983) was presented in italics, as an extensive direct quote by John Paul II. He ends in his own voice, referring to the information that had been leaked regarding the search of his apartment, claiming his own inability to

## The warden's dilemma

Popiełuszko had become dangerous because he was speaking 'the truth', and in the process arousing too much support from the population. The official press had tried to make him out to be a terrorist, but, when this didn't work, someone in the secret service adopted the logic that is often used in relation to terrorists: eliminate them and the problem will disappear. On 19 October 1984 Popiełuszko did disappear – but not the problem. There were different hypotheses about the reason for the kidnapping and who was behind it. The risk in eliminating someone with such a strong following is that he becomes a martyr, thereby increasing support for the cause. Both the Jaruzelski regime and the Soviets would have wanted to avoid this eventuality, given the potential for widespread unrest not only in Poland but the Eastern bloc as a whole. From this perspective, claims that the idea originated with a right-wing faction within the government that wanted to destabilize Jaruzelski are plausible.[40]

Whatever the actual motive behind the kidnapping, following the discovery of Popiełuszko's body the Jaruzelski regime immediately distanced itself from the murder,[41] attributing it to a few bad apples

'tell it like it is' but nonetheless attempting to inform the faithful that the allegations were untrue and that he viewed them as a provocation.

[40] Bratkowski, a friend of Popiełuszko, argued that the killing of the priest was portrayed as an act of aggression against those in power. The death of Popiełuszko was supposed to cause social unrest, a big social or mass revolution. The government of Jaruzelski wouldn't react strongly enough, which would result in a change of government, putting more of a strongman in power. The script takes into account Soviet interests insofar as the conflict in Poland following Popiełuszko's death would justify 'help' from the 'brotherly' nation (Russia) in calming the situation. The West in turn would see the Soviet Union's actions as justified because of the unrest and violence. This reflects the probable thinking of those in the Polish government who didn't agree with Jaruzelski and wanted a harsher line (Litka 2009: 83–6). This line of argument suggests that those responsible for the murder hadn't considered the possibility that the crowd would remain non-violent or, perhaps, that Popiełuszko would be considered a martyr.

[41] According to Piotr Litka (2009: 79), documents and statements from the period leave the impression that the kidnapping of Popiełuszko came as a shock to those in power. For instance, during a meeting between Fidel Castro, the president of Cuba, and Rakowski, the vice prime minister in Jaruzelski's Cabinet, on 25 October 1984, after the kidnapping but before the body was discovered, the Cuban leader advised the Polish regime to find the perpetrators quickly, investigate the case and punish them decisively. Castro claimed that

in the secret service, who were subsequently arrested and subjected to a public trial – an unprecedented move in the Eastern bloc. This was another moment at which the opposition could have plunged into more direct action, or even violence, as Solidarity leaders debated the relative wisdom of a general strike or remaining calm and engaging in dialogue with the government. Wałęsa, who represented the latter view,[42] said at the funeral: 'Solidarity lives because you, Father Popiełuszko, died for it', invoking the metaphor of the seed dying to bear fruit, or Christ's crucifixion. The estimate of numbers attending the funeral at St Stanisław church ranged from 250,000 to a million. Popiełuszko was hailed worldwide as a martyr.[43] The land surrounding his grave at the church came to be referred to as 'Solidarity's sanctuary' and a 'piece of free Poland'.[44] The Pope also spoke of Popiełuszko's death as a beginning, a resurrection, and Father Teofel Bogucki, in the Mass of the fatherland three weeks after Popiełuszko's funeral, referred to his sacrifice, alluding to the idea that just as Christ, the first priest, sacrificed himself, so should other priests.[45] An anonymous poet also referred to Popiełuszko as a martyr, like Christ, who through his death had resurrected the hearts of the Polish people, as Poland became the resurrected chosen nation.[46]

The size of the larger 'body politic' expanded through its identification with Popiełuszko's martyrdom, through a vertical narrative, in which his suffering connected to all the martyrs who had preceded him, and a horizontal narrative, by which the martyr's death expressed the suffering of all those who had suffered and died in the contemporary struggle. These vertical and horizontal dimensions form the symbol of the cross, and the image of Poland as the 'crucified nation'. In so far as Popiełuszko, the martyr, was a victim of the state, who suffered for witnessing to 'truth', his death legitimized the alternative narrative at the expense of the official one, inspiring others to follow his example. By putting 'truth' in quotation marks, I am not suggesting

---

Jaruzelski might come out of the crisis well, without his authority suffering, if he acted speedily. Castro further said he thought the murder had been carried out by the US Central Intelligence Agency (CIA) (Litka 2009: 80).

[42] Pick (1984a).
[43] See, for example, Canine and Seward (1984); Pick (1984b).
[44] While Popiełuszko was still alive, the Church itself was sometimes referred to as 'free Poland' (Litka 2009: 26).
[45] Bogucki (1984a).   [46] 'Tyś symbolem'.

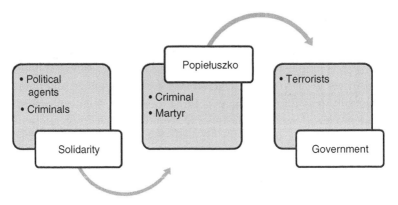

**Figure 5.1** Shifting games in Poland

that it is somehow false or relative but, rather, that its status as truth is reinforced by the social capital attached to it, which was expanded by the martyrdom itself. The speaker, who the state attempted to silence, already symbolized the nation. His voice, and thus the voice of the community he represented, was magnified in death, as the martyred body became the materialization of the ideas he symbolized.

In the period following his death the trial of the secret service members accused of his kidnapping and death took place, during which the Jaruzelski regime endeavoured to show the world that it was a state based on the rule of law, where terrorism of any kind would not be tolerated and where justice would be done. Many viewed the trial as nothing more than a scam, an effort to identify scapegoats and get the government off the hook. The prosecution went so far as to try to portray the victim – Popiełuszko – as the criminal for provoking the secret service. Figure 5.1 summarizes this shift in meaning.

In relation to the warden's dilemma, the trial was interesting in several respects. First, the human rights campaign – the Committee of Social Resistance (KOS) – had long been pointing out the lawlessness of the regime. Members of the state apparatus were now in the dock for having gone too far, and perceived the need to prove to the world that the state was in fact guided by the rule of law. Further, even if responsibility for the crime itself did not go all the way to the top – or was an effort by more extreme factions of the government to undermine Jaruzelski – there was still a huge tear, visible to the entire world, in the veneer of communist unity, on the one hand, and morality, on the other, if socialist humanism could give rise to this kind of 'terrorism'. The most visible tear was the recognition that 'terrorism' in Poland originated from inside the government rather than outside, with Solidarity or the Church.[47]

Finally, the government's dilemma, prior to Popiełuszko's death, was what to do about a priest who, despite martial law, was continuing to fan the spirit of opposition, despite all efforts to humiliate and harass him. This gave rise to a choice, namely to allow him to continue, and watch the numbers of opponents to the regime grow, or to eliminate him,[48] with the possibility that he would become a martyr (Litka 2009: 28–9). The only hope for the government to maintain any legitimacy for itself, after the latter choice had been made, was to engage in dialogue with Solidarity. In no small part influenced by Wałęsa's calming influence, against more vituperative voices calling for a general strike, a dialogue began between Solidarity and the government, and Western leaders as well, which set the stage for further changes in the game that would take place a few years later, when roundtable talks began.

After years of trying to impose conformity on Polish society, culminating with the murder of Solidarity's martyr priest, the warden faced the dilemma that the use of force against a population that refused to hit back, while continuing to resist, was destroying its legitimacy, giving *it* the appearance of being criminal – particularly after the kidnapping and death of Popiełuszko. The dilemma is expressed in an interesting transformation in the discourse following Popiełuszko's death. The regime, in trying to distance itself from the killers, emphasized the rule of law and the importance of justice being done in Poland. It went further, though, in denouncing terrorism in

---

[47] This tear related to a larger tear in society, which was expressed in the biblical metaphor of Cain and Abel, whereby 'Cain' referred to those people servicing the government and 'Abel' referred to those who were persecuted (Popiełuszko 2004: 591). The government, which is supposed to be a source of security, had become a source of insecurity; the Church had replaced it as the source of security and legitimacy, a bastion of the Polish nation (Popiełuszko 2004: 589, 590).

[48] Professor Andrzej Marek (Litka 2009: 102) argues that the aim of the kidnapping was to terrify the Church and priests. Rather than killing him quickly they had to torture someone, which could have been filmed or photographed, so that the films and photos could be shown to priests who wanted to follow in Popiełuszko's steps to indicate what would await them: not only death but extensive suffering. Marek says: 'Quick killing is not enough. It had to be torture. It was designed as the stations of the cross.'

any form. Terrorism, it argued, undermined negotiations and provided an opening for the enemies of Poland to make emotional use of the crime to disrupt peace and stability, thereby destabilizing the Polish revolutionary movement. The acts of the murderers were said to be contrary to the line of the Interior Ministry, the party or the government. Government officials, such as General Czesław Kiszczak, the head of the Ministry of Interior,[49] Jerzy Urban, the government spokesperson,[50] as well as the PUWP[51] and an official Christian publication, all repeated variations on the theme. A statement from university students began with a similar statement but added a different twist,[52] claiming that 'kidnapping is an act of political terror, which targets the core of human ethics (human rights) and also the constitutional foundation of the state, which is freedom of belief and feelings of security in one's own country'. This statement was preceded by references to Popiełuszko as the defender of true value, who awakened social hope and had the courage to speak about things that many people were thinking. This represents a subtle shift away from the terrorism versus dialogue opposition, stated in the official sources, to what for the students is a human rights issue that challenges the constitutional foundation of the state, which is defined as freedom. While the official statements sought to reinforce the rule of law, and to save the current system in the face of this 'terrorism', the student statement used the same claims about terrorism as a point of departure

[49] For instance, on 27 October 1984 Kiszczak stated: 'In the state of law no one can be above the law. Acts like this are unprecedented in the history of political culture. Our country is not and will not be a jungle of lawlessness. One cannot hide the truth, no matter how painful it is. The same goes for the manipulation of truth. One cannot draw conclusions from one individual case as is done by those who are against the government. The kidnappers, members of the security services, were acting contrary to the political line of the department, the party and the government.'

[50] During a press conference, Urban (1984) stated that the 'government is against any methods of political banditry. Methods such as kidnapping are alien to us. The kidnapping of Father Jerzy is a political provocation aimed at the government.'

[51] The Oświadczenia KC PZPR referred to the kidnapping as 'a dangerous provocative crime, alien to Polish culture'. They further stated 'forcefully' that 'there will be no turning a blind eye to anarchy and terrorism of any kind'. The enemies of Poland, usually associated with Solidarity or actors in the West, are now associated with 'terrorists' who are located within the government (Polska Agencja Prasowa 1984).

[52] Uniwersytet Warszawski (1984).

for questioning the current order, which corresponded with a further shift away from concerns about attacks on the revolutionary movement towards recovering 'a fatherland that is great, independent and free'. For Solidarity and the Church, Popiełuszko's death was a martyrdom that resurrected Solidarity and made negotiation possible.[53] Solidarity was above ground and no longer the criminal; the government with criminals in its ranks had to change game and negotiate with Solidarity.

As stated by Professor Andrzej Marek, a specialist in criminal law and observer of the trial of Popiełuszko's killers, held at Toruń (as quoted by Litka 2009: 145),

The year 1984 was a watershed. After Popiełuszko's death, we had a lot of changes inside the government and one can observe a change in the relationship between the government and opposition. In light of this, the death of Popiełuszko had two dimensions, the metaphysical and the martyrdom. One victim pulled down the curtain on the system. When the priest died the whole Soviet system shook. A month after the Toruń trial (which ended on 7 February 1985), Chernenko died (10 March 1985). Gorbachev replaced Chernenko on 11 March 1985 and with that the slow reform of the system began, which in Poland ended symbolically in 1989.[54]

Communist Poland has long since died. Father Popiełuszko, by contrast, was beatified in 2010.

## Conclusion

The convergence of the interests and the actions of the various parties that sought an independent Poland distinguished the resistance of 1980s Poland from previous efforts to bring about reform. We see the sedimentation and consolidation of a form of resistance, coming from the analysis of intellectuals, the inspiration of figures within the Catholic Church and the actions of workers and common people, which was a product of 'talk' over a lengthy period of time. This 'talk' rested on a transformation of historical memories with a deep emotional resonance into a framework for non-violent practice. At several stages this 'talk' played an important role in calming and giving

---

[53] Bogucki (1984a).
[54] This is merely symbolic, given that the Russian army remained in Poland until 1993 and elections were only partially democratic.

perspective to a humiliated population. In this context, the apparent defeat represented by martial law became an opportunity for articulating a victory of continuing solidarity, even under the most extreme conditions. The death of one of the central agents of this message at the hands of the security forces was arguably the final nail in the coffin of the regime, forcing it to change games and switch to dialogue with the Church and the opposition, which eventually resulted in its own non-violent transformation. Popiełuszko, the martyr, became the embodiment of the martyred Polish nation, which, in his absence, was resurrected. The embodiment was less a cause than a re-enactment of the familiar narrative of Christianity, which had been the narrative of crucified Poland throughout its history.

The keys to preserving unity between actors that historically had been divided were an ability to compromise and the construction of social trust (Beyer 2007). The philosopher and chaplain of Solidarity, Father Tischner, wrote in his *Etyka solidarności* (published in 1981) that solidarity requires dialogue. Dialogue is a type of interaction and argument that rests on recognition that one side is never the sole possessor of truth. Dialogue requires a sincere effort to see the world from the perspective of the other (Tischner (2005 [1981]). It was the opening to dialogue presented by Popiełuszko's martyrdom, and the willingness of Solidarity to pursue dialogue with the communists, that eventually led to the historic roundtable meeting in 1989.

Large-scale solidarity in Poland throughout the 1980s rested on the willingness of Poles to come to one another's aid, which arose out of a new sense of trust in the human person. According to Wladyslaw Zuziak (2001: 33), a faith in the other, and mutual trust, are the preconditions for the functioning of solidarity. This renewed faith in the goodness of the human being spawned mutual trust among people and enabled Poles to make great sacrifices for one another during the Solidarity era (Beyer 2007). Given the historical experience of evils such as Auschwitz, Kolyma, Katyń or the 1956 and 1970 massacres, the Poles were less naive than willing to leave space for change, even by the perpetuators of such great evils. Tischner (2005 [1981]) argues that solidarity means dialogue even with those who have betrayed you, in the hope that the latter will look at themselves in the mirror, see themselves as they are and undergo a transformation. The willingness to serve others and the common good meant martyrdom for some, not least Popiełuszko. A 'form of life' constructed around words and actions that assume mutual respect for and the dignity of others is solidarity, and it contributed to a transformation of the Polish nation. Talking non-violence was an important element of trust-building in this case. It was an essential part of the refusal to reproduce the lie. It began with 'acting as if' Polish voices and traditions mattered.

IR scholars have been inclined to look at changes such as the end of the Cold War in terms of the rational calculations or strategic interests of states. So, for instance, the strategic interests of Mikhail Gorbachev, the CPSU general secretary, would be most decisive in explaining his 'new thinking' and his change of strategy. While not denying that state actors have strategic interests and make strategic decisions, the approach of this book is to shift attention to the context of the rules within which these decisions had meaning for domestic and international publics. Poland was not the only consideration for the Soviet Union. Everything from peace movement demands for disarmament in the West to the failed intervention in Afghanistan would have played into Gorbachev's calculations. Although events in Poland, on the front line of the Cold War, were important for the Soviet Union, Gorbachev's new thinking, as I have argued elsewhere (Fierke 1998), was the crystallization of an alternative game that drew together different strands of opposition in both East and West, and thus created a new space for both superpowers to manoeuvre. Gorbachev himself began to act as if dialogue was possible, making unilateral gestures to suspend nuclear testing that drew Reagan into a 'peace' competition. While Poland was the most likely place for widespread resistance to Communism to begin, given the independent status of the Catholic Church there, the non-violent revolutions that followed across eastern Europe relied on similar practices of 'acting as if'. The Polish campaign can, in this light, be seen as an important step in creating the contours of a new game, which later convulsed the whole communist system.

# 6 | *Self-immolation in Vietnam, 1963*

The last chapter focused on the non-violent campaign of Solidarity that culminated in the 'martyrdom' of Father Popiełuszko. This chapter shifts to an Asian context, where a brutal Catholic regime was confronted by Buddhists seeking change at a decisive turning point in what became the Vietnam War. The self-immolation by burning of Thich Quang Duc was a defining moment of this crisis. On 11 June 1964 he sat down on a busy Saigon street, covered himself in gasoline and set fire to his robe. In what follows I explore the meaning and consequences of this act, while situating it in the larger domestic and international context of the time.

Most accounts of the Vietnam War have been written from an American perspective, although in recent years a number of books have appeared that include voices from Vietnam as well. In constructing the various narratives in this chapter, I have tried to weave together these often contesting perspectives to create a more multidimensional context. The aim is to explore how practice was defined and justified within a cultural framework that draws on memories and traditions with emotional resonance but that was also continuously shaped and reshaped as agents engaged in a global space.[1] This engagement was not for the most part face to face but mediated through images and the written word, particularly insofar as acts on one side of the world became a cause of reflection and action on the other.

The body of literature on the Vietnam War is vast, given that the conflict ended forty years ago. My focus is on a very short period in the mid-1960s and a particular form of political self-sacrifice:

---

[1] It needs to be mentioned that the diverse accounts of the same events, as represented in the literature, were not consistent in their portrayal of basic factual information. I have tried to triangulate to be as accurate as possible. This problem with the detail should not, however, detract from the larger picture, whereby differences were a function of the contrast between American or Vietnamese perspectives, both of which I have tried to incorporate.

self-immolation through burning. While a number of authors have dealt with the theological dimensions of the self-burnings, or the political dynamics, this chapter is distinct in three respects. First, I problematize the tendency in existing accounts to conflate suicide and sacrifice, drawing out the distinction between these two ascriptions of meaning. Second, acts of self-immolation by burning are analysed within the framework of the warden's dilemma. Finally, the analysis combines a concern with how the theological and emotional meaning of the act in two distinct contexts, those of Vietnam and the United States, shaped an international conversation.

The first section examines the meaning of self-immolation by burning in Mahāyāna Buddhism. The second section sketches the broad outlines of the international and domestic political context from which the Buddhist crisis emerged, followed by an analysis of the development of this crisis, and the self-burning of Thich Quang Duc. Section three then examines the double warden's dilemma that led to the coup against the Diem regime. Finally, section four explores a conversation over the meaning of self-immolation as suicide or sacrifice, as the practice was imitated in the American context.

## Self-immolation in Buddhism

Self-immolation through burning has a long history in Mahāyāna Buddhism, which is the predominant school of Buddhism in Vietnam. Buddhism came to Vietnam via China and India, but in the Vietnamese context it absorbed elements of Taoism, Confucianism and ancestor worship. In contrast to Theravada Buddhism, which emphasizes monasticism and is more conservative, Mahāyāna Buddhism is a progressive school that is concerned with social justice and change, and emphasizes active 'compassion' (*karuna*) and 'benevolence' (*maitre*) as the most important qualities of the bodhisattva, or enlightened one (Kleine 2006: 160). Non-violence is more than a strategy in this tradition; it is a way of life that respects all life. A central tenet of Buddhism, characteristic of both traditions, is that the Buddha is present in everyone, which means an emphasis on one's inner life but also a responsibility for the peace and well-being of the community (Hanh 1967: 18).

Self-immolation has been a part of the Mahāyāna tradition from the beginning but would seem, on the surface, to be contrary to some of the core teachings of Buddhism, and not least the emphasis on respect for life and non-violence. Self-burning involves violence to the self, though not others, and therefore fits uncomfortably with a tradition of non-violence. While suicide is prohibited in Buddhism, self-immolation, if undertaken with the proper intention, is, in the exceptional case of the bodhisattva, understood as an offering and sacrifice to the Buddha that transcends moral precepts.[2] As discussed in Chapter 1, sacrifice embodies a dialectical tension in that it is at one and the same time the most criminal and most honourable of acts.

The term 'self-immolation', strictly speaking, means 'self-sacrifice', and is derived from the Latin *molare*, 'to make a sacrifice of grain'. The concept thus refers to a broad range of practices, including drowning and death by starvation, as well as self-burning (Benn 2007: 8). Self-burning or auto-cremation has roots in the ancient Chinese practice of moxibustion, which involved igniting a cauterizing cone of herbs or other substance in close contact with the body as well as indigenous practices of burning the body to produce rain (Keown 2005: 105; Benn 2007: 11) – practices that pre-dated the arrival of Buddhism in China. Within Buddhism, self-burning has usually been associated with acts of sacrifice to the Buddha, and has its roots in chapter 23 of the *Lotus Sutra*, a religious scripture[3] that has been seminal in the development of Mahāyāna Buddhism.[4] The lotus flower is one of the most common symbols of Buddhism. Within Mahāyāna Buddhism it symbolizes the bodhisattva as one who is firmly rooted in the mud of the earth and flowering towards

[2] In the Mahāyāna tradition the action itself is secondary to the intention. The deed will be considered pure if the intention was pure, but if the intention was impure the deed will also be (Kleine 2006: 162–3).
[3] The *Lotus Sutra* was probably compiled in the first century of the common era (Reeves 2008: 3). The practice of self-burning has also been reinforced and embellished in biographies of self-burning and the inclusion of these texts in the Buddhist canon as exemplars of heroic practice (Benn 2007: 1–3). Other texts have also been important. The *Brahmajala Sutra*, a Chinese text from the fifth century CE explained how new bodhisattvas should be introduced to ascetic practices such as setting fire to the body, the arm or the finger. If one didn't set fire to oneself as an offering to the Buddhas, one would not be a renunciant bodhisattva (Keown 2005: 107).
[4] The title *Lotus Sutra* is a product of the first Western translation in 1852 by Eugene Bornouf into French (*Le lotus de la bonne loi*). On the basis of direct translation of the Japanese and Chinese characters, the title means 'wonderful Dharma lotus flower sutra' (Reeves 2008: 1).

the sky.[5] The symbol communicates the importance of helping others to awaken within the world while finding meaning in the cosmos (Reeves 2008: 1).

Chapter 23 of the *Lotus Sutra* is the story of the bodhisattva medicine king (Bhaisajyarja), who was a model of enlightened action. The medicine king had studied and practised under a Buddha, and as he progressed he came to a point at which he no longer identified with his physical body and could appear in various bodies in order to help people, such as becoming a child if he needed to be a child, or taking a female form to become a woman, always appearing in the form that was most appropriate to the situation. As a result, he brought great joy to the people he encountered. The medicine king overcame the idea of the body as a fixed and permanent self and, given this insight into his ultimate nature, was able to manifest himself in many transformation bodies in order to help others, relinquishing his body with great ease (Hanh 2008). According to the *Lotus Sutra*, the king poured fragrant oil over himself and allowed himself to be burned by fire as the most perfect offering to the Buddha (Williams 2009: 160) and to demonstrate his insight that the body is not permanent and unchanging – an act that was inspired by deep love (Hanh 2008: 157–8).

In east Asian Buddhism, from the early fifth century CE, burning joints or the whole body was taken very seriously as an act of devotion (Williams 2009: 160). Daodu, a monk with connections to the Ling dynasty, which ruled southern China for the first half of the sixth century, was, according to his funeral inscription, inspired by the *Lotus Sutra*. His story relates to a tradition of 'abandoning the body' that has been part of Chinese Buddhism from the late fourth century to the early years of the twentieth century. Over this 1,600-year period there are hundreds of examples of monks, nuns and laypeople who have offered their bodies.[6] The sacrifice was often witnessed by a large audience, including government officials, and even emperors in one dramatic staged event (Benn 2007: 7). In medieval China, monks

---

[5] A bodhisattva is a saintly human who chooses to act as a helper of humanity rather than entering the final, blessed state of Nirvana (Hope 1967: 151).

[6] Self-immolation was always an exceptional practice, although a tenth-century treatise from the monk Yanshou (904–975) argued that practices of self-burning, either of fingers, entire limbs, or, in more extreme cases, the entire body, should be recommended for ordinary monks and not only great bodhisattvas, as argued by the authorities (Keown 2005: 104).

who made offerings of their bodies were viewed as a potential threat to state control, both because the state couldn't be seen to condone or encourage suicide and because of fears that the monk would become a hero, inspiring a cult that would threaten political stability or draw attention and support away from the emperor (Benn 2007: 5). Self-immolation was also often performed in the face of foreign invasions. A monk named Fahe set himself on fire in 1134, to offer his body to the Buddha and to demand that invaders be driven out of northern China and the empire reunified under the Song emperors (Benn 2007: 167).

The idea that self-burning could have political consequences as well as spiritual ones has had numerous expressions over the centuries. As James Benn (2007: 7) points out, self-immolation was thought to operate according to a mechanism of stimulus-response referred to as 'ganying'. For instance, in the case of Daodu, the miracles surrounding his self-immolation provided evidence that the action had stimulated (gan) a response (ying) from the universe, and was thus 'right'. Ganying was said to operate within human society, in which interactions between rulers and their subjects were based on the responsiveness of rulers to the needs of their people. Rulers could not afford to ignore or condemn the sincerity of the self-burning as this would violate the cosmic and human order. Ganying was based on a belief that human actions and emotions could evoke a cosmic response and transformation. A selfless act by the petitioner was more likely to be followed by a response from the cosmos (Benn 2007: 7).

The self-immolation of Thich Quang Duc and the other Vietnamese monks and nuns in the 1960s has its roots in the *Lotus Sutra*. The Buddhist monk and scholar Thich Nhat Hanh (2008: 158–9) places the act in this context, claiming that, because the monks had, like the medicine king, acquired insight into their ultimate nature, they felt free to use their bodies to deliver a powerful message – that is, 'they transformed their bodies into torches to illuminate the suffering of the Vietnamese people'. The courage to relinquish the body without suffering grows out of a realization that one's current physical form isn't permanent or fixed and can take many forms. The offering in this case was on behalf of the Vietnamese people and nation. In a letter to Diem, which was one of three final letters prepared by Thich Quang Duc, he wrote: 'Before I pass through the Buddha gate, I pray the president will treat his people with compassion so that he may maintain the treasure of the nation forever' (Chanoff and Van Toai 2009: 143).[7]

## The political context

Vietnam has a long history of occupation and subsequent resistance. The country was mostly under Chinese rule for a thousand-year period until its independence in 938 CE, following the defeat of Chinese forces at Bang Dang River. Vietnam was colonized by the French for approximately eighty years from the middle of the nineteenth century, interrupted by the Japanese occupation during World War II, after which the French returned to Indochina. Following the defeat of the French at Dien Bien Phu, the Geneva Agreement of 1954 divided Vietnam along the seventeenth parallel.[8] North of the seventeenth parallel the Viet Minh, who had defeated the French, would establish a 'regroupment area', while France and the United States would organize a 'regroupment area' in the south. Ho Chi Minh, the leader of the Viet Minh, agreed to the temporary partition, with elections to be held in 1956, and became the head of North Vietnam. In South Vietnam, Ngo Dinh Diem, a Vietnamese Roman Catholic who had been living in the United States, was to provide a 'democratic alternative' to the communist north (McNamara *et al.* 1999: 67). The United States and Ho Chi Minh both felt themselves to be losers in this outcome. That the industrial north fell to a 'communist' regime was a loss for the Americans. While gaining the industrial half of the country, Ho Chi Minh lost much of the territory his army had won on the battlefield and was forced to settle for only half the country (Halberstam 2008: 11). The Geneva Agreement contained fundamental clauses about independence and unity, which, according to Luce Doan Huynh (quoted by

---

[7] The above translation comes from a Vietnamese speaker – Thich Giac Duc, one of the key political strategists of the Buddhist movement – who knew Thich Quang Duc. The translation that appears in most English texts is: 'Before closing my eyes to go to Buddha, I have the honour to present my words to President Diem, asking him to be kind and tolerant towards his people and enforce a policy of religious equality' (see, for instance, Keown 2005: 101).

[8] The agreement was an end to the First Indochina War, which brought a withdrawal of French forces and split French Indochina into Laos, Cambodia and Vietnam. The division was supposed to last only until elections could be held, but national elections never took place, due to a refusal by Ngo Dinh Diem and his declaration of leadership in South Vietnam.

McNamara *et al.* 1999: 88), the leader of the southern resistance, helped the North Vietnamese to legitimize their political battle for the liberation of the south.

In the period following the agreement the United States claimed to have only advisors in Vietnam. Their presence was not highly visible in the American media. US involvement in this far-off country arose out of concern about the nuclear threat and the potential spread of communism. The domino theory, a term that was coined by US president Dwight Eisenhower, reflected a concern that, if South Vietnam fell to the communists, other small nations across east Asia would fall like dominoes. As Robert McNamara (quoted by McNamara *et al.* 1999: 27) notes, Vietnam represented a 'special problem' for the United States because it was the only state in south-east Asia that was 'essentially the *creation of the US*' (emphasis added).[9] In the minds of American politicians, what was otherwise a local conflict in a far-off land came to be understood as a threat to fundamental US interests, and linked to the Soviet enemy with nuclear weapons. In the context of Vietnam, John Kennedy, who succeeded Eisenhower as president, redefined the domino theory to refer not to potential occupation by Soviet troops but a communist insurgency that took orders from Moscow and Beijing.

While the United States was engaged in great power politics, the Vietnamese were fighting a 'people's war' – a concept that was a response to millennia of invasion and occupation by outside powers, and a strategy that sought gradually to weaken and 'outlast' the forces of a great power, whether Mongol, Chinese, Japanese or French. The end was purely defensive, to retake control of the Vietnamese people and territory, not to conquer others. According to the military commander of the Viet Minh, General Vo Nguyen Giap (1966: 29), the most famous exponent of Vietnamese people's war, the political objective of independence was necessarily prior to the military objective, given the huge sacrifices that would be required to defeat a larger and more militarily powerful enemy.[10] Ho Chi Minh, the leader of the newly created North Vietnam, was first and

---

[9] See also Laderman (2009: 16); US Department of State (1954). The paternalistic relationship was articulated by President Eisenhower in a 1956 speech in which he stated: 'If we are not the parents of little Vietnam, then surely we are the godparents... [T]his is our offspring' (McNamara *et al.* 1999: 27).

[10] On the centrality of sacrifice as part of the mindset of the struggle to save the country, see Chanoff and Van Toai (2009: 8, 21, 103, 210); Vo Nguyen Giap in McNamara *et al.* (1999: 24).

foremost a nationalist who sought independence for Vietnam. Following Japan's unconditional surrender in 1945, and the August revolution in the following days, he had appealed to the US Declaration of Independence as a model for Vietnam (Nguyen Co Thach, a Vietnamese revolutionary and diplomat, quoted by McNamara *et al.* 1999: 46), and saw common cause with the United States, both historically, given that both were former colonies, and during World War II, in their joint battle against the Japanese.

At the time, the Vietnamese also viewed the United States as a world leader against fascism, as well as the only non-imperialist great power and thus a symbol of potential support in the anti-colonialist struggle (Tran Quang Co, a former first deputy minister in Vietnam, quoted by McNamara *et al.* 1999: 49). This all changed after the Geneva conference. The architects of the agreement were the major powers, including the United States,[11] and the Vietnamese took a back seat to the French.[12] In this respect, the eventual war between the United States and the Viet Cong arose at the intersection of two distinct games. On the one hand, the American intervention was informed by great power politics and concerns, in the first instance, about the power vacuum resulting from the French withdrawal and, in the second instance, about the potential consequences if that power vacuum were filled by a 'communist' regime. On the other hand, Ho Chi Minh, who had led the resistance against the French, was first and foremost concerned with the national independence of Vietnam;[13] he was increasingly moved to seek support from the Soviets and Chinese, however, despite the long history and memories of occupation by the latter.[14] The

[11] The United States was the only great power that refused to sign the Geneva Accords.
[12] According to McNamara (quoted by McNamara *et al.* 1999: 69), the United States saw the French as the principle actor in Indochina while the indigenous Viet Minh movement was viewed as a 'native' bit player.
[13] According to Thich Nhat Hanh (1967: 62), the Vietnamese people viewed Ho Chi Minh as a national hero who had led the struggle against the French, and no one, except a small group of intellectuals, thought of him as communist or as wanting to establish a communist regime in Vietnam.
[14] Indeed, as Nguyen Khai Huynh (McNamara *et al.* 1999: 93) notes, the passage of Resolution 15 in 1959 signalled a shift from a purely political struggle to a military one with the objective of achieving reunification – a change that was seen as necessary due to the brutal tactics of the Diem regime. One of the greatest difficulties was gaining support from the Soviet Union and China for the new policy, given the problems between the Soviets and the Chinese at the time. Obtaining support from both took great skill on the part of Ho Chi Minh.

Vietnamese came to view the United States as another 'imperialist' power that was replacing France (Luu Van Loi, a former senior official at the Ministry of Foreign Affairs, quoted by McNamara *et al.* 1999: 85). The English-language broadcast announcing the creation of the National Liberation Front (NLF – Viet Cong), on 29 January 1961, called on 'the entire people' to rise up and evict the American 'imperialists' who were 'subjugating the southern part of the country through the 'camouflaged imperialist' or 'colonialist regime' of the United States (Tran Van Giau and Le Van Chat 1982: 27–9).[15] About the same time, and one week after taking office, Kennedy approved a counter-insurgency plan for South Vietnam (McNamara *et al.* 1999: 97). That Ho Chi Minh was anything other than a pawn of Communist China and the Soviet Union didn't enter the American imagination. The military intervention was built on a fundamental misperception on the American side, as well as a failure to understand the underlying politics that drove resistance in the Vietnamese context (Hanh 1967: 93; Topmiller 2002).

The Viet Cong were not the only force within Vietnam that sought national independence. The non-violent Buddhist movement became another key player, particularly between 1961 and 1963, prior to the fall of the Diem government. The military strategy of the Viet Cong emerged out of the political objective of independence but became preoccupied with fighting the 'American War'.[16] Given its focus on the military aspects of the 'Vietnam War', the United States failed to understand or properly take account of the political or cultural dimensions. The two together turned Vietnam into a battleground between the United States and Asian communism. The cultural and political elements of the conflict are less easily ignored if one shifts attention to the Buddhist movement.

One consequence of the partition of Vietnam was that 800,000 refugees, primarily Catholic and fearing persecution, left North Vietnam for the south. The Diem regime provided special assistance to the

[15] This transformation of US identity from anti-fascist and anti-imperialist to fascist and imperialist continued and framed the North Vietnamese and Communist Chinese representations by 1963. Diem is presented as a dictator 'more brutal than the fascist Hitlerites' and the 'strategic hamlets', created by the administration, were referred to as 'concentration camps', where 'people are tortured and killed' (Hanoi Radio 1963). The frequent reference to a 'US–Ngo clique' further links the brutal regime to 'US imperialists' (Cheng-Chin 1963).
[16] Although the conflict is referred to as the 'Vietnam War' in the West, the Vietnamese called it the 'American War'.

refugees and to the refugee camps, which became a source of anger among the local population (Hanh 1967: 35). The massive influx of Catholics, and their preferential treatment, heightened tensions with the Buddhist community, which constituted a majority in the south[17] but were treated as second-class citizens by the Diem regime (Halberstam 2008: 120). This was reflected in the naming of Catholicism as a religion while Buddhism was considered legally to be a mere 'association',[18] which, for instance, made Buddhists ineligible to acquire property for their pagodas (Jones 2003: 249). The regime gave priority to Catholics over Buddhists in most areas of life.[19]

In this context, with a majority population feeling excluded and repressed by a Catholic regime, the Buddhist movement became a significant player in the summer of 1963. The conflict was not religious per se but, rather, a result of the Diem family's use of Catholicism as a tool of political control. Allegiance to the Catholic Church meant allegiance to the Diem regime as well (Chanoff and Van Toai 2009: 136). As a result of Diem's misuse of the police to suppress the opposition, consolidate the position of the Ngo family and to spread Catholicism, many people viewed the regime as their enemy (Hanh 1967: 35). The demands of the Buddhist movement targeted a domestic issue relating to the status of Buddhism in South Vietnam, but the emphasis on Buddhism, Vietnamese history and tradition highlighted the association of the regime with a foreign element – Catholicism – and its distance from the people (Topmiller 2002: viii). The Buddhist crisis evolved into something far more serious than its initial demands would suggest, exposing major divisions within South Vietnamese society and almost universal opposition to the dictatorial rule of Diem (Topmiller 2002: 1–3).

---

[17] A 1961 survey conducted in Saigon by the Asian Foundation found that over 80 per cent of the population identified themselves as Buddhists, while only 13 per cent were Catholic and 3 per cent Confucian (Topmiller 2002: viii).

[18] The French had used the law to limit the authority of the Buddhists and to increase the power of their Catholic supporters. The refusal of Diem to abandon this law became a constant reminder to Buddhists of their inferior status in the south (Topmiller 2002: 2).

[19] As Thich Giac Duc (quoted by Chanoff and Van Toai 2009: 134) noted, the only way to get ahead was to become Catholic; the only way to get anywhere in public life was to join Can Lao, the political party started by Diem.

## The Buddhist crisis

The NLF and the Buddhist movement were the only internal challenges to the Diem regime (Topmiller 2002: viii). The non-violent Buddhist peace movement, while often viewed as a mere tool of the communist NLF (Hanh 1967: 58), had a distinct identity and strategy, which was to counteract the influence of both Can Lao, the president's party, and the communists, teaching people the inseparability of Buddhism and the Vietnamese nation, and discouraging people from falling into the hands of foreign ideas (Chanoff and Van Toai 2009: 136). Communism and the Diem regime both belonged to the category of foreign ideas. Although opposition to communism within Buddhism was relatively recent, having developed in the previous ten to fifteen years, resistance to Western imperial domination went back centuries (Hanh 1967: 42). Catholicism was a Western, particularly French, import, and Diem was imported from and backed by the United States. The lack of agency experienced by the Vietnamese in their own land was articulated clearly by Nhat Hanh (1967: 122) in a statement to the *Congressional Record* in Washington, DC, several years into the protests:

The demonstrations, the self-immolations, and the protests which we are witnessing in Vietnam are dramatic reflections of the frustrations which the Vietnamese people feel at being so effectively excluded from participation in the determination of their country's future. Eighty years of French domination over Vietnam were ended by a long and bloody struggle, waged and won by the Vietnamese people against overwhelming odds. During the twelve years since independence, most Vietnamese have remained without a voice in the nation's destiny, and this at a time when the nation is being subjected to a destructive force far surpassing anything ever before seen in our country.

President Diem was the core problem (Richardson 2005: 142–3). As early as 1955 he had begun executing large numbers of people. His security forces had been trained in the United States and there was a widespread perception of him as a US puppet (Nguyen Khac Huynh, a former analyst in the Vietnamese Foreign Ministry, quoted by McNamara *et al.* 1999: 93). US president Kennedy had tried to reinforce the legitimacy of Diem but at the same time had doubts about the wisdom of the US role in Vietnam, and, prior to the escalation of the Buddhist movement, he had developed a strategy of increasing the number of troops in Vietnam for the purpose of eventually reducing the US role (Jones 2003: 246). The policy of supporting Diem and the strategy of eventually decreasing US troop strength both changed as a result of the protests that began on 8 May 1963 in the ancient capital of Hue.

In that year the celebration of Vesak, the Buddha's birthday,[20] coincided with the day of the Lady of La Van,[21] and a visit from a Vatican delegation, which had come to investigate Diem's brother, Archbishop Ngo Dinh Thuc, for candidacy as a cardinal. It was usual practice for the Buddha's birthday to be celebrated with flags and marches, but, because of the visit from the Vatican (Chanoff and Van Toai 2009: 136), a previously dormant law, Decree number 10, which prohibited the display of religious flags without permission from local authorities (Jones 2003: 246), was invoked.[22] In defiance of the law, students in Hue, which was the spiritual centre of Buddhism in Vietnam, marched through the city carrying multicoloured Buddhist flags, which also waved prominently above homes and pagodas.

The peaceful demonstration became violent, resulting in the deaths of nine teenagers. How the demonstration turned violent became a source of controversy. When, a short distance from the confrontation, two explosives went off, Major Dang Sy signalled for his men to employ grenades, and the government forces sprayed fire hoses into the crowd. When the monks refused to evacuate the area, a dozen grenades were thrown into their midst. The government forces later claimed that their grenades were designed only to stun, and that the bombs had come from the Viet Cong. Nevertheless, many doubted whether the well-known plastic bombs of the Viet Cong could have caused so much destruction.[23] The next morning the atmosphere intensified again, as some 6,000 Buddhists attended a meeting at Tu Dam Pagoda, with Army of the Republic of Vietnam (ARVN – South

[20] It was his 2,527th birthday.
[21] There had been a vision of the Madonna in La Van, and the place had become a Catholic shrine.
[22] The insult was magnified because, only the week beforehand, Catholics had carried papal flags in celebration of the twenty-fifth anniversary of Archbishop Thuc.
[23] Viet Cong members denied involvement at the time, and for years afterwards (Jones 2003: 250–1).

Vietnamese) troops and police hovering nearby. Tri Quang, the leader of the Buddhists,[24] repeated pleas to remain non-violent and appealed to the power of martyrdom, encouraging the crowd to 'follow Gandhi's policies' and 'carry no weapons; be prepared to die' (Jones 2003: 252).[25] That the banners of the movement were written in English as well as Vietnamese suggests their strategy was directed not only at the population but at Western photographers as well, in the hope of attracting American sympathy for their cause (Jones 2003: 249).

The Kennedy administration was at the time preoccupied with the civil rights crisis in the US south, but encouraged Diem to make peaceful gestures towards the Buddhists and to respond to some of their concerns. These suggestions fell on deaf ears. When the Buddhist clergy presented him with a manifesto, stating their five demands, Diem argued that the claims of religious oppression had no basis in fact, that there was a constitutional guarantee of religious freedom and that *he* was the constitution. Both Diem and the American ambassador, Frederick Nolting, identified the Buddhists with the Viet Cong; Diem, as a result, ignored any chance of a peaceful settlement (Jones 2003: 255–6).

The defining moment of the crisis came on 11 June 1964, when Thich Quang Duc, a seventy-three-year-old monk, in a yellow robe and with a shaved head, sat down on the pavement in a lotus position on a busy Saigon street and starred quietly ahead. Two companions carrying a five-gallon container of gasoline mixed with diesel fuel emptied the contents over his head and body as the monk, clasping prayer beads, chanted the sacred words 'Nam mo amita Buddha' ('Return to eternal Buddha'). Quang Duc then struck a match and set fire to his robe. This was the first self-immolation during the 1963 Buddhist crisis, but it would be followed by many more. Quang Duc was acting with the consent, albeit reluctant, of

[24] Tri Quang had a well-established reputation as an independent Vietnamese nationalist. The CIA labelled him as 'an ambitious, skilful, ruthless, political manipulator and born demagogue'. He was often referred to as a provocateur and a schemer in the American press (Topmiller 2002: 8).

[25] As Marjorie Hope (1967: 153) notes, many of the Buddhists had read the works of Gandhi and Martin Luther King and followed the civil rights movement in the United States closely. There was a centuries-long tradition of non-violent resistance in Vietnam as well, however – a tradition that included sit-downs, fasting and quiet non-cooperation with the authorities.

the Church authorities, who came to see him as a bodhisattva.[26] During the self-burning the monk was surrounded by a shield of monks and nuns, which made it impossible for onlookers to extinguish the fire. As Quang Duc burned, another priest repeated over and over into a microphone: 'A Buddhist priest burns himself to death, a Buddhist priest becomes a martyr' (as cited by Richardson 2005: 161).

Malcolm Browne (1965), the photographer who captured the self-immolation in a photograph, was notified in advance, although he was not informed of the nature of the act he would later witness. His photo of the self-immolation was quickly circulated worldwide and became an iconic image of the Vietnam War. *The New York Times* correspondent David Halberstam (2008: 128) wrote: 'As he burned he never moved a muscle, never uttered a sound, his outward composure in sharp contrast to the wailing people around him. I had never felt such conflicting emotions: one part of me wanted to extinguish the fire, another warned that I had no right to interfere, another told me that it was too late, another asked whether I was a reporter or a human being.' Many in the Kennedy administration were 'shocked and appalled' by the 'horrifying' self-immolation (McNamara 1995: 49). Browne's photograph of Quang Duc's burning, which ran in the *Philadelphia Inquirer* on 12 June 1963, was on President Kennedy's desk the next morning. He responded to the image of the burning monk by exclaiming 'Jesus Christ!'. He had the photograph on his desk when he briefed Henry Cabot Lodge, the new ambassador, to pressure Diem to compromise with the Buddhists (Browne 1965: 182). Dean Rusk, the Secretary of State, warned the American embassy in Saigon that the White House would publicly dissociate itself from the regime if Diem did not resolve the crisis within a few days (Jones 2003: 271).

Many Americans became aware of the Buddhist crisis as a result of Quang Duc's self-burning (Appy 2008: 61). The event left an 'indelible stamp on America's collective consciousness and rudely awakened the Kennedy administration to the gravity of the Buddhist crisis' (Jones 2003: 268). In Vietnam, the notorious 'Madame Nhu', Diem's sister-in-law, referred to the self-immolation as a 'barbecue' (*Los Angeles Times* 1963b; Richardson 2005: 166, 169), which was received with a horror

---

[26] Buddhist leaders in Vietnam sanctioned Quang Duc's self-immolation as well as that of another elderly monk, Thich Tieu Dieu, but refused permission to many younger monks (Keown 2005: 101).

second only to the burning, but for people throughout Vietnam the event was an emotional one, and Quang Duc was seens as a martyr who witnessed to their suffering. Immediately following the self-burning massive demonstrations broke out. People in Saigon, who had remained passive for years out of fear of Diem's policies, crowded into the pagodas to kneel and weep. They then followed the monks onto the streets, demanding an end to the reign of the Ngo family (Fitzgerald 1972). The Buddhist leaders added to the legend by taking the heart of Quang Duc to the pagoda and placing it in a jar, claiming that, since the heart had not burned, Quang Duc had left this world unsatisfied (Halberstam 2008: 129).

After the burning the government agreed to a number of the Buddhists' demands, and a joint communiqué was released. Within a few days the arrests started up again, and Madame Nhu continued to make speeches denouncing the Buddhists. A massive spontaneous demonstration against the government emerged out of crowd of more than a million people who had gathered for Thich Quang Duc's funeral in Saigon. The police action that followed led to the self-burning of a nun in Nha Trang in protest (Chanoff and Van Toai 2009: 143). In the first week of August there was a massive wave of arrests across South Vietnam, as well as a succession of further burnings in the weeks that followed. The first, on 5 August in Phan Thiet, was followed by comments from Madame Nhu, stating that she hoped there would be more burnings and she would clap her hands if there were (*Los Angeles Times* 1963), which only escalated tensions. On 15 August a Buddhist monk in Hue set himself on fire, and government troops, using bayonets and swinging steel helmets like billy clubs, snatched the body from the other priests. Three days later a Buddhist nun in Ninh Hoa burned herself to death in protest at the government's act of seizing the body of the Hue priest. The next morning a fifty-year-old Buddhist priest burned himself. A few days later Ngo Dinh Nhu, the president's brother, who was the head of the secret police, ordered a raid of the pagodas. The American press was outraged by the events that followed (Richardson 2005: 173).

## The warden's dilemma

Many scholars and practitioners have referred to the period between 1961 and 1963 as a turning point. Halberstam (2008: xiii) calls it 'a crucial moment of truth', during which the ultimate outcome in

Vietnam was determined. Although the Buddhist crisis and the self-immolations of the Buddhist monks and nuns were not the only element of this crucial moment, they were decisive in bringing about an end to the Diem regime and a change in US policy. As the fate of the two were interlinked, both in practice and in the perception of the Vietnamese, the crisis turned into a warden's dilemma for both.

As already mentioned, following the self-immolation of Quang Duc, and under pressure from the Americans, Diem finally met with the Buddhists, and the two sides produced a joint communiqué. Diem soon did an about-face, however, and resumed the repression of his opponents. At the end of June John Richardson, from the CIA, met with Nhu in an attempt to get him to persuade Diem to compromise with the Buddhists, to which he responded with a fit of rage. Several days later the *Times of Vietnam*, a paper associated with Madame Nhu, printed an article suggesting that Quang Duc was on drugs when he burned himself, which enraged the Buddhists and was followed by a cable to Washington from Richardson saying that Diem's enemies had begun plotting coups, and that there was even talk of an assassination (Richardson 2005: 164–6). In the meantime, the Buddhist protests continued. The dilemma for Diem at this point was that, if he cracked down, the protests would increase; if he granted reforms, he would be inviting his enemies into the government, which would lead to his downfall; if he did nothing, the situation could drift into more dangerous territory. Further, a refusal to make changes would cost him US support.

The United States also faced a dilemma, however. In the autumn of 1961 General Maxwell Taylor had been sent by President Kennedy to Vietnam on a special mission to see what could be done to keep Vietnam from falling to the communists. After the visit the US commitment to Diem increased dramatically. What had been only 600 advisors became 16,000 US troops in an advisory and supporting role, with a commitment of $1.5 million a day in economic aid – steps that tied US policy to the Ngo family (Halberstam 2008: 7–8). By 1963 a Comprehensive Plan for South Vietnam, which would have begun US disengagement, was just coming into being. In May, before the Buddhist crisis became known in the United States, the Joint Chiefs of Staff had directed procedures for pulling out 1,000 men by the end of the year. The outbreak of violence brought this programme to a halt (Jones 2003: 248). Because the US administration had been deliberate in praising the Ngo family, its actions were constrained by Diem's movements. It pressured Diem behind the scenes to take a more conciliatory stance, but without great success. Any kind of public statement became very awkward, given the potentially sharp contrast with previous statements and the potential effect on Vietnamese domestic politics. As Halberstam (2008: 127) notes, 'The American officials had little room to manoeuvre in, and while they coaxed the family they watched American prestige being dragged down with it.'

A detailed historical analysis of the events and intrigues leading to the assassination of Diem is beyond the scope and purpose of this chapter. My objective is to highlight how the Buddhist crises more generally, and the self-immolations in particular, created a dilemma for both the Diem family and the United States, and how their interdependent actions culminated in the removal of Diem and an escalation of the US role in Vietnam. That the crisis was decisive and a turning point has been recognized on all sides of the political spectrum in both countries. Why these sacrifices should be considered to have had a significant influence has received less attention.

The Diem family, as already stated, was closely linked in the Vietnamese perception to foreigners. Aside from the association of Diem with Catholicism, Daniel Singal (2008: xvii) notes that the growing dependence on American aid made it appear to the Vietnamese that they had replaced one foreign master for another. The closer the connection between Saigon and the United States, the less political loyalty the regime could command at home. At the same time, the clumsiness of Diem's response to the widespread unrest, the horrifying comments by Madame Nhu and the savage attacks on Buddhist pagodas in August 1963 led to a loss of support for the family from Washington, as well as the development of tacit US support for the coup that removed the Diem regime from power.[27]

The point of no return happened on 21 August, during the transitional period between Nolting's departure and the arrival of the new ambassador, Lodge, when busloads of South Vietnamese soldiers raided the Xa Loi Pagoda, a Saigon temple that was the heart of the Buddhist movement. For two hours the gong tolled as soldiers dragged monks and nuns from the pagoda, arresting some 400 in all

---

[27] As Singal (2008: xx) notes, this support was less tacit than actual. Previously classified documents have revealed that the United States had a special CIA agent who met regularly with the generals and transferred messages between them. A representative of the US government was also present in their headquarters on the night of the coup.

(Richardson 2005: 173). Diem declared martial law and imposed a curfew and press censorship as Buddhist pagodas across the country were raided with great violence and repression (Topmiller 2002: 3). In the days following the pagoda raids Saigon's students, who had not traditionally been interested in politics, took over the protests against the government by going on strike in the schools and inviting mass arrests. Thousands of university students were arrested, and, once they had gone, high school students took their place and began to be arrested in the thousands. For a week the streets of Saigon were filled with students being carted off to indoctrination centres. There were also arrests of professors, lawyers, civil servants and some young officers (Halberstam 2008: 152–3).

As in the case of the Hue demonstrations, there were two stories about the source of this violence. This time it was not the Viet Cong who were alleged to be behind the attacks but, rather, either Nhu, the president's brother, who was said to have planned the whole thing without the army knowing, or, on the other hand, it was the army acting alone. *The New York Times* printed both stories on 22 August, one of which attributed the plot to Nhu, and the other to the army. It later became clear that Nhu had used the army as a front for the strike, in order to hide his involvement and to give the impression that the raid had broader backing than it did. The decision to attack the Buddhist pagodas in South Vietnam had been planned and executed by the president's brother. The army had not seized power and knew nothing about it until the raids were under way. As Halberstam (2008: 148) states: 'The troops involved were under the command of Colonel Tung, and Nhu had acted to teach the Buddhists and the Americans a lesson, and to present Lodge with a *fait accompli*.'[28] The violence of the pagoda raids had shocked most Americans, and the implications were dire. It meant the end of a policy based on a misperception that it was possible to have a conciliatory effect on Diem. Given that American equipment and American-trained troops had been used, there would be even less confidence in the United States on the part of the Vietnamese population (Halberstam 2008: 147).

---

[28] Lodge's appointment had indicated a change in policy towards Diem. Lodge provided asylum to dissidents, which further aggravated relations (Topmiller 2002: 3).

The dilemma for Washington, as stated earlier, was what to do about Diem: whether to continue support for him, and alienate the Vietnamese people, not to mention an increasingly critical US public opinion; or to abandon the Diem government and invite a coup to remove him from power. The response of Washington to the pagoda raids also became a point of no return. McNamara (1995: 52) notes that most of the key decision-makers in Washington, including himself, Kennedy, Rusk, McGeorge Bundy (the national security advisor) and John McCone (the CIA director), were out of town when the events at Xa Loi took place. As the reports of the raid flowed into Washington, several of the officials left behind, and in particular Roger Hilsman, assistant Secretary of State for Far Eastern affairs, set in motion a military coup that, McNamara (1995: 52) claims, was 'one of the truly pivotal decisions concerning Vietnam made during the Kennedy and Johnson administrations'. Kennedy was contacted about the cable that was to be sent to Lodge and agreed to it, conditional on the approval of his top advisors. These advisors were then contacted and agreed, reluctantly, having been given the impression that Kennedy supported the action. General Taylor, who received a copy after it had been sent, was shocked, recognizing it as a major change in the administration's Vietnam policy. The cable read (as cited by Richardson 2005: 176):

24 August – Eyes only Ambassador Lodge. No further distribution. US government cannot tolerate situation in which power lies in Nhu's hands. Diem must be given chance to rid himself of Nhu and his coterie and replace them with best military and political personalities available. If, in spite of all your efforts, Diem remains obdurate and refused, then we must face the possibility that Diem himself cannot be preserved.

Kennedy later regretted the cable, and McNamara (1995: 55) states that 'it shocks and saddens me today to realize that action which eventually led to the overthrow and murder of Diem began while US officials in both Washington and Saigon remained deeply divided over the wisdom of his removal'. In defending Washington's decision to support a coup, the Secretary of State said: 'We cannot stand any more burnings.'[29]

---

[29] As recollected by the former ambassador, Nolting (quoted by Jones 2003: 317).

The clash between Diem and the Buddhists in the end created a US commitment that led eventually to some 58,000 American and 3 million Vietnamese deaths. The irony was that the Buddhists opposed Diem in part because of his connection to the United States. What they hadn't realized was Diem's major efforts to restrain Washington and that the Americans supported the 1963 coup in order to have a regime in South Vietnam that was more amenable to their will. The coup against Diem produced a political vacuum that was filled by the United States, resulting in an escalation of the war, which was an outcome the Buddhists had wanted to avoid at all costs (Topmiller 2002: 4–5).

## Emotion and imitation

The first part of this chapter examined the meaning of self-immolation in the cultural context of Mahāyāna Buddhism, linking this tradition to Quang Duc's self-immolation in the political context of the Buddhist crisis. The monk's act fanned public resistance in Vietnam, involving not only monks and nuns but for the first time ordinary citizens, awakened US public opinion to the repressive nature of the South Vietnamese government and resulted in a double warden's dilemma for the Diem regime and its US supporters, which culminated in a coup and the assassination of the Ngo brothers on 1 November 1963. The final section of this chapter examines the imitation of the Vietnamese self-burnings by Americans in subsequent years. In this respect, the American self-burnings were a response (ying) to the Vietnamese stimulus (gan), but at the same time they were themselves a stimulus for further changes. Quang Duc's act had some sense within the cultural framework of Mahāyāna Buddhism. Giving meaning to an act of self-burning was far more problematic in the context of Judeo-Christian America.[30] While the acts were primarily undertaken by Quakers and Catholics, the emotional resonance was arguably as significant as it had been, and of a somewhat different kind, in Vietnam. These acts fanned the protests against the Vietnam War in the United States, resulted in expressions of appreciation and emotional warmth from the Vietnamese for the sacrifices on behalf of their suffering, and touched deep emotional chords in major US

---

[30] As Hanh (1967: 9) notes, Quang Duc's self-immolation had a greater emotional impact on the West than the East, because of significant differences in their religious and cultural backgrounds.

decision-makers, and not least McNamara, who witnessed the self-immolation of Norman Morrison from his office in the Pentagon.

Michael Biggs (2006a: 22; see also Biggs 2006b) has argued that a series of self-immolations over the last four decades belong to the lineage of Quang Duc,[31] stating that 'almost all acts either copied his act, or copied another act which can eventually be traced back to his act'. He refers to protest by self-immolation as 'monophyletic' – a term from biology meaning that a lineage can be traced back to a single origin. Biggs argues that these imitations did not rely on personal contacts or connections but, rather, images and reports transmitted via the mass media, mediated through photographs and news reports. This raises a further question, as to how an act that has cultural meaning in one context acquires emotional resonance and meaning in a much different cultural context, in which it deviates from existing traditions of self-sacrifice. Although the image of the act and its meaning were conveyed by the media, they also invoked further discussion within religious circles. In what follows, I explore acts of imitation in the United States as the basis for a conversation regarding the dialectical tension embodied in an act of self-burning.

## The conversation

The Vietnamese had a framework for making sense of the self-burnings of Buddhist monks and nuns in 1963.[32] Although Buddhism clearly prohibits suicide, these exceptional acts were considered a form of sacrifice, and Thich Quang Duc was understood to be a bodhisattva. In the American context, the Vietnamese self-immolations, while raising perplexing questions, were generally viewed as simply wrong (Hope 1967: 149).[33] One New York newspaper referred to the suicides by fire

---

[31] He states that individuals in some three dozen countries have chosen self-immolation since 1963. This number has undoubtedly increased since the article was written, given the self-immolations of women in Afghanistan and those across northern Africa in the context of the Arab Spring of 2011.

[32] There was not complete agreement on this, however. While some interpreted the self-immolations as heroic acts of self-sacrifice, others argued that it was contrary to Buddhist teachings insofar as it involved both violence and the squandering of precious human rebirths (Keown 2005: 102).

[33] Hanh (1967) recounts a story of sitting next to an American woman on a flight from New York to Stockholm who referred to Quang Duc's act as 'abnormal'. Self-burning, she argued, was an act of savagery, violence and fanaticism.

as a 'sinister scheme of a group of fanatics' uttering 'hypocritical cries of religious persecution'. Other national magazines said that the self-immolations were the work of Buddhist leaders who were 'naive' yet 'cunning', while implying that those who 'gave themselves to flames must be mentally ill' (Hope 1967: 149). In this respect, the American debate surrounding the Vietnamese self-immolations is not dissimilar to twenty-first-century debates about suicide terrorism.

Nhat Hanh's reflection on the *Lotus Sutra*, mentioned earlier, suggested that self-immolation contains two meaningful actions. The first is an act of offering, which places it in the category of sacrifice. In a context of the persecution and destruction of large numbers of people, the agent sacrifices the self to the Buddha in the hope of bringing all living beings closer to liberation (Hanh 2008: 161). This is the 'gan', or the stimulus, but the offering is also a communicative act. The question is what precisely is communicated, particularly when the burning of the body speaks differently to people in very different cultures, who may be more or less equipped to make sense of an act of this kind.

At face value, the act may appear to communicate that a suicide has taken place. In a letter to Martin Luther King, Hanh (1967: 117–19) explained that Quang Duc's act was not suicide or even a protest, but what I have referred to as an 'act of speech':

What the monks said in the letters left before burning themselves aimed only at alarming, at moving the hearts of the oppressors and at calling the attention of the world to the suffering endured then by the Vietnamese. To burn oneself by fire is to prove that what one is saying is of the utmost importance. There is nothing more painful than burning oneself. To say something while experiencing this kind of pain is to say it with utmost courage, frankness, determination and sincerity. [...] One can, of course, say these things while sitting in a comfortable armchair; but when the words are uttered while kneeling before the community of sangha and experiencing this kind of pain, they will express all the seriousness of one's heart and mind and carry much greater weight... The monk who burns himself has lost neither courage nor hope; nor does he desire non-existence. On the contrary, he is very courageous and hopeful and aspires for something good in the future. He does not think that he is destroying himself; he believes in the good fruition of his act of self-sacrifice for the sake of others... [T]he monk believes he is practicing the doctrine of highest compassion by sacrificing himself in order to call the attention of, and to seek help from, the people of the world... Now in the confrontation of the big powers occurring in our country, hundreds and perhaps thousands of Vietnamese peasants and children lose their lives every day and our land is unmercifully and tragically torn by a war which is already twenty years old.

Hanh's letter contrasts suicide, or even protest, with a concept of sacrifice. As a sacrifice, the act shared more with the tradition of American non-violence or Christian martyrdom.[34] The extent to which self-burning could be understood within the latter traditions became the heart of a conversation as a number of Americans, following Quang Duc's example, also engaged in acts of self-burning. The first, in March 1965, was an eighty-two-year-old woman named Alice Herz, who stood on a street corner in Detroit, covered herself with cleaning fluid and set herself on fire to protest 'a great country trying to wipe out a small country for no reason' (Ryan 1994: 21). She told a Fire Department lieutenant on the way to the hospital, 'I did it to protest the arms race all over the world. I wanted to burn myself like the monks in Vietnam did' (Jones 1965). Both her daughter and her pastor stated that she was not acting out of depression or psychological compulsion, nor was she a crackpot; rather, she was trying to 'stir action', and to 'call attention to the gravity of the situation'. Her act received less publicity than those that took place in symbolically important locations. Of the nine Americans who set themselves on fire in the context of the Vietnam War (Ryan 1994: 36, fn 1; see also Books LLC 2010), Norman Morrison probably made the biggest impact, in part because his self-immolation took place outside secretary of defense McNamara's office and because he was holding a child.

The precipitating event for Morrison's self-immolation is said to have been an interview he had read with a French priest. The priest was recuperating in a Saigon clinic after witnessing and surviving an American bombing raid on a village in Vietnam. The priest said, 'I have seen my faithful burned up in napalm. I have seen the bodies of women and children blown to bits. I have seen all my villages razed'

---

[34] This sentiment was expressed by a young Catholic student in Vietnam, who said: 'It is *not* suicide. It is sacrifice...' Hope (1967: 153) then surmises that the student sensed something in the burning bonze that was akin to the spirit of the Christian martyrs; if they did not raise their hands against themselves, they did act in a way to make death inevitable.

(King 2000: 128). Morrison was particularly unsettled by the account of children being killed. In the letter he left behind to his wife, Morrison wrote, 'Know that I love thee but must act for the children of the priest's village.' Morrison's decision to take his baby daughter with him may have symbolically represented the children who had been bombed in Vietnam, although he did hand her over to someone after setting fire to himself, and she was not harmed. The statement to the press, provided by a close friend of the Morrisons a few hours after his death, said that he had 'given his life today to express his concern over the great loss of life and human suffering caused by the war in Vietnam. He was protesting our Government's deep military involvement in this war' (*New York Times* 1965). While Quakers have a very long tradition of non-violence, they have no tradition of self-inflicted death. After Morrison's death, however, many Quakers did question how large the difference is between a death at one's own hand and a death at the hand of others into which one has walked willingly (King 2000: 129).

A third self-immolation took placed at 5:20 a.m. on the morning of 9 November 1965, when Roger LaPorte, a member of the Catholic Worker movement,[35] covered himself in gasoline in front of the United Nations' (UN's) Dag Hammarskjöld Library in New York to protest against US involvement in the Vietnam War. In the hospital, prior to his death, LaPorte stated: 'I am a Catholic Worker. I'm against war, all wars. I did this as a religious action' (Zaroulis and Sullivan 1984: 5).

The imitation of Quang Duc's self-burning in a Christian context raised three questions in particular. The first, already mentioned, is whether these were acts of suicide. Nhat Hanh, in his letter to Martin Luther King, states that it is not suicide, or even protest, but an offering or sacrifice. By contrast, in referring to the acts of self-burning, American newspapers most often used the language of suicide (Halberstam 1963; *Los Angeles Times* 1963a, 1963b; *New York Times* 1965) or protest (Cameron 1965; Biegel 1965), as distinguished from North Vietnamese newspapers or documents, which consistently referred to the American deaths as a sacrifice or martyrdom (Hanoi Radio 1965a, 1965b; *Nhan Dan* 1965a, 1965b, 1965c).

---

[35] The Catholic Worker movement revolved around a daily newspaper, by the same name, and a series of soup kitchens and houses that provided care to the homeless and needy. It was started by Dorothy Day, a former socialist who underwent a conversion to Catholicism.

The intention behind an act of self-burning is an important consideration in determining whether it is suicide or sacrifice. As Sally King (2000: 141–3) points out, in theory, motivation determines the moral nature of the act, such that a selfless and loving motivation equates to a morally good act.[36] If self-immolation is used as a means to end life, in order to destroy the self, and is motivated by this goal, the act can be considered suicide. This represents an entirely different act, although the same in appearance, from one when the self-immolation is a means to awaken others to suffering human life, in which case it becomes a visual representation of violence committed by an 'other'. In sacrificing the body and life, the agent is not doing so for the purpose of escaping the constraints of earthly life but, rather, seeking to effect social change, and in this respect the motivation transcends the self and is concerned with altering the potential of the community. In this regard, therefore, Quang Duc's self-immolation involved reclaiming agency, not only for himself but for South Vietnamese Buddhists as well.

The second question is whether self-immolation is a sin. In her discussion of LaPorte's act, Day (in Ellsberg 1983: 166), the leader of the Catholic Worker movement, states that the Catholic Church always considered suicide to be a sin, but left some space for mercy by claiming that any people who took their own life were temporarily imbalanced and thus not in full possession of their faculties, in which case they could be considered to be temporarily insane, and thus absolved of guilt. While she acknowledged that everyone would view LaPorte's act as a suicide, she wanted to place it in the Church tradition of 'victim souls', as a way of trying to understand what he 'must have been thinking when he set fire to himself' (in Ellsberg 1983: 167). Identifying LaPorte's action with those of Herz and the Buddhist monks in Vietnam, she concluded that 'all were trying to show their willingness to give their lives for others to endure the sufferings that we as a nation are inflicting upon a small country and its people, to lay down their own lives rather than take the lives of others. It is the teaching of the Church that only in the Cross is there redemption' (167).

---

[36] In Buddhism, negative karma will follow an act of violence towards the self, as it indirectly harms others, such as parents, and breaks the rules of the Buddhist order. If one accepts the negative karma, however, one is in fact freed of its consequences, and thereby can earn merit.

To Buddhists, suicide is a 'transgression', and sin does not exist in the way that it does in Christianity.[37] The eightfold path of right conduct taught by the Buddha showed the way rather than teaching commandments. In that there are always exceptions in life, there can be no moral laws. For Buddhists, suicide would generally be wrong because it is an act against *life*; but self-immolation is not considered an act against life. As stated by one Saigon teacher (quoted by Hope 1967: 162):

The rest of us are not superior beings like Thich Quang Duc and other martyrs – but we understand them. They must have been thoroughly merged with the concept of eternity as a straight line unlimited at both ends, with one human life like a slight ripple before it goes back to the straight line again – their detachment from life is such that life and death are not disconnected.

If it is possible to reach that point where life and death are not disconnected, then self-immolation cannot be an act against life. For Christians, suicide is a sin because, in the words of one priest (quoted by Hope 1967: 161), 'it is an attempt against dominion and the right of ownership of the creator'. Christianity's emphasis on the salvation of the individual soul contrasts with the Buddhist belief that there is no permanent self, and that, like all else in the universe, a person is in a process of continuous change. Although the Western self acquires control *over* nature, this self is no longer in union with it. From this perspective, self-immolation becomes an act of destruction of the individual self rather than a gesture for life, as it is in Buddhism (Hope 1967: 162). As King (2000: 142) argues, however, what differentiates the two religions is the long-established tradition in Buddhism of pardoning the violence of self-immolation if it is based on noble motivation. Buddhists have a habit of thinking of self-immolation as heroic, which is a cultural value that is understood by individuals in Buddhist countries even if they are not themselves religious.

The third question is whether self-burning can be considered a non-violent strategy, given that the body is, in the process, destroyed. Thomas Merton, a Catholic writer and Trappist monk, raised this question in the context of LaPorte's self burning, which he argued (quoted by Ryan 1994: 24) 'contradicted the principles of nonviolence

---

[37] This claim was made by a Buddhist psychiatrist (see Hope 1967: 161).

by turning upon themselves the very fury of the violence they condemn'. Daniel Berrigan, a Jesuit priest, who, along with Merton, formed the Interfaith Coalition against the Vietnam War, came to a different conclusion. Berrigan, like Day, saw self-burning as horrific, but, also like her, couldn't bring himself to condemn it.[38] While Merton, at the time, viewed self-immolation as an act of inflicting violence on the self, and thus suicide, and a sin, and therefore condemned it along with violence in all forms, Berrigan made a distinction between different traditions of non-violence, between doing violence to the self and taking violence upon oneself. This establishes a fine continuum between acts that involve deliberate violence to the self and violence that arises from acts that it can be predicted will result in violence being directed at the self by others, such as when one attempts to prevent violence against a victim by placing one's body between an aggressor and the victim. Absorbing violence wouldn't usually be considered suicide. To view an act of self-immolation as 'taking on' violence is to place it in the category of self-sacrifice rather than suicide.

Day and Berrigan viewed suicide as arising from private despair, while the act of self-immolation had to 'be spoken of in a far deeper context' (in Ellsberg 1983: 166). The latter was a *political* act consistent with the deepest aspirations of non-violent resistance. Day wrote that Herz, Morrison and LaPorte were all trying 'to endure the suffering that their nation was inflicting on others' (167). As Cheney Ryan (1994: 32) notes, Day was not suggesting that these agents suffered *for* the Vietnamese, meaning that they were animated primarily by compassion. Rather, she referred to them as *sharing* the suffering of the Vietnamese, such that it became *their* suffering as well. In this respect, Herz, Morrison and LaPorte were motivated less by compassion for others than by a type of *identification* with them, and thereby embodied some of the deepest impulses of non-violence. This sentiment was expressed by Nhat Hanh (1987: 63–4) in his well-known poem 'Please call me by my true names':

> I am the child in Uganda, all skin and bones
> My legs as thin as bamboo sticks...
> I am the twelve-year-old girl,
> Refugee on a small boat,
> Who throws herself into the ocean after being raped by a sea pirate...

---

[38] Indeed, at a memorial service for LaPorte, his words were so sympathetic that he was exiled by his superiors to Latin America for a time (Berrigan 1987).

The key to these verses is the 'I am'. As King (2000: 132) notes, when the barrier of 'self' falls, the pain of another becomes one's 'own'. In this situation, one is inclined to act quickly and strongly to relieve the intense suffering.

## Conclusion

The acts of self-immolation touched individuals on both sides of the Pacific. The imitation in a foreign environment of an act that had a particular resonance in Vietnam identified with those suffering in Vietnam who were, in the context of war, supposed to be the enemy. While the acts of self-immolation within Vietnam contributed to a *communitas* of the Vietnamese nation, the conversation in a more international space contributed to the construction of a *communitas* of individuals who suffered with those who were the victims of US policy. McNamara noted the profound effect Morrison's self-immolation had on him. In his memoir *In Retrospect*, McNamara writes, 'At twilight that day, a young Quaker named Norman Morrison, father of three...burned himself to death within forty feet of my Pentagon window.....Morrison's death was a tragedy not only for his family but also for me and the country.' He adds, 'I am horrified, horrified by it... And I was also quite aware that my own family was deeply disturbed by the event, and many other members of the public were' (McNamara quoted by Steinbach 1995). Paul Hendrickson (1996: 214), who has carried out an in-depth study of both McNamara and Morrison, writes:

[W]hat I fervently believe, and cannot prove, is that Norman Morrison's act became the emotional catalyst for the secret turn. What I believe, and cannot prove, is that the fire in the garden became the deep sensitizing agent for a revelation that began seeping into the secretary of defense about a fortnight later.

When McNamara published *In Retrospect*, Morrison's widow, Anne Morrison Welsh (as quoted by Hendrickson 1996: 240), wrote to him about the book and released her statement to the press, which said:

To heal the wounds of [the Vietnam] war, we must forgive ourselves and each other, and help the people of Vietnam to rebuild their country. I am grateful to Robert McNamara for his courageous and honest reappraisal of the Vietnam War and his involvement in it. I hope his book will contribute to the healing process.

McNamara is said to have carried a copy of her statement with him, often reading it aloud to the press 'in an emotion-choked voice'. He further expressed his admiration for 'anyone [who] could have gone through what she did and then write the person who, in the mind of her husband, was responsible for the actions that resulted in his killing himself. . . I was deeply grateful to her for expressing forgiveness. . .and I was deeply moved' (Steinbach 1995).

The self-immolations were deeply emotional for the Vietnamese as well. People make pilgrimages, for political as well as religious reasons, to the home temple of Thich Quang Duc. This shrine includes the car in which he rode to his self-immolation, along with a photograph of the actual self-immolation. In North Vietnam, the American self-immolators had a similar status. Morrison was a hero, and poems and songs celebrating his heroic deed were very popular during the war (King 2000: 142). North Vietnam issued a commemorative stamp with his picture on it and a street has been named after him. Pictures of Morrison and Herz hang in the Revolutionary Museum in Hanoi. Anne Morrison recognized that Norman's death was used politically by the Hanoi government, but also that the politicized news of his sacrifice would not alone have had the power to move so many people, even years and years later. She said (quoted by Appy 2008: 151):

It was like an arrow was shot from Norman's heart, which was so broken because of the war, and the arrow sailed all the way across thousands of miles and pierced the heart of the Vietnamese people, in the way that love pierces your heart. One of them said, 'We were such a tiny little country. It was like a gnat fighting an elephant. But someone from that huge country cared enough for us that he gave his life for us.' They really believed Norman gave his live for them.

The use, while political, suggests a cultural resonance and understanding of the meaning of these acts.[39]

The self-immolations in both contexts generated similar dynamics. In Vietnam they fanned the flames of resistance, widening the circle of *communitas* willing to support, identify with or even die for an end to the Diem regime. While the Vietnamese resistance sought to restore a unified Vietnamese nation, self-immolation in the American

---

[39] By contrast, there have been no public honours extended to Morrison in the United States (King 2002: 142).

context pointed towards a more international *communitas* and the potential to suffer with those who had been harmed by US policy. The American self-burnings took place against the backdrop of the US escalation of the war and at the same time fanned the flames of the anti-war movement. The first self-immolation, by Herz, took place on 16 March 1965, just a few weeks after the beginning of Operation Rolling Thunder, an aerial campaign against North Vietnamese targets, followed in the same month by the introduction of US combat troops and the authorization by Lyndon Johnson, Kennedy's successor as US president, of the use of napalm. The protests against US involvement in Vietnam had begun in 1964, with demonstrators numbering in the hundreds, but after the draft was increased from 3,000 a month to 33,000 in October 1965 the protests escalated. Morrison's self-burning followed on 2 November, with Roger LaPorte a week later. The largest demonstration to date took place a few weeks later, on 27 November, when an anti-war rally in Washington drew some 30,000. On the same day President Johnson announced an escalation in US troop numbers from 120,000 to 400,000. While there is an element of 'ganying', or stimulus and response, it was not of a kind that pointed in the direction of any kind of peaceful resolution in the short term. The protests escalated along with the war.

By 1972, with the peace movement gaining ground at home and North Vietnam feeding an endless supply of soldiers into the war, Secretary of State Henry Kissinger (1972) referred to the 'catch-22' of being caught between an 'insatiable peace movement and an implacable enemy' and the huge long-term consequences of a humiliating withdrawal. While it would be difficult to draw any causal link between the 'catch-22' expressed by Kissinger and the self-immolations almost a decade earlier, the latter represented a significant turning point. The self-burnings in Vietnam in 1963 fanned the flames of protest, paving the way for a coup against the Diem regime and an escalation of the US military involvement, and the imitation of these self-burnings in the American context a few years later fanned the flames of the US protest movement against the war and paved the way for McNamara's withdrawal, followed a few years later by a US withdrawal, when the administration of President Richard Nixon finally accepted that it had no choice but to accept defeat.

As with the case of Northern Ireland, the self-sacrifice was followed by an escalation of violence. Unlike Northern Ireland, the catalyst for this escalation was the removal of the existing regime from power. Like Northern Ireland, the self-sacrifice had a counterpart in a group engaged in violent conflict. Although the Northern Irish hunger strikers were imprisoned because of their links to the IRA, however, and placed their actions in the tradition of IRA prison strikes going back to the 1916 Easter Rising, the Buddhist peace movement and the Viet Cong represented two distinct strands of opposition. The one was committed to non-violence and the latter engaged in the violent practices of war, albeit sustained by an ethos of sacrifice in the face of an external power. In both contexts, the self-sacrifice gave rise to a liminal state, in which identities were in flux. In both cases, further war was the consequence, which reinforces Turner's claim that there is no direct relationship between the liminal conditions of anti-structure and what will emerge from it.

# PART III

# Comparisons and Conclusions

# 7 | *Martyrdom in the contemporary Middle East and north Africa*

The previous chapters have focused on earlier examples of political self-sacrifice from the period following World War II. This distance facilitated research, in terms of the availability of archival evidence, on the one hand, but also, on the other, allowed for a somewhat more objective and dispassionate analysis. It is useful to end by bringing insights from these historical examples to bear on more contemporary cases. Variations on the three forms of political self-sacrifice have been part of the contemporary politics of the Middle East and north Africa.

While the previous three chapters analysed distinct expressions of political self-sacrifice within separate cultures, this chapter analyses suicide terrorism, non-violent martyrdom and self-burning as expressed in one regional context. The first, 'suicide terrorism', is a separate category, in that it involves a deliberate decision to destroy the self as well as innocent others. Suicide terrorism does, however, share a family resemblance with the Northern Irish context, where the self-sacrifice of IRA prisoners was connected to a violent IRA campaign outside the prison.[1] The family resemblance grows out of the combination of self-sacrifice and violence, albeit expressed in a very different way in each case. Second, I explore Israel's incursion onto the humanitarian flotilla heading for Gaza on 31 May 2010, which resulted in the deaths of 'martyrs' who were 'acting as if' it were possible to deliver aid to Gaza. The third category was the self-immolation through burning of the Tunisian Mohammad Bouazizi, followed by others, which triggered the massive protests that brought down the leaders of Tunisia and Egypt.

This chapter, like the others, situates the meaning of political self-sacrifice in religious/cultural and political contexts, draws on the

---

[1] The emphasis on the self-sacrifice distinguishes this comparison from the more frequent contrast between the 'old' terrorism of Northern Ireland and the 'new' terrorism of al-Qaida.

warden's dilemma framework to examine the strategic dynamics of each and explores the role of political self-sacrifice in constructing *communitas*. The patterns that were characteristic of the historical cases are also evident here, including the contestation over the identity of the agents as terrorists or martyrs, and their deaths as suicide or martyrdom, and the central role of emotions related to humiliation and dignity. The chapter is distinguished from the others by the comparative engagement within a regional context, which draws on insights from and contrasts with the more historical cases. As in the last chapter, I examine the role of particular religious and cultural traditions in justifying action.[2]

## The *shahid* in Islam

The idea that suffering for faith is a powerful testimonial is as old as Islam, going back to the first revelations of the prophet Muhammad (approximately 610 CE). Unlike Christianity, in which Christ's crucifixion provided the model for martyrdom, it was not the prophet Muhammad's personal experience of suffering that gave rise to the collective Muslim memory of martyrdom but the suffering of helpless slaves in Mecca (Cook 2007: 13). One of the best-known stories of martyrdom from the Meccan period of the Prophet's life was that of an Ethiopian slave named Bilal, who was persecuted for his belief in a monotheistic Islam in a context in which the powers that be were polytheistic. This story reflects an understanding of martyrdom not unlike that of the early Christian martyrs. Bilal was taken by his master into the blazing sun and told to lie down on his back, after which his master placed a heavy stone on his chest, saying to him: 'You will continue like this until you die or you deny [the god of] Muhammad and worship al-Lat and al-'Uzza.'[3] Bilal was eventually rescued by Abu Bakr, the eventual successor to the prophet Muhammad, who bought him and freed him from slavery. Although he survived, Bilal became a powerful symbol of martyrdom, on account of his suffering for the sake of Islam (Cook 2007: 14).

---

[2] Portions of this analysis are drawn from Fierke (2009b) and Fattah and Fierke (2009).

[3] The latter were the two primary deities of pagan Mecca.

The early Muslim community eventually migrated to the oasis town of Medina, not least because of the persecution experienced in Mecca. In 622 CE the Prophet and his followers were invited to settle there by local tribesman who had converted to Islam. Within five years of establishing a community in Medina, almost everyone in the oasis was Muslim. In the Medina period Muhammad became the leader of a military force. From this time onward Islam for the most part occupied a position of power. The result was a different understanding of martyrdom from that in faiths that had been deprived of worldly success during their early development (Cook 2007: 14).

With the eventual split between Sunni and Shia Muslims, the concept of martyrdom took a much more central place among the latter. The Battle of Karbala, which took place in 680 CE, is the centrepiece of Shia rituals of martyrdom.[4] The battle involved Hussein ibn Ali, the Prophet's grandson and third imam of the Shiites, who was defeated by the government militia led by Umayyad Caliph Yazid. Although the battle took place before the formal split of Muslims into Sunni and Shia, it sealed the schism between them. For the Shiites, Hussein's blood was shed unjustly, and those who killed him – the spiritual ancestors of the Sunnis – are guilty of his murder. Shiites, however, suffer the guilt of having abandoned him to his fate, failing to provide him with support at a critical moment (Cook and Allison 2007: 20). Hussein was venerated because he didn't cower in the face of an asymmetry of power, nor was he deterred by this inequality from seeking to redress injustice (Hafez 2007: 124).

While the concept of 'martyrdom' exists in both the Sunni and Shia traditions of Islam, it has a different meaning in each. In the Sunni tradition, martyrdom is closely linked to jihad and a conception of self-sacrifice as the noblest act of witness to the sovereignty of God (Hulmes 1991: 277). For Shiites, martyrdom is more closely linked to rituals of suffering, mourning and redemption (Kermani 2002). This

---

[4] Kermani (2002: 21) further notes that the Shiite cult of martyrdom has never promoted attacks on defenceless or unarmed people. It did lead to a dramatic increase in the number of people prepared to sacrifice themselves, but this applied to situations of militant confrontation, such as that of the Battle of Karbala.

difference reflects the dominant position of Sunnis historically and politically, as well as the suffering of Shiites at their hands.[5]

It is not only that the split between Shias and Sunnis influenced the meaning of martyrdom; its meaning in both traditions has been shaped by changing historical conditions. Daniel Brown (2001: 108) notes that medieval Muslim scholars would not have embraced more modern assumptions that violent death is the most significant expression of martyrdom. The emphasis at the time was on the inward sacrifice of the believer and the jihad against evil within the human spirit. Martyrs included not only those who died in battle but also those who testified to truth through argument or engaged in 'the jihad of the pen', which was a reflection of a time when opportunities for martyrdom on the battle-field were minimal (Brown 2001: 109). By contrast, the ascendency of the West, colonization and the accompanying sense of economic and political upheaval led to a rearticulation of the meaning of jihad and martyrdom by Sunnis. While the initial reaction to colonialism was the emergence of military jihad movements, this was followed in the nineteenth century by a shift back to an emphasis on the jihad of internal spiritual struggle. In the twentieth century Sunni revivalists once against highlighted the importance of physical jihad and armed struggle, and it became the duty of the individual Muslim to participate in jihad to liberate the land in the case of Muslim territory being occupied by an enemy invader. If physical jihad was considered superior, then the true martyr became one who died in battle (Brown 2001: 110–11). In the thinking of Hasan al-Banna, the founder of the Muslim Brotherhood, a martyr was a person who no longer existed as an individual but became the ideal he or she died for. The martyr thus exchanges life for something greater and more lasting (Brown 2001: 12).

---

[5] The term 'Sunni' comes from the word 'Sunnah', meaning the method, custom, practice or path of the Prophet laid out after his death in Islamic tradition and law. 'Shii', on the other hand, is derived from 'Shia', meaning a faction, party or group; 'Shiite' simply means a follower. As such, the term 'Shia' has a meaning only when the leader is specified. Examples from the Qur'an include the prophet Abraham being mentioned as the Shia of Noah (Qur'an 37: 83) and 'the Shia of Moses versus the enemies of Moses' (Qur'an 28: 15). Following the split of Islam, Shiites were the followers of Ali, the grandson of the Prophet of Islam. This means that Sunnis follow a law while Shiites follow a leader. In the latter branch, clergy enjoy a much higher degree of influence and power. There are approximately 1.5 billion Muslims, and only about 15 per cent are Shiites. In the Middle East, they constitute a majority in Iran, Iraq, Azerbaijan and Bahrain.

Much like the Western theory of the just war, most Islamic scholars would argue that any use of violence should only be defensive (Abu-Nimer 2003: 35). Imam Yahya Hendi, a Qur'anic scholar who is the Muslim chaplain at Georgetown University, states that while, 'the Qur'an doesn't condone terrorism', Muhammad used violence as the leader of a military force during the Medina period. Islam is very clear regarding the prohibition, in times of military engagement, on destroying civilian life, advising military commanders and soldiers on the battlefield to be fair, avoid excessive violence and incline towards peace (Kamali 2002: 22). The marriage of martyrdom with a concept of external jihad by contemporary Sunni militants has contributed to a widespread assumption that Islam is fundamentally violent. Although the Qur'an does refer to jihad and fighting (*qital*) against non-Muslims, scholars have pointed out that, in contrast to *qital*, jihad refers more generally to various methods of bringing religion into practice. Even when jihad entails some use of force there are ambiguities in the Qur'anic references. The prophet Muhammad made a distinction between taking up arms against an unbeliever, on the one hand, and the struggle against one's own desires and selfishness, on the other. Upon returning from battle, Muhammad reportedly said: 'We have returned from the lesser jihad to the greater jihad.' When asked which the greater endeavour was, Muhammad is said to have replied, 'It is the struggle against one's self' (as cited by Euben 2002).

While there are passages in the Qur'an, like the Old Testament of the Bible, that celebrate military victory, the overall gestalt of the Qur'an promotes a more restrained view, as expressed in the following passage (Qur'an: 5.32):

We ordained for the Children of Israel that if any one slew a person – unless it be for murder or for spreading mischief in the land – it would be as if he slew the whole people: and if anyone saved a life, it would be as if he saved the life of the whole people.

This passage places a great value on the sanctity of a single life. Hendi (cited by Ateek 2002: 6) argues that many Qur'anic verses say that martyrdom must not cause harm to others, quoting the prophet Muhammad as saying 'Do not attack a temple, a church, a synagogue. Do not bring a tree or a plant down. Do not harm a horse or a camel.'

The *shahid* is a martyr who has suffered death as a witness to his or her faith or the principles he or she stands for.[6] In Arabic, the verb *shaheda* means 'to witness'.[7] While the English word 'martyr' is derived from the Greek word for 'witness', *martys*, the *shahid* almost always refers to a witness as one who observes and can attest and provide proof (Berenbaum and Firestone 2004: 136).[8] In Islam, as in Christianity, martyrdom is associated with bearing witness, which is itself tied up with the idea of struggle against injustice and oppression. 'To witness' means to be present and to testify, which suggests that the martyr lives not only in the afterlife but in the recollections and remembrances of the community of the living (Euben 2002).

This understanding of the martyr as witness to the community contrasts with the logic of suicide, in which the subject and object of death is the individual actor who is disconnected from a social world. 'Suicide' in Arabic is *intihar*, which means 'to kill one's self for personal reasons'. As stated in the Qur'an (4: 29): 'Do not kill yourselves, for God is merciful to you. If any of you does these things, out of hostility and injustice, We shall make him suffer Fire: that is easy for God.' In the Islamic conception, as in the Buddhist, the distinction between suicide and martyrdom is closely linked to the intention of the agent (Lewinstein 2001: 81).[9]

---

[6] Although the word *shahid* does not appear in the Qur'an, the text does refer to 'those slain in the path of God', as, for example, in Qur'an 2: 154; 3: 169. It is in the Hadiths (collections of Islamic traditions containing sayings of the prophet Muhammad) that martyrs are more clearly distinguished from ordinary Muslims.

[7] The word *shahid* (plural *shuhada*), meaning both 'witness' and 'martyr', is influenced by the Syriac *sahido*, which is the word used to translate key Christian concepts related to martyrdom in the Syriac Bible, the Pshitta (such as Acts 1: 8).

[8] Footnote b on page 44 of the Qur'an (2008) states that the noun *shahed* is more complex than the term 'martyr', which is usually the English translation. The root 'sh–h–d' conveys 'to witness, to be present, to attend' but also 'to testify' or 'to give evidence'. The *shahed* is thus chosen by Allah to witness, is given the opportunity to give evidence of the depth of his or her faith by sacrificing his or her worldly lives and will testify with the prophets on the last Day of Judgment.

[9] Keith Lewinstein's focus is on the intentionality of martyrdom in jihad. To be considered a martyr, the intent of fighting should not be for earthly reward but the word of God. While intention is central to the performance of any act of piety, and only Allah can know intention, any warrior who dies at the hands of the enemy should be buried as a martyr.

## *The political context*

The purpose of this section is to provide a framework for making sense of the various acts of political self-sacrifice explored in what follows. The brief structural sketch is complemented by further elaboration of more localized contexts throughout. All the examples thus far have revolved around peoples who 'played with a weak hand', in a situation in which their sovereignty is said to have been curtailed by foreign interference. I use the phrase 'said to have been' to highlight the fact that the question of foreign interference or occupation is often part of the contestation, and embedded within an historical narrative that rests on particular constructions of identity and geography, while situating and justifying forms of action vis-à-vis potential audiences.

Western observers of the Middle East and north Africa might be inclined to make a distinction between the colonial past and the sovereign status of contemporary states in the region, or to identify a 'clash of civilizations' (Huntington 1996) or any number of other differences, such as traditional versus modern (Friedman 2000; Kaplan 2000), that distinguish this region from 'the West'. These narratives often assume the superiority of the latter and are based on orientalist assumptions (Said 1979). As Said (1980) noted over thirty years ago:

Very little of the detail, the human density, the passion of Arab-Muslim life has entered the awareness of even those people whose profession it is to report the Arab world. What we have instead is a series of crude, essentialised caricatures of the Islamic world presented in such as way as to make that world vulnerable to military aggression.

These caricatures establish a set of boundaries distinguishing past and present (colonial versus sovereign), as well as cultural boundaries, that have defined the unique history of each half of the clash.

The spatial and historical division of space is much different in the more regional narratives that have informed resistance, which focus on the relationship between international, regional and national dynamics that are inseparable from the past, as well as an historical experience of humiliation and betrayal. The boundaries and structures of Middle Eastern states were imposed by European colonizers. Colonial penetration by European powers, beginning with Napoleon's invasion of Egypt in 1798, set the stage. The occupation of Egypt by a small French military force revealed to Arabs and Muslims both the power of Western states and the weakness of their Islamic protector, the Ottoman caliphate. The French invasion also made Muslims realize that only another European power, namely the United Kingdom, could get the French out of their lands (Lewis 2001). During World War I the British mobilized Arabs to revolt against the Ottomans on the basis of promises that were not fulfilled. They were promised that they would receive independence and autonomy in return for cooperation. In the end the British stayed in the region for several decades. While states are now formally independent, the international relationship to the United States is often, within this narrative, articulated as the contemporary expression of the historical humiliation, betrayal and subordination of people in the region.

The construction of 'Western' states – the national dimension – began with the secret Sykes–Picot agreement in 1916, which carved up the most ethnically complex and historic portions of the region into British and French zones of colonial influence.[10] The artificial, arbitrary and conflict-laden borders of today's Middle East are largely the result of this secret agreement. Iraq, for instance, which has been torn apart by sectarian conflict over the last decade, is a concrete example of an Arab country 'designed' by a handful of British officers (Hudson 1977).

The more regional dynamic relates to the proclamation of the State of Israel in 1948, followed by the Palestinian *al Nakba* (catastrophe) and the mass expulsion of the Palestinians from their lands. Going back to 1917, the Balfour Declaration, which was a letter from the foreign secretary of the United Kingdom, Arthur James Balfour, to Baron Rothschild, a leader of the British-Jewish community, expressed support for the establishment of Palestine as a national home for the Jewish people, but expressed concern that nothing be done that would prejudice the civil or religious rights of the non-Jewish population in Palestine. The trauma experienced by European Jews during World War II and the Holocaust gave impetus and moral legitimacy to the creation of the Israeli state. Palestinian Arabs and the surrounding Arab states rejected the 1947 UN plan to partition Palestine and

---

[10] As bin Laden stated in 2003, '[O]ur wounds have yet to heal from the Crusader wars of the last century against the Islamic world, or from the Sykes–Picot Agreement of 1916..., which brought about the dissection of the Islamic world into fragments' (Lawrence 2005: 187).

viewed the General Assembly vote as an 'international betrayal' (Beinin and Haijar 2000). The dispossession and expulsion of Palestinians with the creation of Israel has been a primary focus of expressions of anger in the region, and the central loss identified by Islamists (see, for example, Ayman al-Zawahiri in Mansfield 2006: 211). The three examples of political self-sacrifice that follow relate to this division, focusing on the global logic of the War on Terror, the regional dynamics relating to the plight of the Palestinians and the resistance to dictatorial regimes.

This structural division of the political space provides a framework for thinking about how, in a region made up of de jure sovereign states, many would carry not only memories of foreign occupation but a perception of continuing foreign influence. The 9/11 bombers originated not from 'axis of evil' countries or countries perceived to be hostile to Washington, such as Syria, but from those with US-supported governments in the region. Fifteen of the hijackers were Saudis; two were from the United Arab Emirates, one from Lebanon, one from Morocco. They were led by an Egyptian, Mohammed Atta, and aided from Germany by the Moroccan Mounir el Motassadeq. Abu Musab al-Zarqawi, the former al-Qaida leader in Iraq, was Jordanian. In the narratives of militant Islamists, the historical experience of humiliation is the product of a national, regional and international construction, imposed by the West on Arabs and Muslims and lowering their status within it.

Many of these regimes, which have also been a focus of the more secular Arab Spring, have lacked a popular political base and maintained power through a draconian security apparatus. From the lack of basic social infrastructure and political rights, including freedom of speech, to the everyday humiliation by bureaucracies and security forces, a popular image of a corrupt Westernized elite developed among the masses (Roy 1998 [1992]). A further sense of betrayal emerged, not only from the failure of the state to provide protection to its population but from an increasing perception that the state was a source of insecurity. Although the narrative presented above has been most explicitly articulated by Islamists, it has a broader resonance among the populations to which they have appealed.

The War on Terror increased the powers of the state against potential 'terrorists', and many states in the region became the destination for rendition flights carrying suspected terrorists to be tortured. Many would claim that the War on Terror was a Bush administration creation that ended, at least in its extreme form, with the election of Barack Obama as US president. Indeed, the Obama administration, while retaining more of the Bush administration's policies than first hoped, has made an explicit shift away from the stance of 'you are either with us or the terrorists' to that of 'unclenching fists'. Obama made a gesture to the Arab and Muslim world in his inaugural address, and then in a speech in Cairo in June 2009 (Obama 2009a, 2009b). Both speeches signalled a change in the identity of the United States towards the Arab and Muslim world, as well as calling on citizens abroad to hold corrupt and authoritarian governments to account. Thus, while the Bush administration advocated the spread of democracy to the Middle East, often at the barrel of a gun, Obama called on the people themselves to bring this reality into being. The contrast between the two administrations will be one element of the strategic dynamic explored in the following sections.

## Sacrificial violence

Many scholars have argued that suicide bombing has proliferated because it works. The most important precedent occurred in Lebanon in April 1983 with the suicide attacks on the US embassy in Beirut,[11] in which sixty-three people died, and on the US marine barracks six months later, which killed 241 US marines. At the same time, an explosion at the French peacekeeping compound resulted in the deaths of fifty-eight. A further attack four months later was followed by the departure of the Multinational Force from Lebanon. Faced with the shock of this unprecedented event, and a choice between watching further troops die or pulling out, the United States decided to leave. Edward Walker, a senior State Department official at the time, said

---

[11] Some start with 1981, when a sole suicide attack hit the Iraqi embassy. In addition, during the Iran–Iraq War, the Basiji (Popular Mobilization Army or People's Army) carried out 'human wave' assaults, in which men and boys as young as nine used their bodies to clear mines. This sacrifice, which de-mined Iraqi positions and overran them, was essential for the Iranian forces behind them to secure their positions and eliminate the Iraqis (Cook and Allison 2007: 12). Fahmide, a twelve-year-old who threw himself under an Iraqi tank and exploded a grenade on 10 November 1980, became a model for future suicide missions (Saturen 2005). As a situation of military confrontation, however, this was more consistent with the Shiite notion of martyrdom.

that the 'long-term implication [of the subsequent US withdrawal] was it appeared to terrorists that. . .all you have to do is hurt the Americans and you will get what you want. That's been a persistent problem for us' (CNN 2003).[12] While campaigns of this kind have been successful in achieving limited goals, as Pape (2003) points out, they have been less successful in accomplishing the overall objective of removing a foreign power. The US withdrawal from Lebanon is thus the exception rather than the rule.

The legitimacy of martyrdom operations has been a subject of debate within Islam. At the height of the War on Terror, some Islamic scholars distinguished the acts of al-Qaida against a foreign power, which they labelled 'terrorist', from acts within, for instance, Israel/Palestine, which were viewed as a legitimate form of resistance to occupation (Malka 2003: 19). Sheikh Usuf al-Qaradawi, a Sunni religious authority, rejected the term 'suicide operations', maintaining that 'marytrdom operations' should not be attributed to suicide. Distinguishing between 'suicide terrorism' and 'martyrdom', Qaradawi declared (as cited by Esposito 2007: 2):

The Palestinian who blows himself up is a person who is defending his homeland. When he attacks an occupier enemy, he is attacking a legitimate target. This is different from someone who leaves his country and goes to strike a target with which he has no dispute.

Contrary to Qaradawi's argument, al-Qaida used the language of 'martyrdom', and the American presence in Saudi Arabia was presented as one justification for its action.[13]

While religion has acquired a persuasive value in the Middle East, its use in this context is paradoxical. As Navid Kermani (2002) argues, aside from the earlier use of suicide bombers by Shiites in Lebanon, contemporary 'martyrdom operations' tend to be organized by Sunni groups, such as Hamas and al-Qaida. The martyrdom of Islamic militants, such as al-Qaida, marries the Sunni emphasis on jihad, or

---

[12] There are other examples of success short of removing an occupying force. Palestinian suicide terrorism in Israel in 1996 resulted in a change of government and had a major, if deleterious, impact on the Middle Eastern peace process (Merari 2007: 101). It has been successful in derailing sensitive negotiations, such as the Oslo Accords, has strongly impacted political processes (the Madrid train bombings) and has disrupted military activities and humanitarian/ rebuilding efforts (Afghanistan and Iraq) (Speckhard 2005: 1).

[13] The US presence in Saudi Arabia has been dramatically reduced subsequently.

struggle, with the Shia cult of suffering in creating candidates for death. In Iraq the discourse of martyrdom came from Jihadi Salafis, who are Sunnis, and was combined with a virulent anti-Shia discourse that dehumanized targets and justified killing them in suicide operations (Hafez 2007: 111–12).[14] The paradox is that the Jihadi Salafis mimicked Shia martyrdom in attacking their Shia enemy (Hafez 2007: 125).

As the earlier discussion suggests, even a few decades ago the association of martyrdom with taking one's own life and that of bystanders would have been foreign to the Muslim world. The use of martyrdom as a justification for the human bomb is a product of a group of middle-class and Westernized Arabs who underwent a religious conversion, before becoming the leaders of al-Qaida (Kermani 2002). Their narrative of martyrdom weaves together strands of religious discourse in contradictory ways. For instance, the integration of a martyrdom discourse into a Sunni package highlights the experience of humiliation and the need for jihad against non-Muslims in justifying the use of violence. This discourse has had resonance throughout the Middle East given the widespread sense of humiliation among Arab and Muslim populations – a theme that is pervasive in the literature from the region (Moghadam 2002: 27–8; Khashan 2003: 1062; Telhami 2008; Fattah and Fierke 2009).

There has been widespread criticism that the terms 'jihad' and 'martyrdom' have either been misinterpreted or interpreted very narrowly by militant Islamists (Fadl 2005), but the terms nonetheless have had a resonance in the Middle East. Martyrdom locates the act within a social world of injustice, and an ongoing experience of humiliation by a community, as well as a desire to re-establish dignity (Saad-Ghorayeb 2002: 127). Choosing to end one's life with suicide brings an end to earthly life and, given the religious prohibition, is not generally tied to an expectation of afterlife. 'Martyrdom', as expressed by Islamic militants, makes a connection between earthly and divine objectives. The martyr gives up earthly life with the promise of continuing life in paradise. It is the dignity of Allah (God) that is the ultimate justice to be restored, but this dignity also resides in the

---

[14] Unlike other elements of the insurgency, the Jihadi Salafis saw the war in Iraq not just as the mere expulsion of occupation forces but also as an opportunity to establish a genuine Islamic state.

potential for justice towards the ummah (the Islamic community). In the Palestinian context, 'martyrdom' was, at one and the same time, the 'fastest way to immortalise themselves in Allah's heaven and the surest way to achieve a balance of terror with Israel's overwhelming military machine' (Khashan 2003: 1061). It is the social significance of the act, the promise to address a social injustice, as well as the remuneration of the martyr's family (Rabinovich 2002), that provide the social legitimacy for choosing to end one's life. It is not only that organizations behind the acts used it as a coercive strategy but that many Palestinians were convinced that martyrdom operations provide the ultimate weapon for coercing Israel to submit to their demands, given their inability to challenge Israel's devastating military power in a conventional confrontation (Khashan 2003: 1061).[15]

'Suicide bombing' and 'suicide attack' are examples of Western terminology. Suicide is taboo in both Christianity and Islam. It is the act of the non-believer who has given up all hope, in a religious sense. It is, further, the act of the isolated individual, who is alienated from any human or divine community. The terminology of 'suicide' is compatible with explanations that emphasize the irrationality of the act, as it represents the end of life, rather than its continuation with Allah, as assumed by the concept of martyrdom. Like the more general term 'terrorism', it isolates the action from a political context, and thereby depoliticizes and criminalizes it, focusing on the violence rather than the injustice that the 'martyr' hopes to address. The terminology of 'suicide terrorism' dislocates the meaning of the act from the context of its origin. It reinforces the illegitimacy and arbitrariness of the act, as well as the legitimacy of retaliation by states. Insofar as the emphasis on suicide isolates the agent, it is less explicit in recognizing the 'collateral damage' to innocent bystanders. The term 'homicide bomber', as used by Fox News and the Bush

---

[15] This section focuses on the context of the War on Terror. The number of attacks has steadily declined since the peak in 2002, from an average of 105 per year between 2000 and 2005 and twenty-three year per year from 2006 to 2009. The drop between 2006 and 2009 follows on the Israeli withdrawal from Gaza and large parts of the West Bank. The relationship between the Israeli withdrawal and the significant decline in the number of human bombs reinforces the argument that this method of attack is driven mainly by strategic concerns (Pape and Feldman 2010: 240).

administration (Fleischer 2002; Fox News 2003, 2004, 2005),[16] communicates the latter more clearly.

The use of a language of 'martyrdom' constitutes the agency of Islamic militancy and is justified by giving a particular identity to the bystanders who, in the process, become victims. Israel is understood to be 'one big military camp', which obscures the distinction between soldier and civilian, thereby dismissing the latter's deaths as 'collateral damage' and thus acceptable (Malka 2003: 4). Further, the 'martyr', while dying for a just cause, does not in most religious traditions take his or her own life or the lives of others in the process. In this respect, the act of blowing oneself up does fit more closely with the meaning of 'suicide'; nevertheless, the use of 'suicide' to give meaning to an act that is situated in a moral world of martyrdom establishes a tension, which was at the heart of the regional and larger global logic of the War on Terror. 'Suicide' and the possibility of killing civilians or other Muslims are both forbidden in Islamic tradition and law and therefore require flexible interpretations in order to appear legitimate (Allison 2007: 1; Malka 2003: 2). The important issue here, however, is not whether it is more accurate to give meaning to these acts as 'suicide' or 'martyrdom'; it is, rather, to examine how a particular, albeit distorted, use of each *constitutes* a different logic of action. In the one world, the agency of 'martyrdom' was constituted and *had sense* among communities that felt powerless otherwise to address the injustice they experienced. In the other world, the agency of retaliation was a product of attempts to *make sense* of an act of violence in terms of 'suicide'.

## The security dilemma

Within the warden's dilemma model, presented in Chapter 2, 'martyrdom operations' occupy the category of violent resistance. It was argued that, in the absence of an ability to overpower a stronger enemy physically, the weaker party risked reinforcing his or her criminal status, thereby providing a justification for further punishment by the warden. While the successful suicide attacks in Lebanon provided a precedent that encouraged the imitation of this strategy, the logic of

---

[16] Audrey Cronin (2003) notes that 'genocide bombings' and 'homicide attacks' are phrases that are frequently used by those who identify with the victims.

the more sustained campaign in the context of the War on Terror was quite different. In the latter context, the language of 'suicide' terrorism and 'martyrdom' appealed to distinct audiences, which contributed to the construction of a hard boundary between them – a 'clash of civilizations' – and a structural logic of violence. The structural logic was reproduced by the tension between a primarily Western use of 'suicide' terrorism and another of 'martyrdom operations', articulated by Islamic militants, both of which legitimized action to different audiences. To highlight the tension in the relationship between the two concepts, as used in this context, I use the term 'suicide/martyrdom' when pointing to it.

The military logic underpinning violent martyrdom rests on an acknowledgement that negotiations lead to a dead end in a situation of military inferiority, while 'martyrdom operations' have a tremendous impact, because of the fear they inspire in the population of the enemy (Hafez 2006: 174–5). The main objective of the human bomb is to guarantee that the enemy will be traumatized (Sela-Shayovitz *et al.* 2007: 161). 'Suicide/martyrdom', like terrorism more generally, undermines public confidence in the authorities, and specifically their ability to protect citizens, thereby creating a climate of fear (Hoffman 2003: 4). Suicide/martyrdom has accounted for a minority of all terrorist acts, yet has been responsible for the majority of terrorist-related casualties (Atran 2006: 127), killing four times as many people as other terrorist acts (Hoffman 2003: 2).

The military logic that grew out of both language games established what on the surface appears to be a classic security dilemma. Suicide attacks provided a pretext for state retaliation in response to the traumatization of a population; state retaliation reinforced the sense of injustice in the communities that had spawned 'martyrs'. In this environment of insecurity, both sides perceived themselves to be victims, which gave rise to increased public support for extreme measures. In 1999, prior to the beginning of the al-Aqsa Intifada, 26.1 per cent of Palestinians supported 'martyrdom operations' against Israel; this figure had doubled, to 66.2 per cent, three months after the uprising had begun (Hafez 2006: 180), and reached a new high in October 2003, when 74.5 per cent of Palestinians were behind the attacks (172, 180). The Israelis responded to Palestinian violence with aerial and naval attacks on Palestinian police stations and government institutions, and imposed curfews, closures and checkpoints on

Palestinian towns, which were perceived by the Palestinians as unfair collective punishments and an attempt to humiliate them in their own land. 'Martyrdom operations' were fuelled by a combination of a desire for revenge, in the face of perceived victimization, and empowerment in the face of overwhelming threats by a superior adversary (180).

'Martyrdom operations' had wide support, particularly among Palestinians. This support, as argued above, was dependent on a structure of meaning, derived – if in a distorted fashion – from Islam, which constructed rituals and ceremonies that amplified the heroic nature of the sacrifice. Families were encouraged to celebrate rather than mourn the deaths of loved ones (Hafez 2006: 177). The ritual surrounding the act, from videotapes recording a last will and testament, to head bands and banners, were symbols of the empowered individual making a free choice to self-sacrifice for the cause. As Mohammed Hafez (2006: 177) notes, these rituals turned the act 'into *performative* traditions and *redemptive* actions, through which the faithful expressed their devotion'. The rituals constituted the meaning of risks, rewards, means and ends within a religious logic and framework.

While the cultural framework provided the constitutive conditions for martyrdom, it remains unclear why some individuals embraced this agency of death rather than remaining supportive spectators. Studies have shown that neither socio-economic status, educational status, age nor, increasingly, gender determine who will choose to become a human bomb (Bennet 2002; Cronin 2003). Having said this, most who choose this path within conflict zones, according to Anne Speckhard (2006), have experienced trauma, arising from an ongoing experience of loss, of watching the death of neighbours and loved ones, of witnessing countless acts of violence, of losing self value, given their frequent experiences of humiliation and lost opportunities, either of education or employment – and thus a loss of those features of life that constitute a sense of human dignity. In the Palestinian context, many had felt their lives threatened by the Israel Defense Forces or had been incarcerated in Israeli prisons, where they were influenced by members of terror groups (Speckhard 2005).

Insofar as anyone living in a conflict zone may have these experiences, this may not ultimately explain why some choose to become 'martyrs', except perhaps that some people are more susceptible or predisposed to post-traumatic stress than others. The dramatic increase in the number of people who were willing to make this choice as the level of violence rose suggests that the marriage of 'being already dead' with a religious justification and a sense that one was contributing to a better future for the community constituted the conditions under which a choice to give up one's life appeared to be not only a viable option but a heroic one.

A distinction can be made between the strategic, ideological and territorial goals of 'suicide/martyrdom' and the more personal concerns of individual suicide bombers, ranging from revenge, redemption, desperation or eternal reward (Allison 2007: 2). In this respect, a further distinction can be made between the instrumental use of language by those who organize violence, on the one hand, and, on the other hand, the extent to which these language games seep into the everyday discourse of a population and become part of the taken-for-granted assumptions that underpin the decision of agents to become human bombs. One theme unified much of the Islamist discourse supporting militant activity: the global Muslim narrative of Western oppression and humiliation – a sense of persecution that was fuelled by symbols such as Abu Ghraib, Guantanamo Bay and the Iraq War (Allison 2007: 2).

'Martyrs' act against injustice with the aim of re-establishing dignity, which acquired some legitimacy among communities with a long experience of suffering, not least the Palestinians, who viewed the act as a form of social redress otherwise denied by their circumstances (Speckhard 2005). By contrast, in the West, an act of 'suicide' not only lacks legitimacy but helps to constitute the legitimacy of retaliation by Western states. In this respect, the coexistence of the two structures of meaning reproduced a military asymmetry, by reinforcing the legitimacy of the use of force by the state against non-state actors who use illegitimate force. These acts of retaliation then reinforced the very sense of injustice that the 'martyr' seeks to overcome – that is, the increasing humiliation and destruction of the populations they claim to represent. Having said this, the overkill that characterized the War on Terror, as well as the public exposure of the human costs, from Guantanamo Bay to Abu Ghraib, from Fallujah to Palestine, undermined the legitimacy of the United States in particular, not only in the larger world but domestically as well. The approval ratings of the Bush administration were at an all-time low by the time of the US presidential elections in 2008, and candidates were scrambling to define themselves in opposition to its policies. Repairing the US image in the world became one of the central platforms of Democratic Party candidates.

The violent strategies of the War on Terror were, arguably, counter-productive for both sides. What united the West after 9/11 was the humiliation of the United States by al-Qaida. What united Arabs and Muslims in the post-9/11 geopolitical climate was a collective feeling of humiliation. What divided the West was the excessive violence, particularly of the Iraq invasion, as well as the public exposure of humiliating acts directed at Arabs and Muslims, which was a violation of core Western values of dignity and human rights. What divided Arabs and Muslims was the attempt by al-Qaida to regain dignity through the taking of innocent lives. In this respect, the 'clash' was driven less by Arab and Muslim opposition to Western values of democracy, human rights and freedom (Khouri 2004), or by civilizational, cultural, ideological or religious motives, than by the US violation of Western values and principles, on the one hand, and, on the other hand, by the violation of militant Islamist groups of the core values of respecting human life as advocated by Islam. The big losers were Arab and Muslim populations in the Middle East, north Africa and the West, as well as Western populations confronted with the increased threat of terrorist attack and restrictions on civil liberties.

The macro-logic of the War on Terror was not qualitatively different from the classic security dilemma between states. It was different, however, in that the conditions that were reinforced and exacerbated as a result impacted more directly on innocent civilians than states, reproducing a political culture of fear and trauma on both sides. Insofar as the classic security dilemma presumes a focus on states, it further implies a separation between military and civilian life, and the responsibility of the state and its armed forces for shielding the latter from harm, although this distinction has become blurred since the advent of total war in the late nineteenth century. In the interaction between 'martyrs' and state retaliation for 'suicide terrorism', it has been primarily civilians who have suffered on both sides, either because they were in the wrong place at the wrong time, or lived in a state that was targeted because of its military actions or became victims in an armed confrontation in which insurgents and civilians were not easily distinguished. It is the injustice or trauma experienced by civilians that differs from the traditional security dilemma, in which the state acts in defence of a population.

Questions of recognition and legitimacy were at the core of the asymmetric logic of 'suicide/martyrdom'. Retaliation against 'suicide terrorists' is seen to be legitimate because of the injustice of killing innocent civilians and the resulting traumatization of Western society. The legitimacy of the martyrdom operation, by contrast, rests on the injustice and traumatization that has been suffered by communities in the Middle East and the adoption of an interpretation of Islam that gives meaning to that experience. A more consistent logic of survival would rest on the recognition that both sides ultimately seek an end to fear, trauma and injustice and the adoption of non-violent means to that end.

## The body of sacrifice

What Farhad Khosrokhavar (2005 [2002]) refers to as 'defensive' martyrdom has its roots in another strategy that has been used by those in an asymmetric power situation, who play with a weak hand: a non-violent strategy, as put to use by Gandhi against the British in India or in Solidarity's campaign in Poland, to name a few notable historical examples. The focus of these strategies was more the earthly experience of injustice and oppression, and the objective of change, than the desire to leave this world, as it was for the Christian martyrs, but these campaigns did involve 'bearing witness' to a higher principle through the refusal to comply with the authorities or prevailing laws. 'Bearing witness' potentially led to 'martyrdom' insofar as the 'witness' suffered or absorbed violence as a result of his or her refusal to comply, while also refusing to retaliate or use violence. In this respect, it is compatible with themes in Islam such as the principle that to kill one person is to kill all of humanity.

It was often assumed, at the height of the War on Terror, that non-violence is incompatible with Islam. A strand of Islamic scholarship argues that Islam is compatible with non-violence, highlighting the emphasis on equality, human dignity, the sacredness of human life and speaking out against injustice (Abu-Nimer 2003). These scholars tend to accept the hypothesis, articulated by Patout Burns (1996: 165), that 'there is no theological reason that an Islamic society could not take a lead in developing nonviolence today, and there is every reason that some of them should'. These scholarly arguments about its compatibility are reinforced by a range of historical examples of non-violent campaigns. For instance, Abdul Ghaffar Khan's 'Army of God', located in the Pashtun region of the north-west Indian subcontinent, now Pakistan, involved some 100,000 people in a non-violent resistance movement against the British that lasted twenty years. As Eknath Easwaran (1984: 103) states:

There is nothing surprising in a Muslim or a Pashtun like me subscribing to the creed of non-violence. It is not a new creed. It was followed fourteen hundred years ago by the Prophet all the time he was in Mecca, and it has since been followed by all those who wanted to throw off an oppressor's yoke. But we had...forgotten it.[17]

A non-violent strategy is often discounted, for several reasons. First, it is often presumed to be successful only against liberal democracies. The Polish case, examined in Chapter 5, raises questions about this conclusion. Second, non-violence is often viewed as submission and passivity in the face of injustice and aggression, which is the perspective that was held by secular militants in Palestine, Northern Ireland and South Africa (Abu-Nimer 2003: 54). Nonetheless, the strategies of non-violence employed, for instance, by Gandhi and Solidarity were just that: strategies.[18] These strategies had the aim not merely of defusing tensions temporarily, while preserving or even reinforcing the structural violence, as is often the case with violent militancy, but of dissolving the structural violence underlying conflict and creating the conditions for dialogue. A non-violent strategy, like any other strategy, can be employed with greater or lesser degrees of skill and with greater or lesser amounts of discipline.

In the Indian and Polish cases, the agency of 'defensive martyrdom' contributed to the overall objective of ending 'occupation' in a much shorter time than the 'terrorist' campaigns in the Middle East or Northern Ireland – neither of which achieved this goal – and with less death and traumatization among the population. In Northern Ireland, the brief civil rights movement in the 1960s was followed by a bloody terrorist operation that continued for thirty years, with severe

---

[17] After Pakistan achieved independence, the movement vanished because of the policies adopted by the Pakistani president, but it nonetheless contributed directly to the liberation of the region from British colonial control.

[18] See Sharp (2005).

consequences for civil society and democracy. Other conditions also contributed to the withdrawal of the British from India, of course, but the non-violent strategy of Gandhi revealed the moral bankruptcy of the British presence, thereby undermining its legitimacy. While an historical experience of humiliation was also a motivating factor in these cases, the focus of the protagonists' strategy was the achievement of dignity through 'acting as if' they were free.

The conceptual network surrounding suicide terrorism/martyrdom, explored in the last section, includes a relationship between humiliation and dignity. A Hamas activist who rejected the idea that hunger or 'hatred of humanity' drives suicide bombers argued that the primary factor is the loss of 'dignity' that comes with living under Israeli occupation (Collins 2004: 181). In their marriage of humiliation to dignity, militant Islamists have argued that the latter can be established through violence.[19]

In international law, or more traditional Islamic thought, these two concepts suggest a different relationship. The right of all human beings to dignity is enshrined in international law (United Nations 1948: article 1) and is the opposite of humiliation, which is clearly prohibited. Dignity relates not only to a right to life but to the quality of life. Mohammad Kamali (2002), a Malaysian professor of law, provides an enlightening analysis of the place of this word in Islamic thought. While sharia law upholds and sanctifies measures that are devised to protect human dignity, Allah is said to reward self-restraint and patience in the face of evil and adversity, strongly discouraging extremism and excess in all matters. Kamali (2002: 68) quotes the Prophet: 'Avoid extremism, for people have been led to destruction because of extremism.' Dignity is further tied to compassion, insofar as the cry of the oppressed has to be heard and attended to (77), as dignity is absent when there is crushing poverty and degradation (95). Although 'evil' may, in his argument, require an exception to self-restraint and patience, the emphasis is placed on speaking out, not violence. Kamali quotes (42) from a Hadith:

'Let no one humiliate themselves.' Upon hearing this, the Companions asked: 'How does one do that, O Messenger of God?' Then the Prophet said: 'When someone sees an occasion in which he should speak out for the sake of God but he

---

[19] A similar conflation was made indirectly by US President Bush when he suggested that the practice of waterboarding was compatible with human dignity (MacAskill 2008).

does not, then God Most High will tell him on the Day of Judgment: 'What stopped you from speaking on that issue?' And when the person answers: 'The fear of people,' then God says: 'You should have feared me and put Me above fearing others.'

Like the concept of human rights in international law, dignity (*karamah*) in Islam is an absolute and a natural right for every human being. The word *karamah* is derived from *karam* (generosity). In this sense, dignity is connected with the capacity to give rather than receive. In Arab culture, *karamah* is a fundamentally social concept (Gabriel 2007) and a 'highly charged emotional frame through which the individual determines the worthiness of his or her life' (Ayish 2003).

A concept of universal dignity rests on an acceptance of difference (Abu-Nimer 2003: 58). On the one hand, all people belong to a single community. On the other, the Qur'an (49:13) notes that the division of the world into nations and tribes was also intended as God's will so that 'you may know one another (not that ye may despise each other)'. No regime can take dignity away from an individual, and, in this respect, the Islamic concept is compatible with the Western doctrine of human rights and dignity. Kamali suggests that dignity rests on one's own sense of value and an ability to exercise not just self-restraint but agency in speaking out in the face of injustice. Dignity and compassion are inseparable.

In the context of Gaza, *Dignity* was the name of a boat that regularly sailed to Gaza to deliver medical supplies and other humanitarian aid to victims of the siege there. The language of dignity in this use relies on a framework that highlights the humanitarian problem and a non-violent path to its resolution. This example not only points to a way to rethink the distortions in the humiliation/dignity narratives of Islamic militants, but also involves shifting from a military logic to a humanitarian one.

The act of bringing aid to Gaza on ships is not in and of itself an act of political self-sacrifice. The agents in this case were explicit in situating their action in a humanitarian framework, in which they are attempting to bring aid to a desperate population. The act had general meaning within the larger context of the ongoing conflict between Israel and the Palestinian territories and, as discussed in the previous section, the security concerns of Israel in the face of 'suicide terrorism' and the experience of injustice and humiliation expressed by Palestinian 'martyrdom'. The act had more specific meaning in the context of the Israeli blockade of Gaza following the victory of Hamas in the 2006 legislative election in Palestine, which severely limited the goods flowing to the Gazan population. In December 2008 the fragile ceasefire between Hamas and Israel broke down, as Hamas fired rockets into Israel and the Israelis responded with Operation Cast Lead, the bombardment of Gaza that resulted in the death of some 1,400 Gazans and the injury of thousands more. Given the use of white phosphorus and the disproportionate number of deaths, many, after this incident, claimed that Israel had committed war crimes – a conclusion that was reinforced by the Goldstone Report (Goldstone 2009), which also refers frequently to the 'humiliation' of the Gazans.[20] During the onslaught, the tunnels that had brought goods into Gaza from Egypt were largely destroyed and the Israelis limited the humanitarian aid allowed into what was referred to by many as the open air 'prison' of Gaza. Materials for rebuilding, such as cement, were denied access, which meant that, even a year and a half after the bombardment, many Gazans were still living in tents, and many injured or disabled Gazans were without basic medical supplies such as wheelchairs.

Despite the restrictions imposed by Israel, the humanitarian ships that sailed towards Gaza were 'acting as if' the delivery of aid was possible. The dilemma for the Israelis was what to do about these ships, which, they feared, would transport arms into Gaza, yet sailed under a banner of humanitarian aid and dignity. The Turkish *Mavi Marmara*, the largest ship in the 'Freedom Flotilla' that set sail for Gaza at the end of May 2010, was attempting to bring supplies to Gaza to alleviate an increasingly desperate situation. The flotilla included over 600 citizens from thirty-two countries, and its goods had been cleared through Turkish customs before setting off. On 31 May, in the middle of the night, Israeli soldiers intercepted the ship in international waters, some seventy-two nautical miles from the coast of Gaza. The soldiers went on board and, in the conflict that ensued, nine passengers on the Turkish ship were killed.

---

[20] See references to humiliation in sections 540, 1100, 1395, 1507, 1578, 1597, 1672, 1689, 1705, 1742 and 1745.

In the media coverage that followed, the identity of the humanitarian aid workers who were killed became the object of contestation.[21] Israel's deputy foreign minister, Danny Ayalon, said of the ship (as quoted by Black and Siddique 2011: 1):

The armada of hate and violence in support of the Hamas terror organisation was a premeditated and outrageous provocation. The organisers are well known for their ties to global Jihad, al-Qaida and Hamas. They have a history of arms smuggling and deadly terror. On board the ship we found weapons that were prepared in advance and used against our forces. The organisers' intent was violent, their method was violent, and unfortunately, the results were violent.[22]

The contestation revolved around the question of whether the humanitarian workers were 'terrorists' or whether the act of the Israeli soldiers in boarding the ship was illegal, given that it took place in international waters. Those supporting the flotilla, not least the Turkish prime minister, Recep Tayyip Erdoğan, referred to the attacks as a 'massacre' and an act of 'terror' (Erdoğan 2010a), 'barbarism' (Davutoglu 2010), 'banditry and piracy' (Erdoğan 2010b) involving the 'murder of civilians' who became 'martyrs' (see, for instance, Sherwood 2010; Sheehan 2010; Facebook 2010; 'Palestine Citizen 2009' 2010). As the word 'martyr' had in Palestine traditionally referred to anyone who was killed by Israeli forces, the latter usage was more consistent with a longer history of use than that of Hamas in the context of 'martyrdom operations'.[23] While the images shown in the visual media showed aid workers using sticks to keep the soldiers at bay, and thus a breakdown of non-violent discipline, outside Israel the claim that they were terrorists was questioned, given that the contents of the ship had been checked by the Turkish authorities before departing and that the Turkish prime minister had spoken out

[21] One very interesting element of this contestation was the media coverage, during which even the images shown by, for instance, Al Jazeera or Fox News could tell a very different story of who was culpable.

[22] Israel further claimed that the Insani Yardim Vakfi, the Turkish organization that sponsored the trip, also known as the IHH (Humanitarian Relief Fund), was a dangerous Islamic organization with terrorist links (Kershner 2011).

[23] Rashmi Singh (2011) demonstrates how Hamas drew on this longer tradition of martyrdom to construct the legitimacy of martyrdom operations for the Palestinian population. Laleh Khalili (2007) provides an in-depth analysis of how narratives of martyrdom and nation in Palestine have changed over time as they are reproduced through practices of commemoration.

strongly on behalf of the aid workers. Erdoğan claimed that the attack was a clear violation of international law and demanded a formal apology from Israel.

It was not only the identity of the humanitarian aid workers that was contested; the legitimacy of the Israeli action was as well. The central question was whether Israel had engaged in a criminal act, by boarding a ship in international waters, or whether it was engaged in a legitimate act of self-defence against 'terrorists'. Its moral legitimacy had already been damaged by the disproportionate number of Gazan deaths during Operation Cast Lead, and the indictment of the Goldstone Report. The message that Israel was engaged in unlawful acts to prevent the delivery of aid to the suffering people of Gaza was magnified by the event. Israel rejected a proposal by Ban Ki-Moon for an international inquiry and appointed its own internal commission to investigate into the matter. The report of the Turkel Commission (Turkel 2010), which was composed of five Israelis and two observers,[24] concluded that the actions of the Israel Navy during the raid and Israel's naval blockade of Gaza were both legal under international laws. Erdoğan rejected the conclusions of the commission, stating that they had 'no value or credibility' (Ravid 2011).

The Israeli inquiry attracted widespread international condemnation, as did Israel's refusal to cooperate with the international inquiry. The UN Human Rights Council appointed an international, independent fact-finding mission, chaired by Judge Karl Hudson-Phillips, a former judge at the International Criminal Court in The Hague, which reached very different conclusions from the Israeli commission. Its fifty-six-page report found that the interception of the *Mavi Marmara* on the high seas by the Israel Defense Forces was 'clearly unlawful,' and disproportionate (United Nations 2010). The debate surrounding the group that organized the humanitarian mission of the *Mavi Marmara*, the IHH, has also continued. The IHH has been listed as a terrorist organization by the Netherlands and Germany, for alleged connections to Hamas and al-Qaida. The Obama administration's State Department, after being asked by a bipartisan group of Senators to investigate the organization, said that it could not validate any relationship or connection between

---

[24] The outside observers were David Trimble, the Northern Irish politician and Nobel Peace Prize laureate, and Canadian jurist Ken Watkins.

IHH and al-Qaida, but did confirm that members of the group had contacts with Hamas (Krieger 2010).

The main point of this analysis is to highlight the *contestation* surrounding the death of the Turkish 'martyrs'. As in other chapters of this book, and particularly the Polish case, the sacrifice of the Turkish 'martyrs' led to questions about their identity as terrorists, but the 'criminal' nature of Israeli acts also became a focus. Although there have been no formal changes in the status quo, there has since been some symbolic momentum. In September 2011 the Palestinian leader, Mahmoud Abbas, introduced a proposal to the United Nations for the state of Palestine to be considered a full member.[25] The US veto was anticipated, but a range of alternative strategies have since been under consideration, including a change from Palestine's current observer mission status to the possibility of the State of Palestine becoming, like the Vatican, an observer state.[26] In October 2011 Palestine was admitted as a member state of UNESCO (the United Nations Educational, Scientific and Cultural Organization), which formally raised the Palestinian flag in December, in the presence of Abbas. At the time of this writing (March 2012) there have been no further developments.

## The human torch

The dramatic changes brought about by the Arab Spring in Tunisia and Egypt were all the more surprising given the degree of scepticism that had earlier existed within the Middle East regarding non-violence. There is even less precedent in Arab or Islamic culture, however, for making sense of the self-immolation by burning of Mohammed Bouazizi, the Tunisian fruit and vegetable vendor, in early 2011. The debate within Islam regarding the legitimacy of 'martyrdom operations' contrasts with the speedy condemnation of the copy-cat self-immolations across north Africa. Immediately following the self-burning of an Egyptian restaurant owner near the parliament building in Cairo on 17 January 2011,[27]

---

[25] As only states can be members of the United Nations, acceptance of the proposal would have represented a recognition of Palestinian sovereignty.

[26] For a discussion of the strategic options being considered, see Whitbeck (2012).

[27] This was preceded by the self-burning of a fifty-two-year-old lawyer, who shouted slogans about food price rises in central Cairo and then set himself on fire, followed by another man in Alexandria (Mason 2012: 11).

Mohammad Rifa al-Tahtawi, the spokesman of Al-Azhar University (2011), Egypt's most prestigious centre of learning, said to the state news agency that 'Sharia law states that Islam categorically forbids suicide for any reason and does not accept the separation of souls from bodies as an expression of stress, anger or protest'. As one blogger (Bridget 2011) stated in response:

How hypocritical of Islamic clerics to declare suicide 'forbidden' under Sharia law when they refuse to publicly condemn suicide bombers who kill themselves and innocent others in the name of Allah. Perhaps they don't consider it suicide if they are also killing the infidel?

Although Bouazizi's mother (Bouazizi family 2011), as well as many activists and much of the press, referred to him as a 'martyr', this somewhat more official assignment of the term 'suicide' raises questions, against the background of a decade of 'martyrdom operations' in the region. On the one hand, the distinction may relate to the marriage of 'martyrdom operations' to a concept of jihad and the death of infidels, as suggested by the blogger. On the other hand, given the threat posed by acts of self-burning to the status quo in the region, rather than the Israelis or Americans directly, the focus on 'suicide' can be seen as an attempt to depoliticize the act by making it appear to be simply an act of self-destruction by psychologically disturbed individuals.

Ahmad Okasha (2011), president of the Arab Federation of Psychiatrists, reflects on how Arab members of the profession interpreted acts of self-burning. Okasha states that he doesn't believe that the self-immolations had anything to do with 'martyrdom fantasies'. Instead, he views suicide as a cry for help, a plea against powerlessness, desperation and frustration, noting also that 70 per cent of suicides worldwide are the result of depressive disorders. In his view, Bouazizi burned himself because 'he could see no other way out'. Okasha acknowledges that the act was a protest against unemployment and rampant injustice, and that many people saw Bouazizi as a role model because they understood how he felt, given the lack of any outlet for their own frustration, despair and helplessness. He further acknowledges that the suicides usually took place in front of public buildings, but his conclusion about this location was more religious than political. He said that it is as if they were saying '"We are wretched and unhappy! If you cannot help us, then we will turn to God!" In this respect, it is [a] kind of escape from suffering, helplessness and oppression.'

While recognizing both the political context and political impact, Okasha is unequivocal in referring to acts of self-burning as suicide. In comparison to the self-burning of Thich Quang Duc in Vietnam, there is some basis for this claim. Quang Duc acted within a tradition in which self-burning could be a life-affirming act of a bodhisattva, if it grew out of right intention, rather than representing a desperate attempt to end life. He acted with the approval of religious authorities and within the context of an organized effort that involved the support of a large number of Buddhist monks and nuns. Bouazizi's self-immolation was much different. He was a struggling fruit seller, who was insulted and humiliated by a local female bureaucrat. His request to complain directly to the governor was ignored, after which he threatened to burn himself if the issue wasn't immediately resolved (Haiba 2011). A half-hour later he doused himself with gasoline and set himself on fire outside the governor's office (Laub 2011), in what appeared to be a spontaneous act born of desperation. Given the centrality of intention in both Buddhism and Islam, it is reasonable to assume that Bouazizi intended to commit suicide. It was a suicide committed in protest and in full public view, rather than in isolation, but there is no reason to think that he would have envisaged, or even imagined, either the copycat self-immolations or the political avalanche that followed.

Bouazizi stated his intention to burn himself if his complaint was not addressed, and in this respect his intention was embedded in the act (Wittgenstein 1958). Whether he intended to commit suicide or be a martyr is more difficult to ascertain, as he is no longer here, and, regardless of what he might have said, we can't know what was going on in his head. What we can see is that, even though he appeared to act with very different intentions from, for instance, Quang Duc, the effect was similar, in that it was followed by copycat self-burnings and a firestorm of protest that brought down dictatorial leaders within a very short space of time. In this light, it is less the intentions of Bouazizi than the effect of his act, and how it was given meaning, that are of interest.

While leading authorities analysed and/or condemned the act as a suicide, the message that was inscribed on the act by Bouazizi's mother, by the protesters, by bloggers and the social media was very different. Bouazizi was a 'martyr' (Meehan 2011; Belayachi 2011; Mejia 2011), a 'human torch' (Laub 2011), a 'candle who illuminated' the nation and the whole world, who 'released a spark' that triggered a crisis (Haiba 2011; Ben Mhenni 2011), who 'sacrificed himself for freedom' and 'spread the flame of freedom' to the Arab world (Agence France Presse 2011). He 'ignited the victory' of the Tunisian people (Meehan 2011) and is 'still ablaze' within many Arab regimes. The fire that swallowed Bouazizi became the fire of revolution.

Bouazizi's protest was a response to being 'humiliated' by the authorities (Meehan 2011; Agence France Presse 2011; Laub 2011; Haiba 2011; Khouri 2011), but, contrary to the psychiatric assessment, this was less because 'he could see no other way out' than because he sought to 'demonstrate that he remains master of his own self' and thereby reminded others that 'they too remain masters of themselves' (Mneimneh 2011) and 'inspired other Tunisians into self-determination' (Jones 2011). He 'chose, in the most public manner, death over fear' (Mejia 2011), and inspired a nation to do the same. While his experience was one of humiliation, his message to the nation and the region – a message that was taken up by protestors – was one of dignity (Marquand 2011; Mejia 2011; *Daily News Egypt* 2011). Although Bouazizi was Muslim, he was said not to have been political, and the revolutions themselves were largely secular, though taking place in Islamic cultures. While the term 'martyrdom' is usually associated with a religious framework, in this context there was some sentiment that martyrdom was not a religious phenomenon but a universal one that symbolized a 'desire to live a dignified life' (*Daily News Egypt* 2011).

Two further contrasts are interesting in this representation of acts of self-immolation and the largely secular revolutions that followed. Consistent with the other cases in this book, the authorities viewed the protesters as criminals or terrorists. After Bouazizi's act had sent thousands of protesters into the streets, Zine Ben Ali, the president of Tunisia, blamed hooded gangs and spoke of a 'terrorist act that cannot be tolerated' (Lalami 2011). Egyptian president Hosni Mubarak blamed the Muslim Brotherhood and 'infiltrators' for instigating plots to shake the foundation of stability in the country (Lalami 2011). Despite this naming, there was a sharp contrast between the 'civility and dignity' of the protesters and the violent and bloody response of the regimes (Haiba 2011). While the protestors confronted snipers, tear gas and imprisonment in an effort to remove their leaders, the leaders were complicit in using violence against their own populations.

Radical Islamists claimed to represent the poor and oppressed, but in fact they had alienated people with the bloodiness of their terrorist attacks (Wood 2011). By contrast, Bouazizi, in his act of self-burning, 'reflected the pain and vulnerability of millions' (Khouri 2011), and, in abandoning their fear, the protesters made this pain visible to the light of day as they absorbed the blows of the state; and the social media brought these images to the world. The relationship between humiliation and dignity was at the heart of the message of both the militant Islamists, as discussed earlier, and the protesters in Tunisia and Egypt, but the meaning and emphasis was different. For the militant Islamists, restoring dignity was linked to an intention to humiliate the West, as Arabs had been humiliated in the past (bin Laden 2001; Abu Gheith 2002). Dignity thus came from evening the score and harming what was said to be the source of one's humiliation. While the experience of humiliation pervaded the language of the protesters in Tunisia and Egypt, dignity was an act of reclaiming self-respect, which involved overcoming fear and 'acting as if' one were free (Jones 2011). The centre shifts in the latter case to the self; one's acts are not defined in response to the power of others but arise out of a sovereign decision, namely 'becoming master of one's self'.

The social media played a crucial role in facilitating the organization of the protests and the spread of information (Asali 2011). The Arab Spring is distinguished from the cases in earlier chapters by the greater sophistication and speed with which a message or an image could be circulated across the globe, given the existence of technologies such as mobile phones, the internet, Twitter and Facebook. It was the various acts of self-sacrifice that ignited the human will to resist, but the media constituted a crucial medium for mobilizing and making this known to a larger audience. Rashid Khalidi, professor of Arab studies at Columbia University, has noted an important change in the Western media (as cited by *Jordan Times* 2011):

The same Western media that habitually conveys a picture of a region peopled almost exclusively by enraged, bearded terrorist fanatics who 'hate our freedom' has begun to show images of ordinary people making eminently reasonable demands for freedom, dignity, social justice, accountability, the rule of law and democracy.

Al Jazeera's almost continuous coverage, particularly of the events in Tahrir Square, contributed to the 'liberation of mindsets' that made the revolutions possible (Jones 2011), as 'yes we can' became a self-fulfilling prophecy for younger people in the region (Ben Mhenni 2011). Although the regimes were inclined to retaliate with violence, both Ben Ali in Tunisia and Mubarak in Egypt stepped down within a relatively short period of time and did not bring the full force of their military power down on the protesters, as has been case in other countries in the region. Many have put this down to the persuasive powers of the United States, which had less influence on historical enemies of Washington, such as Libya and Syria.

The situation for the United States was more complicated, however. While any US administration may have found itself pulled between a population demanding freedom and democracy, on the one hand, and loyalty to long-time US allies, on the other hand, Obama's position was particularly sensitive given the message he had sent to the region in his inaugural address and Cairo speech just a few years earlier. In his inaugural address, Obama (2009a) stated: '[T]hose who cling to power through corruption and deceit and the silencing of dissent, know that you are on the wrong side of history, but that we will extend a hand if you are willing to unclench your fist.' The focus of this metaphor was less that of an hostile relationship between the United States and another power than the relationship between corrupt powers and their own people – that is, the fact that they silence dissent. The preceding clause refers first to the Arab and Muslim worlds, with which the United States 'seeks a new way forward, based on mutual interest and mutual respect', as contrasted with 'those leaders around the globe who seek to sow conflict or blame their society's ills on the West', which is followed by a claim that '*your people* will judge you on what you can build, not what you destroy' (Obama 2009a, emphasis added). As such, Obama extended a hand of friendship to the Muslim world, while pointing out a barrier to 'unclenching fists', which is a particular form of government that silences dissent but will ultimately be held accountable to its people.

President Bush, following on his ill-fated reference to a 'clash of civilizations', made a clear distinction between Muslims more generally and violent extremists. Obama (2009b) relied on this same distinction in his Cairo speech, but was much more explicit in building on the shared values and identity of the United States and the Muslim world. He acknowledged a past of colonialism, the Holocaust, the dislocation and humiliation of Palestinians and 9/11, as well as invoking an element of his own identity relating to the history of black America. Pointing to the 'lash of the whip of the slave' and the 'humiliation of segregation', he claimed that it was not violence that won full and equal rights but 'a peaceful and determined insistence upon the ideals at the centre of America's founding'– that is, moral authority is not claimed through violence but, rather, surrendered through violence.

While Obama's speeches may have been directed primarily at Iran, where the Green Revolution broke out shortly after his Cairo speech, it was presented to a larger Arab and Muslim audience across the region. Having stood on the world stage, encouraging populations to call their corrupt leaders to account, Obama was placed in a difficult position when they began to do so in relation to long-term US allies who had been key to stability in the region. At the time, Obama was criticized for not being sufficiently vocal in his support for the protestors. Nonetheless, the speeches simultaneously served as a facilitating condition of the protests and constrained the president's room for manoeuvre. The US president was encouraging people in the region to call their corrupt leaders to account, but he was constrained, on the one hand, as the leader of a country that had for decades propped up these dictatorial regimes, and had many interests in the regions for doing so. On the other hand, he could not be too visible a presence in these transformations, both because of these interests and his position as president, and because it would have run counter to the message that the people themselves should hold their leaders to account. In the end, he was praised for his handling of the balancing act in relation to Egypt.

Obama's was, in several respects, a very different kind of warden's dilemma from the other cases. He was criticized when the revolutions were under way for reacting too slowly and for not speaking out against the human rights violations and torture of the Mubarak regime, but, as already suggested, his main message was that it was the people in the region who needed to bring about democracy themselves. Too loud a voice from Washington would have had the potential to undermine the protests, particularly in countries that are less friendly to the United States, such as Libya, Syria and Iran. In these cases, direct involvement from Washington would only have increased the potential for the regimes to vilify the protesters, claiming that they were simply the arm of a foreign power. As Aaron David Miller (quoted by Landler 2011), a public policy fellow at the Woodrow Wilson International Centre for Scholars, states, 'The challenge for the administration is to find the right balance between identifying the US too closely with these changes and thereby undermining them; and not finding ways to nurture them enough.'

Ben Ali and Mubarak, on the other hand, faced the dilemma of whether to continue punishing those who resisted, at the risk of creating martyrs, which they both did, or to engage in dialogue with them, at which point the game would have changed. The latter course, as in Vietnam, was precluded by their past history of oppression and their violence against the protesters. They were branded as criminals, and eventually stepped down from power, at the urging of the United States. Mubarak, rather than the protesters, has become the criminal, and is in dock for his violence against them.

## Conclusion

The War on Terror built on assumptions about the incompatibility of Islam with non-violence and, in the United States, a further assumption that 'suicide terrorism' was an irrational act of religious fanatics. Pape and Feldman (2010) have disputed the claim that religious fundamentalism is the primary cause of suicide terrorism, illustrating the central role of resistance to occupation. While agreeing with their conclusion about foreign interference, this chapter has also examined the way in which a religious symbolism, related to the historical use of a language of martyrdom, humiliation and dignity, was repackaged to give meaning and emotional resonance to acts involving both self-destruction and the destruction of others. Martyrdom was also a framework for giving meaning to other forms of political self-sacrifice, however, in terms of self-burning and the martyrdom of Turkish aid workers on the *Mavi Marmara*. This reinforces the point, which is evident throughout the cases in this book, that meaning is not static. It has resonance because of a history of use but can be repackaged in new circumstances to justify new acts. Suicide terrorism, non-violence and self-burning are all forms of action that diverge from more historical understandings of martyrdom in the Middle East. Suicide terrorism drew on the successful precedent of Lebanon, which led to a withdrawal of US troops. There are a number of historical examples of non-violent campaigns coming out of Islamic communities, albeit not widely recognized. Self-immolation has no real political precedent in the Middle East and north Africa, although it has become a common practice among women, particularly in Afghanistan. The use of self-burning within the context of more secular movements potentially draws on a more global structure of meaning that has developed since Quang Duc's precedent in the 1960s, which has since been imitated in a range of different places across the world.

In the context of the War on Terror, the United States and militant Islamists both went too far in their dependence on hard power, which resulted in a loss of soft power for both. The use of violence by each of them resulted in a security dilemma that reinforced the trauma of populations on both sides. The loss of US soft power created the space for Obama's presidency and a reframing of the American approach to the Arab and Muslim worlds. Obama did not cause the uprisings, but he did send a signal in his inaugural and Cairo speeches that placed the United States, which had historically propped up dictators in the region, in the position of having to balance support for these revolutions, which were 'calling corrupt leaders to account', with the US interest in stability in the region.

The 9/11 bombers and the uprisings in Tunisia and Egypt both originated in countries with US-supported regimes. While the former sought the withdrawal of the United States and the creation of an Islamic ummah, the latter had a more secular orientation and goals of democracy and dignity. Humiliation and the need to restore dignity were the focus of the protests, just as they were the focus of the message attached to suicide terrorism, and the message in both cases was directed at the draconian security apparatus of these countries. The two differed, however, in the meaning attached to the humiliation/dignity relationship. For militant Islamists, dignity came with revenge against those who were said to be the source of humiliation. For the protesters, dignity came from abandoning their fear and acting as if they were free.

The various acts of self-sacrifice contributed to the construction of community and the nation. The dying body became the embodiment of a more widespread suffering, calling others to imitation, or at least support. The community was a liminal *communitas*, 'betwixt and between' the old order and what might eventually emerge in its place.

In this respect, the uprisings in north Africa need to be distinguished from the more stabilized order that will follow. Having said this, there is one difference between the non-violent forms and the violent forms that may prove significant. 'Acting as if' one is free can be understood as a performance that contributes to the construction of a new set of rules and practices, capable of imitation by large numbers and based on respect for the dignity of others and dialogue. Both features underpin democracy. By contrast, the turn to violent performance, in Libya, for instance, did eventually bring down the regime but was dependent on outside powers to do so. In the process, the blood that has been spilled on both sides, and the trauma experienced by civilians and children in the process, potentially sets the stage for a continuing cycle of revenge and division. In this respect, the means by which a regime is brought down do not contribute to the ultimate end: democracy.

The outcomes remain to be seen, but the historical comparison with the route to peace and democracy in Poland and Northern Ireland may be instructive. In the Polish case, the Solidarity activists 'acting as if' they were free, and the subsequent martyrdom of Father Popiełuszko, constituted a performance that contributed to the writing of a democratic script that would prove significant in the move towards dialogue with the government and the eventual transformation to a democratic system. In Northern Ireland, the connection of the hunger strikers to IRA violence made any kind of move towards dialogue by Thatcher's government highly problematic, and, although the strikes did provide a political foundation for the peace process that would emerge ten years later, the time in between was characterized by a bloody escalation of tit-for-tat violence.

# 8 | *The public diplomacy of suffering*

Diplomacy has traditionally been conceived as a dialogue or conversation between states. The more recent phenomenon of public diplomacy broadens this tradition to incorporate a conversation between states and foreign audiences. The public diplomacy of suffering is one further incarnation of a globalizing media. Since the 1990s televised images of civilian suffering, whether in relation to war, repressive regimes or natural disasters, have given rise to concepts such as the CNN effect (Robinson 2002), which highlights the subsequent public pressure on governments to act, or, alternatively, compassion fatigue (Moeller 1999), which refers to the media saturation of these images and consequent feelings of powerlessness to act. Since 11 September 2001 we have also seen the emergence of the Al Jazeera effect (Seib 2008) with the increasing mobilization of Arab and Muslim populations in response to images of suffering in the Palestinian territories, Iraq, Afghanistan and, more recently, the Arab Spring. Images of suffering often depict helpless victims. The suffering of political self-sacrifice is distinguished by the agency of the act. This final chapter is an attempt to make sense of the public diplomacy of suffering as it relates to political self-sacrifice.

These concluding thoughts have three objectives. The first is to summarize the overall argument of the book. The second is to engage in some further analysis across the cases, as part of an attempt to draw out the similarities and differences. The third is to reflect on some of the issues raised by this project. In all these steps I place political self-sacrifice in the context of a conversation that has become increasingly global.

## The argument

This exploration began with a theoretical problem and an empirical problem. The theoretical problem was the increasing emphasis on the individual at the international level, as evidenced by the emergence of a concept of human security and a concern about suicide terrorism. Within the study of international relations, the levels of analysis problem has emphasized the state and the international system rather than the individual, as well as drawing fixed boundaries around individuals, states and structures. A concept of political self-sacrifice brings the individual back in and seeks a more fluid understanding of the relationship between individual, community and the 'international' in a globalizing world. The empirical problem arose from several observations, regarding the contestation surrounding the identity of the agent of self-sacrifice as a criminal/terrorist or martyr, and his or her death as a suicide or martyrdom; foreign occupation or interference, as well as an ongoing experience of humiliation, as the reason for the act; and the objective of restoring the dignity of communities that have suffered a loss of political subjectivity and agency. Although state action in the international system is governed by the desire to protect an already exiting sovereignty, the logic looks much different for those who are sovereign-less. The sovereign state is recognized as having a legitimate right to defend itself with force, but the relationship between legitimacy and violent or non-violent resistance by those outside sovereignty is more complicated. A further problem, which is both theoretical and empirical, regards the relationship between the self-sacrifice of the body, the emotions that move out from it and the subsequent potential for imitation by others.

The theoretical focus of this book has been a concept of political self-sacrifice. Sacrifice is a symbolic structure that involves consecration or the transformation of something into a symbol of the community for which the sacrifice is made (Beattie 1980: 30). Consecration presupposes a system of rules and ritual conventions specifying the possible effects of the sacrifice, what is to be sacrificed and how it is transformed into a symbol (Dalferth 1991: 307). The tension between the 'bad' death and the 'good' death suggests a *process* of consecration by which the good death *becomes* sacred and generates life. The self-sacrifice is an 'act of speech' that communicates political meaning. The circulation of emotions surrounding the body out towards a political community is redemptive. Redemption has religious as well as secular meanings, relating to repaying a debt, getting something back that has been lost or restoring life.

The agency of self-sacrifice is, at one and the same time, the most individual of acts, involving destruction of the body, and a potential catalyst for the restoration of community. Agency, as discussed in Chapter 2, is expressed by 'acting as if' one is free against the background of a dominant structure. The intrusion of a subordinate game becomes the source of contestation between two distinct worlds of action, the one defined by a hierarchy and the other by a refusal to conform and a performance of political subjectivity. The contestation regards the identity of the agent as a criminal/terrorist or martyr, and the nature of the death as a suicide or martyrdom. In this hierarchical context, the prisoner had a choice to conform, to refuse to conform or to use violence. The warden's dilemma was most significant in those situations in which the agent refused to conform but also refused to hit back. As the warden continued the punishment for this refusal to conform, he or she increasingly appeared to be the criminal, given the disproportionate use of force against prisoners who refused to acknowledge their humiliation, but who also did not react with violence.

The symbolic nature of the act of political self-sacrifice highlights the potential to disrupt everyday assumptions surrounding the moral legitimacy of agents and to 'create a conversation with the human conscience' (Bleiker 2000: 90). Several inversions, which were explored in Chapter 3, are at the heart of this conversation. The first inversion is the performance of an act of speech, as distinct from a speech act, in which the materiality of the dying body communicates a political message. Second, the bodily sacrifice becomes a symbolic inversion and a materialization of the historical experience of humiliation and suffering by the body politic. Third, the visualization of 'bare life' carries the power to disrupt assumed relationships of legitimacy and to inspire imitation. As emotions circulate out from the dead body, the boundaries between different audiences are transformed. Whether audiences are 'attracted' to the cause communicated by the act, the core of soft power, or repelled, resulting in a loss of soft power, may be a function of the extent to which responsibility for the death is attributed to the agent or the powers that be.

These dynamics were explored in relation to three post-World-War-II contexts, namely the 1980–1981 hunger strikes in the Long Kesh prison in Northern Ireland (Chapter 4), the martyrdom of Solidarity's priest, Jerzy Popiełuszko, in 1984 (Chapter 5) and the self-burning of the Vietnamese monk Thich Quang Duc in 1963, followed two years later by a series of self-burnings in the United States (Chapter 6). Chapter 7 shifted to the contemporary regional context of the Middle East, drawing on insights from the historical chapters to examine suicide terrorism during the War on Terror, the 'martyrdom' of Turkish humanitarian aid workers on the *Mavi Marmara* and the self-burning of Mohammed Bouazizi in Tunisia, which sparked the Arab Spring.

## The cases

It may seem counter-intuitive at best, and outrageous at worst, to identify acts such as 'suicide terrorism' or hunger strikes by 'terrorists' with a sacred or redemptive quality. How one judges a particular act of political self-sacrifice may be a reflection of one's position in geographical, political or social space, however. As Turner (2008 [1969]: 106–7) suggests, any manifestation of anti-structure, or *communitas*, is likely to appear dangerous to those involved in maintaining the dominant structure. In the contemporary cases, and in particular those involving violence against others, the sacrifice remained a 'bad' death for some audiences, although for others it was an act of dignity. One significant difference between the various cases covered here was the degree to which the sacrifice divided audiences, either leaving a question of whether the agents were criminals/terrorists or martyrs, on the one hand, or, on the other hand, expanding the audience of identification with the latter. In all the cases the agents were hailed as martyrs, but they were distinguished by how widespread the acceptance of this status was.

While some might make a clear distinction between martyrdom involving soldiers in war and suicide terrorism, both fit within Farhad Khosrokhavar's (2005 [2002]) category of offensive martyrdom. Suicide terrorism is seen to be reprehensible by Western audiences given the indiscriminate deaths of innocents. The combination of self-sacrifice and the killing of others is also characteristic of war, although the killing of civilians is in principle forbidden – and conjures up a power of sacrifice that lies in the 'willingness to give up one's own life, while taking the lives of others' (Gilley 1991: 218). For both the soldier in war and the 'martyr', who inflicts harm to the self, the legitimacy of the sacrifice is granted by a community of support, albeit more formal in the one case and more loosely defined in the other. In both types of context involving violence against others, the division of the audience between friend and foe is reinforced.

This can be distinguished from more defensive forms of martyrdom, either involving only death to the self, as in self-burning, or death inflicted on the agent by others for a refusal to cooperate, which was, in the cases explored here, more likely to construct a unity that delegitimized the existing authorities.

## The act of speech

Self-sacrifice of the material body, rather than the sacrificial ethos of movements, has been the focus of this study, which narrowed its analytic scope. The deaths of figureheads such as Bobby Sands, Jerzy Popiełuszko and Thich Quang Duc were a defining moment of each case. One can ask why these deaths should have more impact than the deaths of those killed in the process of resistance more generally. The literature on securitization provides one potential answer to this question. One of the conditions of a successful securitization is, according to Ole Wæver (2000: 252–3), the social capital of the speaker. This means that the illocutionary force of the threat, as a speech act, will be greater if it is articulated by someone in a position of authority, such as a US president, rather than the average person on the street.[1] One could similarly argue that the perlocutionary effect of the martyrdom of Jerzy Popiełuszko – that is, the ability of the 'act of speech' to communicate without words and to persuade or inspire an audience – derived from his status as a symbol of the Polish nation. Equally, in the Vietnamese context, the assumption that Thich Quang Duc was a bodhisattva distinguished his act on behalf of the community from other self-burnings, which may have been viewed as suicides.

For a number of reasons, the securitization argument goes only so far. First, there is a difference between a speech act, such as threatening or promising, and what I refer to as an 'act of speech', such as self-immolation. The speech act is illocutionary, or an act *in*

---

[1] Thierry Balzacq (2005: 176–7) has argued that Wæver's approach reduces securitization to the acts of the speaker, and pays insufficient attention to the audience of securitization. While Wæver is clear about the need to persuade an audience of the validity of his or argument, Juha Vuori (2008) provides a more in-depth exploration of the potential perlocutionary intentions and effects of state securitization in non-democratic societies. Given his focus on the perlocutionary effects of state acts, his argument contrasts with the focus of this argument on the perlocutionary effects of political self-sacrifice.

saying something, which relies on historical conventions and social and cultural factors for its meaning and a certain *force* in the act of saying (Austin 1962: 121). The 'act of speech', by contrast, is perlocutionary, which means a shift of emphasis towards the *effects* achieved by the act. The perlocutionary act can be undertaken without a verbal utterance and is unconventional in the sense that the meaning cannot be determined in advance or on the basis of rules of language use and meaning (Austin 1962: 122). The illocutionary force of the threat articulated by a president rests with the authority of the speaker. The extent to which an act of political self-sacrifice persuades, inspires or convinces may be related to the agent's identity, but flows first and foremost from the emotions generated in various audiences and the extent to which the agent *becomes* a symbol of the suffering community. In this respect, it may be only in hindsight that we recognize these individuals as figureheads. Quang Duc was recognized as a bodhisattva only in the context of his self-burning. Adams (1996) has often referred to Sands as an ordinary 'bloke'. Both were ordinary people who undertook extraordinary acts in extraordinary times. Their identities were *transformed* from ordinary to extraordinary in the consecration surrounding the self-sacrifice. It remains to be seen what status Bouazizi will have in the historical record.[2]

Second, the greater focus on figureheads in the historical cases may be a result of the newness of these acts at the time. What distinguishes the historical and contemporary cases is the importance of the cultural resonance of, for instance, self-burning in the Vietnamese case, and the absence of this cultural framework for understanding Bouazizi's act in the Middle East. In the historical cases, religious traditions were drawn on to give meaning to acts of self-sacrifice. Historically and culturally specific memories and ideas were mobilized, but then often transformed in the justification of either violent or non-violent action. By contrast, Bouazizi in Tunisia had no symbolic status prior to his death, and there was no framework within Islam or Arab culture for making sense of his act of self-burning in any positive sense. In the contemporary world, the meaning of acts of self-immolation or non-violence may be more reliant on the global diffusion of these tactics, given a

---

[2] It may be that, in retrospect, Bouazizi and others will be immortalized and be seen as figureheads similar to those in the older cases. The context is still too fresh to draw conclusions.

long line of self-burnings across the world since the precedent set by Quang Duc, as argued by Biggs (2006a), or, in the case of non-violence, the precedents set by Gandhi in India and Martin Luther King in the United States. In this respect, Gandhi, Quang Duc and King have become part of a more global memory of resistance.

Third, the difference may be a consequence of the evolution of the global media context. The diffusion of forms of internet technology – and possibilities such as Facebook or Twitter with it – or mobile phones have increased the speed with which images and emotions circulate, making resistance less dependent on specific leaders. Indeed, the absence of figureheads was one of the hallmarks of the Arab Spring (Ghonim 2012). Not one of the three forms of political self-sacrifice explored in the Middle East was associated with the sacrifice of a figurehead.[3]

## 'Acting as if'

The warden's dilemma model begins with an assumption that political prisoners seek independence and the ability to engage in negotiation over the rules by which a sovereign-less community lives. From this perspective, sovereignty was less about a set of territorial boundaries or a formal legal category than the capacity to act as political agents. Sovereignty is ultimately a question of who decides, whether it is the people, a head of state, or an outside power. On the most funda-mental level, sovereignty resides in 'acting as if' one is free even in circumstances in which this freedom is denied. In the 'betwixt and between' of *communitas*, this 'acting as if' comes into direct conflict with dominant structures, which demand conformity to someone else's rules. Democracy, by contrast, is a societal formation in which participants are always acting as if they are free but in conditions that encourage and facilitate an ongoing process of negotiation. As such, the distinction between individuals and the institutions that enable participation cannot be clearly separated. Margalit (1996) argues that a decent society is one in which people are not humili-ated; in the context of this discussion, this means a society in which

---

[3] Osama bin Laden was a symarty/martyrdom but did not himself become a human bomb, although his death at the hands of Americans was undoubtedly understood by some as a martyrdom.

power is an expression of acting together, rather than geared to the perpetuation of fear and conformity.

The warden's dilemma model links these possibilities to the action of the prisoners – that is, whether, through their conformity, they doubled the voice of the humiliator or whether, in refusing to conform, and absorbing the blows of retaliation, the voice of the martyr was doubled. The self-sacrifice communicates 'I am sovereign', even in the face of death. As Gandhi said, in the early stages of his South Africa campaign (Attenborough 1982):

> They may torture my body,
> Break my bones,
> Even kill me.
> Then they will have my dead body,
> Not my obedience.

At the time the statement was considered radical, by the British for the disobedience it encouraged and by many in the 'coloured' audience because Gandhi was arguing for a form of resistance that did not involve hitting back. One can ask how this desire for sovereignty differs, for instance, from the sentiment expressed by some Americans during the Cold War that they were 'better dead than red', or the sacrifices that countless soldiers have made over the years on behalf of the nation state. It would seem to be more radical only because it rests on an acknowledgement that the sovereignty that is taken for granted within democratic nation states has been denied to those who for one reason or another, and often due to great power politics, have 'fallen through the cracks'.

Chapter 1 argued that there is a family resemblance between more ancient forms of sacrifice and contemporary forms of political self-sacrifice. The emphasis on the self and the objective of sovereignty for the latter distinguishes the modern from the pre-modern. Sacrifice is a 'form of life' (Wittgenstein 1958: paras. 19, 23, 241) that is evident across human history and in most societies, but self-sacrifice for the nation state is a historically specific phenomenon. Political self-sacrifice by marginalized communities is the flip side of the more common preoccupation with the sacrifice of soldiers of the state in war. The main difference is that the latter is defending that which has already been attained, while the former is attempting to reclaim that which has been lost.

Something more is happening here, however. Although sacrifice has taken a variety of forms, extending back centuries, and sacrifice for the nation state is a modern phenomenon, all the cases in this book have taken place against the backdrop of a globalizing media, whereby the audience neither stopped at the water's edge nor with potential members of the nation, but was international as well. The contestation relied on cornerstones of international law, and the often conflicting principles of sovereignty and human rights. Neither the *communitas* nor the broader audience were confined to the territorial boundaries of the nation state but occupied a more global space, whether as members of the Irish diaspora in the United States, as agents of self-burning in the United States who identified with those who suffered from the Vietnam War, or the people across eastern Europe who were inspired to 'act as if' they were free, following in the footsteps of Solidarity. The successes of the Arab Spring in Tunisia and Egypt were followed by uprisings across north Africa and the Middle East, and also inspired a global 'occupation' movement.

## The suffering body politic

Pape (2006: 46) defines foreign occupation as 'boots on the ground', or the ability of a foreign power 'to control the local government independent of the wishes of the local community'. Al-Qaida's understanding of occupation is much broader, and rests on a long history of injustice manifest in the humiliation of the larger Muslim world by the 'Crusader–Zionist' alliance. Moghadam (2008: 56), in a critique of Pape's work, argues that the latter 'ideologically inspired definition of occupation' is what matters most for al-Qaida and what is missing from Pape's analysis. According to Moghadam, while occupation is part of the publicly presented rationale for suicide terrorism by both local groups and more global Salafi jihadi, what needs to be explained is the presence of suicide terrorism in locations that haven't experienced 'boots on the ground'.

The historical cases in this book focused on agents who defined the reason for resistance as one of occupation or foreign interference, and this claim was often bound up in the political contestation surrounding the meaning of the sacrifice. The notion, for instance, that Northern Ireland was occupied, even in the 1980s, when British 'boots were on the ground', was contested. While 'occupation' was central to republican claims to legitimacy, it was acknowledged neither by Thatcher nor loyalist/unionist populations, who viewed Northern Ireland as an integral part of the United Kingdom. Poland was led by 'Poles', and the potential for foreign 'boots on the ground' was more an ever-present threat than an actuality,[4] although memories of past Soviet interventions in the Eastern bloc, such as Hungary in 1956 and Czechoslovakia in 1968, provided some substance to these fears. Nonetheless, communist Poland was more a Soviet invention than a Polish one, even while it rested on the leadership of Poles. As Longina Jakubowska (1990) notes, Solidarity presented itself as the sole representative of the Polish nation. The government was portrayed as of foreign origin and its domination as a form of foreign domination. The number of American 'boots on the ground' in Vietnam in 1963, when the Buddhist crisis took place, was minimal. The conflict focused on a repressive Vietnamese ruler, supported by the US administration, who, given his Catholic identity, was associated with a long history of outside interference. Despite the historical influence of the United States over Tunisia and Egypt, this has not involved 'boots on the ground'. Occupation or foreign interference has been more *an intersubjective understanding* than a case of actual 'boots on the ground' in all the cases, with the exception of Palestine, which does also have Israeli 'boots on the ground'.

Occupation is a formal legal category defined in the Geneva Conventions. Pape provides a further definition for the purposes of his analysis. The focus of this book has been on the use of 'occupation' in political language as a reason for action. Priority has been given to mapping processes of *contestation* in order to identify whether the family resemblances between cases represent a relationship of distant, twice-removed cousins or a more close-knit extended family. A central methodological claim is that any attempt to transform these family resemblances into a more coherent nuclear family is fraught with even greater problems, which are exacerbated by the fluctuations of identity that have accompanied the process of globalization. The common traits that tie the cases together are memories of humiliation by an 'occupying' power, contestation surrounding the deaths as suicide or martyrdom and the identities

---

[4] The Soviet Union did have a regular military presence in Poland until 1993, which, according to a treaty signed in 1956, was limited to 66,000 troops and thirty-nine military bases. The actual number of troops was not disclosed, but there were in fact seventy-nine military bases, and Soviet nuclear weapons were also installed in the country.

of the agents as criminal/terrorists or martyrs, and the role of a globalizing media. If the relationship between body, emotion and community is
fluid rather than fixed, then there is no reason why the claim to be
'occupied' is purely a question of 'boots on the ground'.

Within Moghadam's framework, to compare local and more
globalized forms of martyrdom – his focus is the human bomb – is
like comparing distant twice-removed cousins rather than a close-knit
extended family. A claim of this kind would seem to be even more true
of this book's comparison of different types of political self-sacrifice.
There is a large body of literature on suicide terrorism. There
is a somewhat smaller one, at least within the field of international
relations, on non-violent resistance.[5] Even less has been written about
contemporary political acts of self-burning,[6] and almost nothing that
examines the relationship between these different tactics.[7] It thus
seems counter-intuitive to argue that there is a sufficient family resemblance between the different cases to justify comparison.

In presenting this work to different audiences, critics have made
conflicting arguments about which case is the potential outlier. One
argument is that suicide terrorism doesn't fit because, unlike the others,
it is a weapon of war that involves the killing of innocents. If one accepts
Carl von Clausewitz's definition of war as politics by other means,
however, then the body was arguably, in all the cases explored here, a
weapon of political battle, if not technically war. In the Long Kesh prison
in Northern Ireland the suffering body was a political extension of the
weapons used by the IRA outside the prison. Gandhi was also very clear
that he was engaged in a form of fighting, although one that was strictly
non-violent. Solidarity used the language of war as a metaphor for non-
violent struggle while engaging with a state of war involving the full force
of the state. The body was in all cases a political weapon; the key issue
was the extent to which this weapon was a source of physical harm,
either to the self or to others, and harmed the legitimacy of the opponent.

The second argument is that non-violent martyrdom doesn't fit
because it isn't really *self*-sacrifice, given that suffering and death are

---

[5] For a useful overview of the literature on non-violence, see Carter (2011), as well
as the book as a whole (Roberts and Garton Ash 2011), which provides analysis
of a number of historical cases of civil resistance.

[6] See, in particular, the work of Michael Biggs (2006b).

[7] Chenowith and Stephan (2011) have paved the way with a large-N study
comparing violent and non-violent resistance.

inflicted by someone other than the agent. The latter, however, fits more closely with definitions of martyrdom as witnessing to injustice than self-inflicted death does. Here Khosrokhavar's reference to the Romans is worth remembering: they saw the Christian martyrs as irrational, and all the more so because they 'caused' their death to be inflicted by others (2005: 6). The discussion among Catholics and Quakers following the US self-burnings, discussed in Chapter 6, suggested a fine line between self-immolation and knowingly undertaking acts that would invite retaliation. Whether or not they fit neatly together, all the cases have provoked discussion about the difference between suicide and martyrdom.

Does agency lie only in lighting the match or detonating the fuse, or does it lie first and foremost in the refusal to cooperate with what is understood to be an unjust order? The film *Gandhi* (Attenborough 1982) depicts the salt marchers approaching a line of soldiers, row by row, only to be bludgeoned until they collapsed to the ground. Was this organized march, which deliberately put the participants in harm's way, and led to their injury and death, any less *self*-sacrifice because the suffering was inflicted by soldiers of Her Majesty's government? The notion of self-sacrifice suggests some degree of agency, but that agency must be viewed as a process rather than a distinct moment in time. The hunger strikes in Northern Ireland are a case in point. The refusal of food was the last resort after a process of refusing to conform to the rules of the prison over a five-year period. The hunger strike was also not a single act, but extended over weeks before the ultimate sacrifice was made.

These are all cases that involve destruction of the material body and a people who have experienced humiliation and seek to restore dignity. The central difference is how the body was sacrificed. Although this is an in-depth study of a small number of cases, one conclusion might provide a point of departure for examining further cases. On the one hand, accepting violence, as a consequence of refusing to conform, is more likely to result in a warden's dilemma, in which the legitimacy of the powers that be is called into question. On the other hand, the use of violence against others as well as the self is more likely to result in a security dilemma, which, given an asymmetry of power, is likely to legitimize retaliation against 'terrorists'. As already stated, the former doubles the voice of the martyr while the latter, like conformity, doubles the voice of the warden.

Self-burning has a somewhat unusual relationship to these propositions. Unlike the human bomb, self-burning involves violence only against the self. While this may be identified as suicide rather than martyrdom, thereby depoliticizing the act, self-burning does not so easily communicate terrorism. In addition, unlike the case of the non-violent witness, self-burning and hunger strikes are self-inflicted. In the case of the non-violent witness, death is a consequence of retaliation for the refusal to conform and acting as if one is free. Popiełuszko was carrying out the duties of an ordinary priest in extraordinary times. The participants in the Gaza flotilla were attempting to bring aid to a suffering people. The self-burning and the non-violent witness are both symbolic, yet the symbolism of the former highlights the current suffering of a people but does not communicate any particular message about the hoped-for future. 'Acting as if' one is free, by contrast, involves participants in a rehearsal of the hoped-for future.

Any kind of conclusion from this comparison may be unsatisfying insofar as there is a desire to draw a line and conclude that if, under certain conditions a particular action is performed, a particular consequence can be expected. Chenowith and Stephan (2011), in a major study of civil resistance, find that non-violent campaigns succeed more often than those employing violence. The point here is that the process and outcome of any one of these scenarios are likely to be as different as the process and outcome of any game of chess – indeed, more so, given that the degree of contingency is greater. The analogy suggests, however, that there is some continuity that ties the cases together, that they are all cases involving self-sacrifice, embedded in a context of social resistance that sought greater freedom to negotiate the rules by which a community would live. The resistance sought to change the game such that they became political agents. If we compare the historical cases to the contemporary cases in the Middle East and north Africa, there is some overlap, but not completely. In part this is difficult to judge because the contemporary cases are still in process.

In the historical cases, the martyrdom of Popiełuszko and the self-burning in Vietnam both led to conclusions that the warden was a criminal. In the former case, this resulted in negotiations that, over time, and in the context of transformation in the Eastern bloc, contributed to a change of games. In the Vietnam case, the warden was assassinated, to be replaced by a new warden, followed by an escalation of the war. In the Northern Irish case, the death of Sands – and others – gave rise to questions of whether Thatcher was a criminal, but she remained inflexible, given the association of the hunger strikers with the violent campaign of the IRA. The result was a stalemate, followed by an escalation of violence and a renewed security dilemma.

In the contemporary Middle East, the deaths of the Turkish aid workers on the *Mavi Marmara* were followed by contestation over whether the Israeli act of boarding the ship was criminal or the aid workers were terrorists, but there has been no significant change in the status quo. While this was one episode in a much larger context that is still unfolding, the aid workers did not display a consistent non-violent spirit and discipline, as evidenced by the images of some protesters wielding sticks. Just as one can play a game with greater or lesser degrees of skill, the same is true of strategic engagement, whether violent or non-violent. The self-burnings that set off the Arab Spring, like Vietnam, led to the warden being replaced in Tunisia and Egypt. Human bombs in the context of the larger War on Terror or in the context of Israel/Palestine provided justification for retaliation by states and a security dilemma. Both sides suffered a loss of soft power as a result. These family resemblances speak more to process and probabilities than to definitive outcomes.

Turner's (2008) notion of *communitas*, or the liminal state of 'betwixt and between' that arises out of the confrontation between structure and anti-structure, has provided one insight from the anthropological literature. In applying these concepts to more contemporary cases, this book has conceptualized *communitas* as an expression of 'acting as if' an alternative set of rules, an anti-structure, was in place, which provided a framework for marginalized communities to understand themselves as political agents. When I have presented the various cases in this book to different academic audiences there has sometimes been a tendency to assume that 'anti-structure' refers to an end state, in which the objective of the new game is realized in practice, with a new set of more formalized structures, but this is to confuse *communitas*, as a liminal state, with the more established structures that might emerge from a change. Anti-structure is defined against the background of structure. Once structure evaporates there is no guarantee that anti-structure will evolve into a stable order. While self-sacrifice may expand the *communitas* supporting change, the path to a stable self-governing community is fraught with potential pitfalls along the way.

## Global questions

In the introduction I stated that it was not my intention to pose the normative question of whether communities in this position have a right to resist but, rather, to begin with the empirical observation that they often do, and that self-sacrifice has been an important element of that resistance. While the normative questions are important and unavoidable, an in-depth examination of these issues must be left for another time. Here I would just like to mention a few points in the hope of avoiding unwanted conclusions in the absence of any discussion.

The first is that society would be impossible if people refused to conform whenever they felt like it or willingly inflicted harm on themselves. The question is one of when non-cooperation or self-sacrifice is justified. The answer, however unsatisfying, is that it is justified when the audience accepts it to be so. There is no ultimate point of reference for determining the most just course of action other than the moral, legal and political resources that are mobilized in the process of 'conversation'. Conversation is silenced in a situation in which rules and the expectation of conformity are imposed on a society. What distinguishes the various forms of self-sacrifice is the extent to which they 'speak', either by breaking through or by hardening everyday assumptions about what is moral or just and who the agents of morality and deviance are. The act speaks to the emotions and represents an encounter with our humanity. To the extent that the objective of non-violence is to create the space for this conversation by accepting harm to the self, rather than inflicting it on others, it can, much like the medical ethos of 'Do no harm', be a source of healing and morality, opening a space for humility – as distinct from humiliation – on all sides.

A non-violent stance raises moral questions of another kind, however, insofar as innocents are placed in harm's way in a situation in which there is no guarantee of success. Is non-violent self-sacrifice moral in a context in which a leader is shameless, and willing to kill large numbers of his or her population in an attempt to hold on to power, as has been evident in many countries of the Arab Spring, but most dramatically in Libya and Syria? Should members of a repressive society engage in non-violent resistance if there is some chance that things will become worse, at least before they become better? This question has to be asked about resistance of any kind, including violent resistance, and particularly in a context of asymmetry, when the use of violence may legitimize retaliation by the authorities. Both are questions that communities in specific locations have had to answer for themselves. I would be inclined to reframe the questions. First, how long can a regime govern if its only source of power is the ability to employ violence against its own citizens? Second, to what extent does the use of violence, from a position of weakness, reinforce the ability of a repressive regime to legitimize retaliation? Third, does the performance of violence, as distinct from 'acting as if', contribute to the objective of a self-governing community, given that the former doesn't involve a rehearsal of practices relating to self-governance, and given that success may depend on outside intervention?

The final point regards the normative underpinnings of the argument. Are we to conclude that people *should* engage in forms of political self-sacrifice, and that if they do they will achieve their objectives? This is definitely not the point. However moral the objective, none of these 'tactics', any more than those of war, are always successful. Success, as with any strategy or tactic, is a measure of timing, context and how skilfully the game is played. There may be unintended consequences of action, as illustrated in the Vietnam case, when the removal of Diem led to an escalation of the US presence and all-out war. There may be significant challenges, in the context of a non-violent campaign, of maintaining non-violent discipline. Given the potential loss of life, whether of the agent or innocent bystanders, a decision to undertake acts of self-sacrifice cannot be taken lightly and may be morally objectionable, at least in some contexts. Indeed, most religious traditions, to the extent that they condone self-sacrifice at all, attach conditions to the legitimacy of the act. In Vietnam an act of self-burning would generally be considered suicide unless undertaken with right intention by a bodhisattva, for instance. The legitimacy of non-violent non-cooperation rests on the injustice of particular laws or power structures. This is not an argument about what communities or individuals should or should not do but, rather, an exploration of some of the dynamics surrounding different expressions of political self-sacrifice for the sake of encouraging greater reflection and reflexivity.

## Restoring community

The study raises epistemological and ontological challenges alike to IR theory, which reveal several tensions for further exploration. This study began with the dialectical tension surrounding the identity of the agent of political self-sacrifice, as a criminal/terrorist or martyr, and the meaning of the act, as a suicide or martyrdom. This represents a challenge, in that concepts that may be the site of political contestation are often treated as labels for an objective reality. From the latter perspective, 'terrorists' simply 'are', and there is no acknowledgement of the extent to which the 'terrorist' label is often used to marginalize those resisting injustice, even those whose actions are strictly non-violent. This is less a problem of the misuse of language per se than a lack of attention to the contestation that is a part of politics itself. The point is nonetheless compatible with Wittgenstein's (1958) claim that many of our (philosophical) problems, or in this case analytical problems, disappear once we recognize them as puzzles that arise out of the misuse of ordinary language and mischaracterization of ordinary practices.

A second tension regards the relationship between some notion of a bounded community and a more global context of what Nira Yuval-Davis (2011: 6) refers to as 'intersectionality'. Intersectionality is a metaphor that suggests a road intersection, or an indeterminate and contested number of intersecting roads. The tendency within IR theory to treat states as fixed bodies or as if they are 'persons' conflicts with the potential transformation of communities and the more fluid processes of globalization. That which is often assumed to be stable and unchanging, whether community identity or power blocs, can be and often is destabilized. This conclusion is being written in Scotland at a time when the independence of this historic nation from the United Kingdom has become a topic of heated debate. Fortunately, this conversation involves engagement with words rather than injury and death, but the destabilization of an affiliation that has been taken for granted for centuries is no less because of it. Sovereignty is a social construct that most often involves the drawing of boundaries, spatial definitions and the occupation of space. Political self-sacrifice calls forth a more fluid conversation.

A third tension regards a distinction between membership in a bounded community and our moral perspective as human beings. This relates to a further challenge, which is both epistemological and ontological, regarding the need to bring emotion into the study of international relations. It points to a contrast between 'occupation' and 'hospitality' as two distinct encounters with the other. Emmanuel Levinas and Jacques Derrida discuss hospitality as an ethical encounter with others, which is fundamentally welcoming and receptive to them, though, for Derrida, it also represents a liminal condition that may be interlaced with hostility (Benhabib 2006: 157–8). While 'occupation' suggests a relationship of imposition, 'hospitality' suggests more of a conversation between actors who are differently positioned in social space, as host or guest. For a field such as IR, which has been primarily concerned with questions of order and war, and the territorial demarcation of space, hospitality highlights the importance of conversation, of the simple question of how we engage with the other as human being, the importance of recognizing the dignity and subjectivity of the other and the dangers that arise from relationships of humiliation. Self-sacrifice is a confrontation with 'bare life', which brings us face to face in an encounter with our humanity, raising questions about the social artefacts at the core of conversation and whether they are first and foremost life-creating or life-destroying. They point to the need for a radical rethinking about the extent to which we are all 'occupied' or need to reoccupy those areas of life that, through the construction of barriers, walls of silence and fear, have denied human or political agency.

The fourth dialectic is that of the 'good' death and the 'bad' death, which is at the heart of sacrifice and redemption. Can a field that prides itself on its scientific status account for more transcendent phenomena? Can a concept of agency, a distinctly modern notion that, according to Bleiker (2000), arises from the death of God, coexist with the sacred, the inexplicable, 'whereof we cannot speak' (Wittgenstein 1922: prop. 7)? Hubert and Mauss (1964 [1898]: 99) claim that all sacrifice involves an element of redemption. An answer to a question as to why sacrifice should be redemptive is less than straightforward. Redemption is shrouded in mystery within religious traditions and is even more incomprehensible from the perspective of science. The idea that the martyr witnesses to injustice is perhaps a point of entry. To witness to injustice is to make visible that which has been hidden or denied, such that the veneer of legitimacy by which repressive practices have been maintained is stripped away and leaders are held to account. The self-sacrifice is a spectacularized symbol of the injustice suffered by a community, which speaks to the fear that allows for the continuation of a status quo and conformity with it. The most individual of acts, the destruction of the body, becomes the expression of a community's struggle for recognition.

In the endeavour to become a science, the contestation that is a part of politics has been replaced by a more static picture, for the sake of measurement and testing, or, as critical theorists have argued, one that reinforces the legitimacy of those in power (Cox 1981). Normative questions about how we should organize life have been replaced by theoretical representations of how things are. The science of international relations was formed, in the aftermath of World War I, to try to explain the occurrence of inter-state war in the hope of avoiding it in the future. This enterprise, while important, has often ignored the movement and dislocation of populations or serious questions about those communities that have been the victims of inter-state politics. Internationally recognized boundaries do not necessarily correspond to community ideas about belonging, however. They have often been the outcome of negotiations between imperial powers, often without any involvement of more local populations or national movements. The acts of political self-sacrifice analysed here express the desire of communities, and individuals within them, to be involved in negotiation over the rules by which they will live.

## New beginnings

Order has been a defining problem of the study of politics and international relations. The desire to fix or hold the state in place is a reflection of the insecurity that has so long plagued human existence and that gave rise to Hobbes' argument in *Leviathan*. This book has contrasted the image on the cover of this classic, in which the body of Leviathan contains the peoples of a state, with an image of the martyr as a symbol of a people in resistance when the state has violated its commitment to protect.

This project began with a question about those who have fallen through the cracks of inter-state politics and how they fight back from a sovereign-less position. The point of departure was a structure of anarchy that divides the world into territorial spaces that, as noted earlier, were often imposed by imperial powers. Anti-structure, in the various cases, called this territorial construction into question, beckoning towards a conversation regarding the rules by which we live – a conversation that has been facilitated by the emergence of a global media. The various conversations now traverse these territorial places and involve a range of actors. This discussion of political self-sacrifice, in a context of 'international' relations, ends with a question about what it means to converse in a global space. What would it mean to occupy a global space in which human bodies matter? Self-sacrifice is a performance of speech in a context in which speech has been silenced. It expresses a desire to have a voice. Dignity is in part a matter of replacing what has been written over with writing of one's own. The question of who 'one' is or where one belongs has become more complex, however. The nation state is no longer the sole container of the conversation over the rules by which we live. In the global space, wealth and power are concentrated in the hands of a small minority, which influences the ability to be heard. Occupying a global space in which human bodies matter, and speak, means reconfiguring a global space in which humanity matters.

# Bibliography

*Note*: 'FBIS-FRB' stands for Foreign Broadcast Information Service – Foreign Radio Broadcast. Since 1947 the FBIS, as part of the CIA, has monitored radio broadcasts and press agency releases around the world.

Abu Gheith, Suleiman 2002. 'In the shadow of the lances', Center for Islamic Research and Studies (reprinted in '"Why we fight America": Al-Qa'ida spokesman explains September 11 and declares intentions to kill 4 million Americans with weapons of mass destruction', Special Despatch no. 388, Middle East Media Research Institute, 12 June).

Abu-Nimer, Mohammed 2003. *Nonviolence and Peacebuilding in Islam: Theory and Practice*. Gainsville: University of Florida Press.

Ascherson, Neal 1981. *The Polish August*. New York: Penguin Books.

Adams, Gerry 1996. *Before the Dawn: An Autobiography*. London: Heinemann.

Adler, Emanuel 1997. 'Seizing the middle ground: constructivism in world politics', *European Journal of International Relations*, 3(3): 319–63.

2010. 'Damned if you do and damned if you don't: performative power and the strategy of conventional and nuclear defusing', *Security Studies*, 19(2): 199–229.

Agamben, Giorgio 1998. *Homo Sacer: Sovereign Power and Bare Life*. Stanford University Press.

2005. *State of Exception*. University of Chicago Press.

Agence France Presse 2011. 'Tunisia protest icon is now world's son: mother', Agence France Presse – English, 5 March.

Ahmed, Sara 2004. *The Cultural Politics of Emotion*. London: Routledge.

2010. 'Orientations matter', in Diana Coole and Samantha Frost (eds.), *New Materialisms: Ontology, Agency, and Politics*, 234–57. Durham, NC: Duke University Press.

Al-Azhar University 2011. 'Suicide is against Islam', Egyptian Gazette Online, 19 January.

Allison, Olivia 2007. 'Understanding suicide attacks', OpenDemocracy, 21 June, www.opendemocracy.net/understanding_suicide_attacks.

Anderson, Benedict 1983. *Imagined Communities: Reflections on the Origin and Spread of Nationalism*. London: Verso.

Appy, Christian G. 2008. *Vietnam: The Definitive Oral History, Told From All Sides*. London: Ebury Press.

Arendt, Hannah 1986 [1970]. 'Communicative power', in Steven Lukes (ed.), *Power*, 59–74. New York University Press.

Asali, Ziad 2011. 'Washington must not be a global policeman or dictators' patron', *Daily Star* (Lebanon), 4 March.

Ateek, Naim 2000. 'Suicide bombers: what is theologically and morally wrong with suicide bombings? A Palestinian Christian perspective', *Cornerstone*, **25**: 1–19.

Atran, Scott 2006. 'The moral logic and growth of suicide terrorism', *Washington Quarterly*, **29**(2): 127–47.

Attenborough, Richard 1982. *Gandhi*. Columbia Pictures.

Austin, John 1962. *How to Do Things with Words*. Oxford University Press.

Ayish, Muhammad 2003. 'Beyond Western-oriented communication theories: a normative Arab-Islamic perspective', *The Public*, **10**(2): 79–92.

Baldwin, David 1980. 'Interdependence and power: a conceptual analysis', *International Organization*, **34**(4): 471–506.

Balzacq, Thierry 2005. 'The three faces of securitization: political agency, audience and context', *European Journal of International Relations*, **11**(2): 171–201.

Barnett, Michael, and Raymond Duvall 2005. 'Power in international relations', *International Organization*, **59**(1): 39–75.

Bean, Kevin, and Mark Hayes (eds.) 2001 *Republican Voices*. Monaghan: Seesyu Press.

Beattie, J. H. M. 1980. 'On understanding sacrifice', in M. F. C. Bourdillon and Meyer Fortes (eds.), *Sacrifice*, 29–44. London: Academic Press.

Beinin, Joel, and Lisa Hajjar 2000. 'Palestine, Israel and the Arab–Israeli conflict', Middle East Research and Information Project, www.merip. org/Palestine-Israel_primer/intro-pal-isr=primer.html.

Belayachi, Daniel 2011. 'Arab world's revolutionary immolations and "martyrdom" change', Afrik-News, 15 March.

Bell, Catherine 2009a [1992]. *Ritual Theory, Ritual Practice*. Oxford University Press.

   2009b [1997]. *Ritual: Perspectives and Dimensions*. Oxford University Press.

Bell, Vikki 2005. 'The scenography of suicide: terror, politics and the humiliated witness', *Economy and Society*, **34**(2): 241–60.

Ben Mhenni, Lina 2011. 'My country, Tunisia: "for years, the regime kept up appearances"', *Toronto Star*, 13 March.

Benhabib, Seyla 2006. *Another Cosmopolitanism* (ed. Robert Post). Oxford University Press.

Benn, James A. 2007. *Burning for the Buddha: Self-Immolation in Chinese Buddhism*. Honolulu: University of Hawai'i Press.

Bennet, James 2002. 'Rash of new suicide bombers exhibit no patterns or ties', *New York Times*, 21 June: A1.

Bennett, Andrew, and Colin Elman 2006. 'Qualitative research: recent developments in case study methods', *Annual Review of Political Science*, 9: 455–76.

Berenbaum, Michael, and Reuven Firestone 2004. 'The theology of martyrdom', in Rona M. Fields (ed.), *Martyrdom: The Psychology, Theology, and Politics of Self-Sacrifice*, 117–46. London: Praeger.

Beresford, David 1994. *Ten Men Dead: The Story of the 1981 Irish Hunger Strike*. London: HarperCollins.

Berko, Anat 2007. *The Path to Paradise: The Inner World of Suicide Bombers and Their Dispatchers*. Westport, CT: Praeger Security International.

Berrigan, Daniel 1987. *To Dwell in Peace: An Autobiography*. San Francisco: Harper & Row.

Beyer, Gerald J. 2007. 'A theoretical appreciation of the ethic of Solidarity in Poland twenty-five years after', *Journal of Religious Ethics*, 35(2): 207–32.

Bially Mattern, Janice 2005. *Ordering International Politics: Identity, Crisis and Representation*. London: Routledge.

2011. 'A practice theory of emotion for International Relations', in Emanuel Adler and Vincent Pouliot (eds.), *International Practices*, 63–86. Cambridge University Press.

Biegel, William 1965. Letter to the editor, 'Pacifists' sacrifice', *New York Times*, 16 November: 46.

Bieler, Andreas, and Adam Morton 2001. 'The Gordian knot of agency–structure in international relations: a neo-Gramscian perspective', *European Journal of International Relations*, 7(1): 5–35.

Biggs, Michael 2006a. 'The transnational diffusion of protest by self-immolation', paper presented at 'Crossing borders' conference, Wissenschaftszentrum Berlin für Sozialforschung, 6 October.

2006b. 'Dying without killing: self-immolations, 1963–2002', in Diego Gambetta (ed.), *Making Sense of Suicide Missions*, 173–208. Oxford University Press.

Bin Laden, Osama 2001. 'Bin Laden's warning: full text', Al Jazeera, 7 October.

Black, Ian, and Haroon Siddique 2011. 'Q & A: the Gaza Freedom Flotilla', *Guardian*, 15 May: 1 & 3.

Bleiker, Roland 2000. *Popular Dissent, Human Agency and Global Politics*. Cambridge University Press.

Bleiker, Roland, and Emma Hutchison 2008. 'Fear no more: emotions and world politics', *Review of International Studies*, 34(1): 115–35.

Bloch, Maurice, and Jonathan Parry (eds.) 1982. *Death and the Regeneration of Life*. Cambridge University Press.

Bloom, Mia 2005. *Dying to Kill: The Allure of Suicide Terror*. New York: Columbia University Press.

Books LLC 2010. *Self-Immolations in Protest to the Vietnam War: Norman Morrison, Roger Allen LaPorte, Alice Herz, George Winne, Jr., Florence Beaumont*. Memphis: Books LLC.

Booth, Ken 1991. 'Security and emancipation', *Review of International Studies*, 17(4): 313–26.

Booth, Ken, and Nicholas Wheeler 2007. *The Security Dilemma: Fear, Cooperation and Trust in World Politics*. Basingstoke: Palgrave Macmillan.

Bouazizi family 2011. 'Bouazizi family's message to Libya', YouTube, www.youtube.com/watch?v=61m567lqL74&feature=player_embedded.

Bourdieu, Pierre 1990. *The Logic of Practice* (trans. Richard Nice). Stanford University Press.

Bridget 2011. 'Egyptian cleric says that suicide is strictly forbidden in Islamic law', Hillbuzz, hillbuzz.org/2011/01/22/egyptian-cleric-says-that-suicide-is-strictly-forbidden.

Brink, Cornelia 2000. 'Secular icons: looking at photos from Nazi concentration camps', *History and Memory*, 12(1): 135–50.

Brown, Daniel 2001. 'Martyrdom in Sunni revivalist thought', in Margaret Cormack (ed.), *Sacrificing the Self: Perspectives on Martyrdom and Religion*, 107–17. Oxford University Press.

Browne, Malcolm 1965. *The New Face of War: A Report on a Communist Guerrilla Campaign*. London: Cassell.

Burgis, Michelle 2008. 'The promise of solid ground: Arab states, territorial disputes and the discourse of international law', *International Community Law Review*, 10(1): 73–99.
    2009. 'A discourse of distinction: Palestinians, international law, and the promise of humanitarianism', *Palestine Yearbook of International Law*, 15: 41–68.

Burkert, Walter 1996. *Creation of the Sacred: Tracks of Biology in Early Religions*. Cambridge, MA: Harvard University Press.

Burns, J. Patout (ed.) 1996. *War and Its Discontents: Pacifism and Quietism in the Abrahamic Traditions*. Washington, DC: Georgetown University Press.

Butler, Judith 1993. *Bodies that Matter: On the Discursive Limits of Sex*. London: Verso.
    2004. *Precarious Life: The Powers of Mourning and Violence*. London: Verso.

Buzan, Barry, Ole Wæver and Jaap de Wilde 1998. *Security: A New Frame-work of Analysis.* Boulder, CO: Lynne Riener.

Cameron, James 1965. 'From Hanoi: premier says, "Let US go, and the war is over"', *New York Times*, 11 December: 16.

Carter, April 2011. 'People power and protest: the literature on civil resistance in historical context', in Adam Roberts and Timothy Garton Ash (eds.), *Civil Resistance and Power Politics: The Experience of Non-Violent Action from Gandhi to the Present*, 25–42. Oxford University Press.

Chanoff, David, and Doan Van Toai 2009. *Vietnam: A Portrait of Its People at War.* London: I. B. Tauris.

Cheng-chin, Liao 1963. 'Speeches, message at rally on Vietnam', Radio Peking, Domestic Service broadcast, 30 August (reprinted in 'China communist international affairs', FBIS-FRB-63-172: BBB8–10).

Chenowith, Erica, and Maria J. Stephan 2011. *Why Civil Resistance Works: The Strategic Logic of Nonviolent Conflict.* New York: Columbia University Press.

Clark, Liam 2009. 'Thatcher offered IRA hunger strike deal', *Sunday Times*, 5 April.

CNN 2003. 'Twenty years later, Lebanon bombing haunts', CNN, 23 October, www.cnn.com/2003/WORLD/meast/10/21/lebanon.annw.ap.

Coakley, Sarah (ed.) 1997. *Religion and the Body.* Cambridge University Press.

Collins, John 2004. *Occupied by Memory: The Intifada Generation and the Palestinian State of Emergency.* New York University Press.

Confino, Alon, and Peter Fritzsche (eds.) 2002. *The Work of Memory: New Directions in the Study of German Society and Culture.* Urbana: University of Illinois Press.

Coogan, Tim Pat 1987. *The IRA.* London: HarperCollins.

Cook, David 2007. *Martyrdom in Islam.* Cambridge University Press.

Cook, David, and Olivia Allison 2007. *Understanding and Addressing Suicide Attacks: The Faith and Politics of Martyrdom Operations.* London: Praeger.

Cowan, Geoffrey, and Nicholas J. Cull 2008. *Public Diplomacy in a Changing World.* London: Sage.

Cox, Robert 1981. 'Social forces, states and world orders: beyond international relations theory', *Millennium – Journal of International Studies*, 10(2): 126–55.

Crawford, Neta 2000. 'The passion of world politics: propositions on emotion and emotional relationships', *International Security*, 24(4): 116–56.

Cronin, Audrey 2003. *Terrorists and Suicide Attacks.* Washington, DC: Congressional Research Service.

Dahl, Robert 1957. 'The concept of power', *Behavioral Science*, **2**(3): 201–15.

*Daily News Egypt* 2011. '"It's dignity, stupid"', *Daily News Egypt*, 15 March.

Dalferth, Ingold U. 1991. 'Christ died for us: reflections on the sacrificial language of salvation', in Stephen Sykes (ed.), *Sacrifice and Redemption: Durham Essays in Theology*, 299–325. Cambridge University Press.

Danchev, Alex 2006. '"Like a dog!": humiliation and shame in the War on Terror', *Alternatives: Global, Local, Political*, **31**(3): 259–83.

Davies, Norman 2001. *The Heart of Europe: The Past in Poland's Present*. Oxford University Press.

Davutoglu, Ahmet 2010. 'Turkish FM addresses at the Security Council', *Turkish Weekly*, 1 June.

Dawson, Graham 1994. *Soldier Heroes: British Adventure, Empire and the Imagining of Masculinities*. London: Routledge.

Dessler, David 1989. 'What's at stake in the agent–structure debate?', *International Organization*, **43**(3): 441–73.

Diplock, Kenneth 1972. *The Report of the Commission to Consider Legal Procedures to Deal with Terrorist Activities in Northern Ireland*, Cmnd. 5186. Belfast: Her Majesty's Stationery Office.

Doty, Roxanne 1997. 'Aporia: a critical exploration of the agent–structure problematique in international relations theory', *European Journal of International Relations*, **3**(3): 365–92.

Dreyfus, Hubert L., and Paul Rabinow 1983. *Michel Foucault: Beyond Structuralism and Hermeneutics* (2nd edn). University of Chicago Press.

Durkheim, Émile 2006 [1897]. *On Suicide* (trans. Robin Buss). New York: Penguin Books.

Edkins, Jenny 2003. *Trauma and the Memory of Politics*. Cambridge University Press.

Edkins, Jenny, and Véronique Pin-Fat 2005. 'Through the wire: relations of power and relations of violence', *Millennium – Journal of International Studies*, **34**(1): 1–24.

Ellsberg, Robert (ed.) 1983. *By Little and by Little: The Selected Writings of Dorothy Day*. New York: Alfred A. Knopf.

Elster, Jon 1996. 'Rationality and emotions', *Economic Journal*, **106**: 1386–97.

English, Richard 2003. *Armed Struggle: The History of the IRA*. London: Pan Books.

2006. *Irish Freedom: The History of Nationalism in Ireland*. Basingstoke: Macmillan.

2009. *Terrorism: How to Respond*. Oxford University Press.

Erdoğan, Recep Tayyip 2010a. 'Turkish premier: "What Israel has done is a massacre deserving every kind of curse"', *Turkish Weekly*, 1 June.

2010b. 'Turkish PM Erdoğan says Israel "must be punished" for raid on Gaza aid ship', *Turkish Weekly*, 1 June.

Easwaran, Eknath 1984. *A Man to Match His Mountains: Badshah Khan, Nonviolent Soldiers of Islam*. Petaluma, CA: Nilgiri Press.

Esposito, John 2007. 'Partners in humanity: legitimate, illegitimate acts of violence', Common Ground News Service, www.commongroundnews. org/article.php?id=21505&Ian=en&Sid=1&sp=0.

Euben, Roxanne L. 2002. 'Killing (for) politics: jihad, martyrdom and political actions', *Political Theory*, 30(1): 4–35.

Facebook 2010. 'Martyrs of the Mavi Marmara', Facebook, www.facebook. com/media/set/?set=a.179490858748774.38536.162060917158435.

Fadl, Khaled Abou El 2005. Interview with Khaled Abou El Fadl, 'Jihad gone wrong', Qantara, 27 October, www.qantara.de/webcom/show.

Fanon, Frantz 2001 [1963]. *The Wretched of the Earth*. New York: Penguin Books.

Fattah, Khaled, and K. M. Fierke 2009. 'A clash of emotions: the politics of humiliation and terrorism in the Middle East', *European Journal of International Relations*, 15(1): 67–93.

Feldman, Allen 1991. *Formations of Violence: The Narrative of the Body and Political Terror in Northern Ireland*. University of Chicago Press.

Fierke, K. M. 1998. *Changing Games, Changing Strategies: Critical Investigations in Security*. Manchester University Press.

2004. 'Whereof we can speak, thereof we must not be silent: trauma, political solipsism and war', *Review of International Studies,* 30(4): 471–92.

2006. 'Bewitched by the past: social memory, trauma and international relations', in Duncan Bell (ed.), *Memory, Trauma and World Politics: Reflections on Past and Present*, 116–34. London: Palgrave Macmillan.

2007. *Critical Approaches to International Security*. Cambridge: Polity Press.

2009a. 'Constructivism', in Tim Dunne, Milja Kurki and Steve Smith (eds.), *International Relations Theory: Discipline and Diversity*, 166–84. Oxford University Press.

2009b. 'Agents of death: the structural logic of suicide terrorism and martyrdom', *International Theory*, 1(1): 155–84.

2009c. 'Terrorism and trust in Northern Ireland', *Critical Studies on Terrorism*, 2(3): 497–511.

Fitzgerald, Frances 1972. *Fire in the Lake: The Vietnamese and the Americans in Vietnam*. Boston: Atlantic Monthly Press.

Fleischer, Ari 2002. Press briefing by Ari Fleischer, White House, 12 April; available at www.whitehouse.gov/news/releases/2002/04/print/20020412-html.

Fontan, Victoria 2006. 'Polarization between occupier and occupied in post-Saddam Iraq: colonial humiliation and the formation of political violence', *Terrorism and Political Violence*, 18(2): 217–38.

Foucault, Michel 1979 [1975]. *Discipline and Punish: The Birth of the Prison* (trans. Alan Sheridan). New York: Random House.

Fox News 2003. 'Arafat swears in new Palestinian Cabinet', Fox News, 7 October.

  2004. 'Bomber kills 10 soldiers in Fallujah', Fox News, 6 September.

  2005. 'Holy Day blasts leave 55 dead in Iraq', Fox News, 22 February.

Fraser, Mariam, and Monica Greco 2005. *The Body: A Reader*. London: Routledge.

Friedman, Thomas 2000. *The Lexus and the Olive Tree: Understanding Globalization*. Norwell, MA: Anchor Press.

Gabriel, Jane 2007. 'Karama: women's activities across the Middle East', OpenDemocracy, 28 November, www.opendemocracy.net/blog/5050/karama.

Gambetta, Diego (ed.) 2006a. *Making Sense of Suicide Missions*. Oxford University Press.

  2006b. 'Can we make sense of suicide missions?', in Diego Gambetta (ed.), *Making Sense of Suicide Missions*, 259–300. Oxford University Press.

Gandhi, Mohandas 1951. *Nonviolent Resistance*. New York: Schocken Books.

George, Alexander, and Andrew Bennett 2005. *Case Studies and Theory Development in the Social Sciences*. Cambridge, MA: MIT Press.

Ghonim, Wael 2012. *Revolution 2.0: The Power of the People Is Greater than the People in Power: A Memoir*. London: HarperCollins.

Giap, Vo Nguyen 1966. *Once Again, We Will Win*. Hanoi: Foreign Languages Publishing House.

Giau, Tran Van, and Le Van Chat 1982. *The South Vietnam Liberation National Front*. Hanoi: Foreign Languages Publishing House.

Gilley, Sheridan W. 1991. 'Pearse's sacrifice: Christ and Cuchulain crucified and risen in the Easter Rising, 1916', in Stephen Sykes (ed.), *Sacrifice and Redemption: Durham Essays in Theology*, 218–34. Cambridge University Press.

Girard, René 2008 [1972]. *Violence and the Sacred*. London: Continuum.

Goffman, Erving 1961a. *Two Studies in the Sociology of Interaction*. Indianapolis: Bobbs-Merrile.

1961b. *Asylums: Essays on the Social Situation of Mental Patients and Other Inmates*. New York: Penguin Books.

1967. *Interaction Rituals: Essays on Face-to-Face Behavior*. Garden City, NY: Doubleday.

Goldsmith, Benjamin E. 2005. *Imitation in International Relations: Observational Learning, Analogies and Foreign Policy in Russia and Ukraine*. New York: Palgrave Macmillan.

Goldstone, Richard 2009. *Human Rights in Palestine and Other Occupied Arab Territories: Report of the United Nations Fact Finding Mission on the Gaza Conflict* (Goldstone Report). New York: United Nations.

Guzzini, Stefano 2005. 'The concept of power: a constructivist analysis', *Millennium – Journal of International Studies*, 33(3): 495–521.

Hafez, Mohammed M. 2006. 'Rationality, culture and structure in the making of suicide bombers: a preliminary theoretical synthesis and illustrative case study', *Studies in Conflict and Terrorism*, 29(2): 165–85.

2007. *Suicide Bombers in Iraq: The Strategy and Ideology of Martyrdom*. Washington, DC: US Institute of Peace Press.

Haiba, Mohamed el Moktar Sidi 2011. 'Revolutionary uprisings in the Middle East', *Daily News Egypt*, 3 March.

Halberstam, David 1963. 'Nun plans suicide', *New York Times*, 24 July.

2008. *The Making of a Quagmire: America and Vietnam during the Kennedy Era*, rev edn. Lanham, MD: Rowman and Littlefield.

Halbwachs, Maurice 1978 [1930]. *The Causes of Suicide* (trans. Harold Goldblatt). New York: Free Press.

1992 [1925]. *On Collective Memory* (trans. Lewis A. Coser). University of Chicago Press.

Hanh, Thich Nhat 1967. *Vietnam: The Lotus in the Sea of Fire*. London: SCM Press.

1987. *Being Peace* (ed. Arnold Kotler). Berkeley, CA: Parallax Press.

2008. *Peaceful Action, Open Heart: Lessons from the Lotus Sutra*. Berkeley, CA: Parallax Press.

Hanoi Radio 1963. 'US-Diem will mislead UN observers', Hanoi Radio, VNA International Service broadcast, 15 October (reprinted in FBIS-FRB-63–202: JJJ5–6).

1965a. 'Vietnam martyr's wife writes Mrs Morrison', Hanoi Radio, VNA International Service broadcast, 4 November (reprinted in FBIS-FRB-65–215: KKK2).

1965b. Youth Federation letter, 'Reportage on Norman Morrison's immolation', Hanoi Radio, VNA International Service broadcast (reprinted in FBIS-FRB-65–217, 9 November: JJJ2).

Hansen, Lene 2011. 'Theorizing the image for security studies', *European Journal of International Relations*, 17(1): 51–74.

Harlan, Lindsey 2001. 'Truth and sacrifice: *satī* immolations in India', in Margaret Cormack (ed.), *Sacrificing the Self: Perspectives on Martyrdom and Religion*, 118–31. Oxford University Press.

Harre, Rom (ed.) 1989. *The Social Construction of Emotions*. Oxford: Basil Blackwell.

Havel, Václav 1985 [1978]. 'The power of the powerless', in John Keane (ed.), *The Power of the Powerless: Citizens against the State in Central-Eastern Europe,* 10–59. Armonk, NY: M. E. Sharpe.

Harvey, A. D. 2007. *Body Politic: Political Metaphor and Political Violence.* Newcastle: Cambridge Scholars Publishing.

Hendrickson, Paul 1996. *The Living and the Dead: Robert McNamara and Five Lives of a Lost War.* New York: Alfred A. Knopf.

Hertz, Robert 1960 [1907]. *Death and the Right Hand* (trans. Rodney Needham and Claudia Needham). Glencoe, IL: Free Press.

Hobbes, Thomas 1968 [1651]. *Leviathan* (ed. C. B. Macpherson). New York: Penguin Books.

Hoffman, Bruce 2003. 'The logic of suicide terrorism', *Atlantic Monthly,* **291**(5): 1–10.

Hogan, Gerard, and Clive Walker 1989. *Political Violence and the Law in Northern Ireland.* Manchester University Press.

Hollis, Martin, and Steven Smith 1990. *Explaining and Understanding International Relations.* Oxford: Clarendon Press.

1991. 'Beware of gurus: structure and action in international relations', *Review of International Relations,* **17**(4): 393–410.

Holzgrefe, J. L., and Robert Keohane (eds.) 2003. *Humanitarian Intervention: Ethical, Legal and Political Dilemmas.* Cambridge University Press.

Honneth, Axel 1995. *The Struggle for Recognition: The Moral Grammar of Social Conflicts.* Cambridge: Polity Press.

Hope, Marjorie 1967 'The reluctant way: self-immolation in Vietnam', *Antioch Review,* **27**(2): 149–63.

Howson, Alexandra 2004. *The Body in Society: An Introduction.* Cambridge: Polity Press.

Hronick, Michael S. 2006. 'Analyzing terror: researchers study the perpetrators and the effects of suicide terrorism', *NIJ Journal,* **254**: 8–11.

Hubert, Henri, and Marcel Mauss 1964 [1898]. *Sacrifice: Its Nature and Functions* (trans. W. D. Halls). University of Chicago Press.

Hudson, Michael C. 1977. *Arab Politics: The Search for Legitimacy.* New Haven, CT: Yale University Press.

Hughes, Derek 2007. *Culture and Sacrifice: Ritual Death in Literature and Opera.* Cambridge University Press.

Hulmes, Edward D. A. 1991. 'The semantics of sacrifice', in Stephen Sykes (ed.), *Sacrifice and Redemption: Durham Essays in Theology*, 265–81. Cambridge University Press.

Huntington, Samuel P. 1996. *The Clash of Civilizations and the Remaking of World Order*. London: Simon Schuster.

International Commission on Intervention and State Sovereignty (ICISS) 2001. *The Responsibility to Protect*. Ottawa: International Development Research Centre.

Iqbal, Razia 2008. 'Hunger's forceful look at Ireland', *BBC News*, 16 May; available at newsvote.bbc.co.uk/mpapps/pagetools/print/news.bbc.co.uk/1/hi/entertainment/7405.

*Irish Times* 2001. 'Hunger strikers who survived', *Irish Times*, March 16: 3.

Jabri, Vivienne, and Stephen Chan 1996. 'The ontologist always rings twice: two more stories about structure and agency in reply to Hollis and Smith', *Review of International Studies*, 22(1): 107–19.

Jackson, Patrick Thaddeus 2004. 'Is the state a person? Why should we care?', *Review of International Studies*, 30(2): 255–316.

Jackson, Richard 2005. *Writing the War on Terrorism: Language, Politics and Counter-Terrorism*. Manchester University Press.

Jakubowska, Longina 1990. 'Political drama in Poland: the use of national symbols', *Anthropology Today*, 6(1): 10–13.

John Paul II 1979. *Return to Poland: The Collected Speeches of John Paul II*. London: Collins.

Jones, Clayton 2011. 'The slap heard round the world', *Christian Science Monitor*, 5 March.

Jones, David R. 1965. 'Woman, 82, sets herself afire in street as protest on Vietnam', *New York Times*, 18 March: 3.

Jones, Howard 2003. *The Death of a Generation: How the Assassinations of Diem and JFK Prolonged the Vietnam War*. Oxford University Press.

*Jordan Times* 2011. 'Another tidal wave needed', *Jordan Times*, 4 March (reprinted in BBC Monitoring Middle East).

Juergensmeyer, Mark 2003. *Terror in the Mind of God: The Global Rise of Religious Violence*. Berkeley: University of California Press.

Kamali, Mohammad Hashim 2002. *The Dignity of Man: An Islamic Perspective*. Cambridge: Islamic Texts Society.

Kaplan, Robert D. 2000. *The Coming Anarchy: Shattering the Dreams of the Post Cold War*. New York: Random House.

Keown, Damien 2005. *Buddhist Ethics: A Very Short Introduction*. Oxford University Press.

Kermani, Navid 2002. 'Roots of terror: suicide, martyrdom, self-redemption and Islam', OpenDemocracy, 21 February, www.opendemocracy.net/faith-europe_islam/article_88.jsp.

Kershner, Isabel 2011. 'Deadly Israeli raid draws condemnation', *New York Times*, 31 May.

Khalili, Laleh 2007. *Heroes and Martyrs of Palestine: The Politics of National Commemoration*. Cambridge University Press.

Khashan, Hilal 2003. 'Collective Palestinian frustration and suicide bombings', *Third World Quarterly*, **24**(6): 1049–67.

Khosrokhavar, Farhad 2005 [2002]. *Suicide Bombers: Allah's New Martyrs* (trans. David Macey). London: Pluto Press.

Khouri, Rami 2004. 'Politics and perceptions in the Middle East after September 11', Social Science Research Council; available at conconflicts. ssrc.org/archives/Mideast/khouri.

   2011. 'Faida Hamdi messed with the wrong man', *Daily Star* (Lebanon), 2 March.

King, Sally 2000. 'They who burned themselves for peace: Quaker and Buddhist self-immolators during the Vietnam War', *Buddhist–Christian Studies*, **20**: 127–48.

Kissinger, Henry 1972. Interview, in *The Killing Zone: The Vietnam War*. History Channel DVD box set, GRD1839.

Kleine, Christoph, 2006. '"The epitome of the ascetic life": the controversy over self-mortification and ritual suicide as ascetic practices in east Asian Buddhism', in Oliver Freiburger (ed.), *Asceticism and Its Critics: Historical Accounts and Comparative Perspectives*, 153–78. Oxford University Press.

Kohn, Marek 2008. *Trust: Self-Interest and the Common Good*. Oxford University Press.

Kramer, Martin 1990. 'The moral logic of Hizballah', in Walter Reich (ed.), *Origins of Terrorism: Psychologies, Ideologies, Theologies, States of Mind*, 131–59. Cambridge University Press.

Kratochwil, Friedrich 1991. *Rules, Norms and Decisions: On the Conditions of Practical and Legal Reasoning in International Relations and Domestic Affairs*. Cambridge University Press.

Krause, Keith, and Michael C. Williams (1997). *Critical Security Studies: Concepts and Strategies*. London: Routledge.

Krieger, Hilary Leila 2010. 'US concerned over IHH–Hamas ties', *Jerusalem Post*, 3 June.

Kubik, Jan 1994. *The Power of Symbols against the Symbols of Power*. University Park: University of Pennsylvania Press.

Laderman, Scott 2009. *Tours of Vietnam: War, Travel Guides, and Memory*. Durham, NC: Duke University Press.

Lachkar, Joan 2002. 'The psychological make-up of a suicide bomber', *Journal of Psychohistory*, **29**(4): 349–67.

Lakoff, George, and Mark Johnson 1980. *Metaphors We Live By*. University of Chicago Press.

Lalami, Laila 2011. 'Who's responsible for the Arab uprisings? A non-exhaustive list', *The Nation*, 25 February.

Landler, Mark 2011. 'A region's unrest scrambles US foreign policy', *New York Times*, 25 January.

Laub, Karin 2011. 'In birthplace of Arab uprising, discontent lingers', Associated Press, 12 March.

Lawrence, Bruce 2005. *Messages to the World: The Statements of Osama bin Laden*. New York: Verso.

Lebow, Richard Ned 2008. *A Cultural Theory of International Relations*. Cambridge University Press.

Leep, Matthew Coen 2010. 'The affective production of others: United States policy towards the Israeli-Palestinian conflict', *Cooperation and Conflict*, 45(3): 331–52.

Lewinstein, Keith 2001. 'The revaluation of martyrdom in early Islam', in Margaret Cormack (ed.), *Sacrificing the Self: Perspectives on Martyrdom and Religion*, 78–91. Oxford University Press.

Lewis, Bernard 2001. *What Went Wrong? Western Impact and Middle Eastern Response*. Oxford University Press.

Lincoln, Bruce 1986. *Myth, Cosmos and Society: Indo-European Themes of Creation and Destruction*. Cambridge, MA: Harvard University Press.

Litka, Piotr 2009. *Ksiadz Jerzy Popiełuszko: Dni, ktore wstrzasnely Polska*. Kraków: Wydawnictwo sw. Stanislawa.

  2010. *Zak zginal Popiełuszko*. Dobrze udokumentaowane, DVD.

*Los Angeles Times* 1963a. 'Monk, 71, burns himself', *Los Angeles Times*, 16 August.

*Los Angeles Times* 1963b. 'Diem vs. Mme. Nhu', *Los Angeles Times*, 18 August: L4.

Louth, Andrew 1997. 'The body in Western Catholic Christianity', in Sarah Coakley (ed.), *Religion and the Body*, 111–30. Cambridge University Press.

Luxmoore, Jonathan 2010. 'Unfinished legacy of a martyr', *The Tablet*, 29 May.

MacAskill, Ewen 2008. 'Bush references London attacks to defend waterboarding', *Guardian*, 15 February.

Malka, Haim 2003. 'Must innocents die? The Islamic debate over suicide attacks', *Middle East Quarterly*, 10(2): 19–28.

Mansbridge, Jane (ed.) 1990. *Beyond Self-Interest*. University of Chicago Press.

Mansfield, Laura 2006. *His Own Words: A Translation of the Writings of Dr Ayman al Zawahiri*. Irvine, CA: TLG Publications.

Margalit, Avishai 1996. *The Decent Society* (trans. Naomi Goldblum). Cambridge, MA: Harvard University Press.

  2002. *The Ethics of Memory*. Cambridge, MA: Harvard University Press.

Marquand, Robert 2011. 'At the heart of the Arab revolts: a search for dignity', *Christian Science Monitor*, 3 March.

Mason, Paul 2012. *Why It's Kicking Off Everywhere: The New Global Revolutions*. London: Verso.

McCrory, Marie Louise 2006. 'Memories from the Maze of the last days of Bobby Sands', *Irish Times*, 5 May.

McEvoy, Kieran 2001. *Paramilitary Imprisonment in Northern Ireland: Resistance, Management and Release*. Oxford University Press.

McKeown, Laurence 2001. *Out of Time: Republican Prisoners, Long Kesh 1972–2000*. Belfast: Beyond the Pale.

McNamara, Robert S. 1995. *In Retrospect: The Tragedy and Lessons of Vietnam*. Times Books.

McNamara, Robert S., James G. Blight, Robert K. Brigham, Thomas J. Biersteker and Herbert Y. Schandler 1999. *Argument without End: In Search of Answers to the Vietnam Tragedy*. New York: PublicAffairs.

Meehan, Sumayyah 2011. 'Alarming trend: self-immolation for human rights', *Muslim Observer*, 27 January; available at muslimmedianetwork.com/mmn/?p=7907.

Mejia, Paula 2011. 'The revolution has just begun: Tunisia's Jasmine Revolution', *The Majalla*, 14 February.

Melissen, Jan (ed.) 2005. *The New Public Diplomacy: Soft Power in International Relations*. Basingstoke: Palgrave.

Merari, Ariel 1990. 'The readiness to kill and die: suicidal terrorism in the Middle East', in Walter Reich (ed.), *Origins of Terrorism: Psychologies, Ideologies, Theologies, States of Mind*, 192–208. Cambridge University Press.

   2007. 'Psychological aspects of suicide terrorism', in Bruce Bongar, Lisa M. Brown, Larry E. Beutler, James N. Breckenridge and Philip G. Zimbardo (eds.), *Psychology of Terrorism*, 101–15. Oxford University Press.

Mercer, Jonathan 2005. 'Rationality and psychology in international politics', *International Organization* 59(1): 77–106.

Milliken, Jennifer, and Keith Krause 2003. 'State failure, state collapse and state reconstruction: concepts, lessons and strategies', in Milliken, Jennifer (ed.), *State Failure, Collapse and Reconstruction*, 1–21. Oxford: Blackwell.

Milton, Kate, and Maruska Svasek (eds.) 2005. *Mixed Emotions: Anthropological Studies of Feeling*. London: Berg.

Minois, Georges 1999. *History of Suicide: Voluntary Death in Western Culture*. Baltimore: Johns Hopkins University Press.

Mitzen, Jennifer 2006. 'Ontological security in world politics: state identity and the security dilemma', *European Journal of International Relations*, 12(3): 341–70.

Mneimneh, Hassan 2011. 'The Bou-Azizi effect, the failure of Islamist mobilization, and global dialogue', Center for Global Engagement, 24 January, www.centerforglobalengagement.org/articles/tunisia.php.

Moeller, Susan 1999. *Compassion Fatigue: How the Media Sell Disease, Famine, War and Death*. London: Routledge.

Moghadam, Assaf 2002. 'Suicide bombings in the Israeli-Palestinian conflict: a conceptual framework', Project for the Research of Islamist Movements; available at e-prism.com.

   2003. 'Palestinian suicide terrorism in the second Intifada: motivations and organizational aspects', *Studies in Conflict and Terrorism*, 26(2): 65–92.

   2006a. 'The roots of suicide terrorism: a multi-causal approach', in Ami Pedahzur (ed.), *Root Causes of Suicide Terrorism: The Globalization of Martyrdom*, 81–107. London: Routledge.

   2006b. 'Suicide terrorism, occupation, and the globalization of martyrdom: a critique of *Dying to Win*', *Studies in Conflict and Terrorism*, 29(8): 707–29.

   2008. 'Motives for martyrdom: Al-Qaida, Salafi Jihad, and the spread of suicide attacks', *International Security*, 33(3): 46–78.

Moore, Cerwyn 2006. 'Reading the hermeneutics of violence: the literary turn and Chechnya', *Global Society*, 20(2): 179–98.

   2009. 'Tracing the Russian hermeneutic: reflections on Tarkovsky's cinematic poetics and global politics', *Alternatives*, 34(1): 59–82.

Moore, Cerwyn, and Laura J. Shepherd 2010. 'Aesthetics and international relations: towards a global politics', *Global Society*, 24(3): 299–309.

Morris, Errol 2004. *The Fog of War: Eleven Lessons from the Life of Robert S. McNamara*. New York: Sony Pictures.

Morrison, Catherine 2006. 'Republicans commemorate hunger strikes after 25 years', *Irish News*, 3 March: 12.

Morrison, Danny (ed.) 2006. *Hunger Strike: Reflections on the 1981 Hunger Strike*. London: Brandon.

Neumann, Iver 2004. 'Beware of organicism: the narrative self of the state', *Review of International Studies*, 30(2): 259–67.

*New York Times* 1965. 'War critic burns himself to death outside Pentagon', *New York Times*, 3 November: 1.

*Nhan Dan*, 1965a. 'Nhan Dan hails sacrifice of Detroit woman', Hanoi Radio, VNA International Service broadcast, 19 March (reprinted in FBIS-FRB-65–055, 23 March: JJJ7).

   1965b. Editorial, 'Morrison immolation hailed by people, press', Hanoi Radio, VNA International Service broadcast, 4 November (reprinted in FBIS-FRB-65–214, 4 November: JJJ4–5).

1965c. Editorial, 'Reportage on war protest movement in US', Hanoi Radio, VNA International Service broadcast, 13 November (reprinted in FBIS-FRB-65–220, 15 November: JJJ8).

Nussbaum, Martha 2001. *Upheavals of Thought: The Intelligence of Emotions*. Cambridge University Press.

Nye, Joseph S. 2004. 'The decline of America's soft power', *Foreign Affairs*, 83(3): 16–20.

2005. *Soft Power: The Means to Success in World Power*. New York: PublicAffairs.

2008. 'Barack Obama and soft power', *Huffington Post*, 3 July.

Oates, Joyce Carol 1992. 'The cruelest sport', *New York Review of Books*, 19 February: 3–6.

Obama, Barack 2009a. 'Barack Obama's inaugural address', *New York Times*, 20 January.

2009b.'Barack Obama's Cairo speech', *Guardian*, 4 June.

Okasha, Ahmad 2011. Interview conducted by Amira Muhamma, 'Escape from suffering and oppression', Dialogue with the Islamic World, 4 February, qantara.de.

Onuf, Nicholas 1994. 'The constitution of international society', *European Journal of International Law*, 1(1): 1–19.

O'Malley, Padraig 1990. *Biting at the Grave: The Irish Hunger Strikes and the Politics of Despair*. Boston: Beacon Press.

O'Rawe, Richard. 2005. *Blanketmen: An Untold Story of the H-Block Hunger Strike*. Dublin: New Island.

Ornatowski, Cezar M. 2009. 'Rhetoric of Pope John Paul II's visits to Poland, 1979–1999', in Joseph R. Blaney and Joseph P. Zompetti (eds.), *The Rhetoric of Pope John Paul II*, 103–50. New York: Lexington Books.

Overvold, Mark Carl 1980. 'Self-interest and the concept of self-sacrifice', *Canadian Journal of Philosophy*, 10(1):105–18.

'PalestineCitizen 2009' 2010. 'In memory of the nine martyrs of the MV Mari Marmara', 'PalestineCitizen 2009', www.facebook.com/media/set/?set=a.179490858748774.38536.162060917158435.

Pape, Robert A. 2003. 'The strategic logic of suicide terrorism', *American Political Science Review*, 97(3): 343–61.

2006. *Dying to Win: The Strategic Logic of Suicide Terrorism*. New York: Random House.

Pape, Robert A., and James K. Feldman 2010. *Cutting the Fuse: The Explosion of Global Suicide Terrorism and How to Stop It*. University of Chicago Press.

Pedahzur, Ami 2005. *Suicide Terrorism*. Cambridge: Polity Press.

(ed.) 2006. *Root Causes of Suicide Terrorism: The Globalization of Martyrdom*. London: Routledge.

Pitcher, Linda 1998. '"The divine impatience": ritual, narrative and symbolization in the practice of martyrdom', *Medical Anthropology Quarterly*, **12**(1): 8–30.

Popiełuszko, Jerzy 2004. *Ofiara spelniona: Msze Swiete za Ojczyzne odprawiane w kosciele sw. Stansilawa Kostki w Warszawie w latach 1982–1984* . Warsaw: Wydawnictwo Siostr Loretanek.

Post, Jerrold M. 1990. 'Terrorist psycho-logic: terrorist behavior as a product of psychological forces', in Walter Reich (ed.), *Origins of Terrorism: Psychologies, Ideologies, Theologies, States of Mind*, 25–41. Cambridge University Press.

Procter, Paul (ed.) 1995. *Cambridge International Dictionary of English*. Cambridge University Press.

Qur'an, The 2008. The Qur'an (trans. M. A. S. Abdel Haleem). Oxford University Press.

Rabinovich, Abraham 2002. 'Suicide bombers' psyches studied: support, revenge seen as motives', *Washington Times*, 30 December: A8.

Ravid, Barak 2011. 'Turkey: Israel's probe of Gaza flotilla has no value or credibility', Haaretz.com, 23 January, www.haaretz.com/news/diplomacy-defense/turkey-israel-s-probe-of-gaza-flotilla-has-no-value-or-credibility-1.338741.

Reeves, Gene 2008. 'Translator's introduction', *The Lotus Sutra: A Contemporary Translation of a Buddhist Classic*, 1–19. Somerville, MA: Wisdom Publications.

Richardson, John H. 2005. *My Father the Spy: An Investigative Memoir*. New York: HarperCollins.

Ringmar, Eric 1996. *Identity and Action: A Cultural Explanation of Sweden's Intervention in the Thirty Years War*. Cambridge University Press.

Roberts, Adam 2010. 'Lives and statistics: are 90% of war victims civilian?', *Survival*, **52**(3): 115–35.
  2011. 'The civilian in modern war', in Hew Strachan and Sibylle Scheipers (eds.), *The Changing Character of War*, 357–80. Oxford University Press.

Roberts, Adam, and Timothy Garton Ash (eds.) 2011. *Civil Resistance and Power Politics: The Experience of Non-Violent Action from Gandhi to the Present*. Oxford University Press.

Robinson, Piers 2002. *The CNN Effect: The Myth of News Media, Foreign Policy and Intervention*. London: Routledge.

Ross, Andrew G. 2006. 'Coming in from the cold: constructivism and emotion', *European Journal of International Relations*, **12**(2): 197–222.

Rothberg, Michael 2009. *Multidirectional Memory: Remembering the Holocaust in the Age of Decolonization*. Stanford University Press.

Roy, Olivier 1998 [1992]. *The Failure of Political Islam* (trans. Carol Volk). Cambridge, MA: Harvard University Press.

Ruzicka, Jan, and Nicholas J. Wheeler 2010. 'The puzzle of trusting relationships in the Nuclear Non-Proliferation Treaty', *International Affairs*, 86(1): 69–85.

Ryan, Cheyney 1994. 'The one who burns herself for peace', *Hypatia*, 9(2): 21–39.

Saad-Ghorayeb, Amal 2002. *Hizbu'llah: Politics and Religion*. London: Pluto Press.

Said, Edward W. 1979. *Orientalism*. New York: Vintage Books.

  1980. 'Islam through Western eyes', *The Nation*, 26 April.

Sands, Bobby 1981. *The Diary of Bobby Sands*. Dublin: Sinn Féin.

Sarraj, Eyad el, and Linda Butler 2002. 'Suicide bombers: dignity, despair, and the need for hope', *Journal of Palestine Studies*, 31(4): 71–6.

Saturen, Valerie 2005. 'Divine suffering in Shi'ism: origins and political implications', *Iran Analysis Quarterly*, 2(4): 22–42.

Saurette, Paul 2005. *The Kantian Imperative: Humiliation, Common Sense, Politics*. University of Toronto Press.

  2006. 'You dissin me? Humiliation and post 9/11 global politics', *Review of International Studies*, 32(3): 495–522.

Scarry, Elaine 1985. *The Body in Pain: The Making and Unmaking of the World*. Oxford University Press.

Seib, Philip 2008. *The Al Jazeera Effect: How the Global Media Are Reshaping World Politics*. Dulles, VA: Potomac Books.

Sela-Shayovitz, Revital, David Yellin College and the Institute of Criminology, Hebrew University of Jerusalem 2007. 'Suicide bombers in Israel: their motivations, characteristics, and prior activity in terrorist organizations', *International Journal of Conflict and Violence*, 1(2): 160–8.

Sen, Amartya K. 1990 [1977]. 'Rational fools: a critique of the behavioral foundations of economic theory', in Jane Mansbridge (ed.), *Beyond Self-Interest*, 25–43. University of Chicago Press.

Seth, Sanjay 2011. 'Postcolonial theory and the critique of international relations', *Millennium – Journal of International Studies*, 40(1): 167–83.

Sharp, Gene 2005. *Waging Nonviolent Struggles: 20th Century Practice and 21st Century Potential*. Boston: Extending Horizons Books.

Sheehan, Cindy 2010. 'Peace heroes: the martyrs of the Mavi Marmara', Free Gaza Movement, 6 June, www.freegaza.org/en/all-passengers/75-ninth-trip-to-gaza-in-may-2010/1219-peace-heroes-the-martyrs-of-the-mavi-marmara.

Sherwood, Harriet 2010. 'Flotilla raid: Turkish jihadis bent on violence attacked troops, Israel claimed', *Guardian*, 2 June.

Singal, Daniel J. 2008. 'Introduction', in David Halberstam, *The Making of a Quagmire: America and Vietnam during the Kennedy Era*, rev edn, xi–xiii. Lanham, MD: Rowman and Littlefield.

Singh, Rashmi 2011. *Hamas and Suicide Terrorism: Multi-Causal and Multi-Level Approaches*. London: Routledge.

Smidt, Corwin E. 2005. 'Religion and American attitudes toward Islam and an invasion of Iraq', *Sociology of Religion*, 66(3): 243–61.

Smith, Pamela Hyde 2007. 'The hard road back to soft power', *Georgetown Journal of International Affairs*, 8(1): 115–23.

Speckhard, Anne 2005. 'Understanding suicide terrorism: countering human bombs and their senders', in Jason S. Purcell and Joshua D. Weintraub (eds.), *Topics in Terrorism: Toward a Transatlantic Consensus on the Nature of the Threat*, 1–22. Washington, DC: Atlantic Council Publications.

  2006. 'Defusing human bombs: understanding suicide terrorism', in Jeff Victoroff (ed.), *Social and Psychological Factors in the Genesis of Terrorism*, 277–91. Amsterdam: IOS Press.

Sprinzak, Ehud 2000. 'Rational fanatics', *Foreign Policy*, 79(5): 67–73.

Stearns, Peter N., and Carol Z. Stearns 1985. 'Emotionology: clarifying the history of emotions and emotional standards', *American Historical Review*, 90(4): 813–36.

Steele, Brent J. 2008. *Ontological Security in International Relations: Self-Identity and the IR State*. London: Routledge.

Steinbach, Alice 1995. 'The sacrifice of Norman Morrison', *Baltimore Sun*, 30 July: 4K–5K.

Stephan, Maria J., and Erica Chenowith 2008. 'Why civil resistance works: the strategic logic of nonviolent conflict', *International Security*, 33(1): 7–44.

Svasek, Maruska (ed.) 2006. *Post-Socialism: Politics and Emotions in Central and Eastern Europe*. Oxford: Berghahn Books.

Sweeney, George 1993a. 'Irish hunger strikes and the cult of self-sacrifice', *Journal of Contemporary History*, 28(3): 421–37.

  1993b. 'Self-immolation in Ireland: hungerstrikes and political confrontation', *Anthropology Today*, 9(5): 10–14.

Tambiah, Stanley J. 1990. *Magic, Science, Religion and the Scope of Rationality*. Cambridge University Press.

Telhami, Shibley 2008. 'It's not about faith', Brookings Institution; available at www.brookings.edu/opinions/2011/1010middleeast_telhami.aspx.

Thompson, Simon 2006. *The Political Theory of Recognition: A Critical Introduction*. Cambridge: Polity Press.

Thucydides 1951 [431 BCE]. *The Peloponnesian War: The Unabridged Crawley Translation* (introd. John H. Finley). New York: Modern Library.

*Times* 2001. 'The story of the hunger strikes that changed the course of the Troubles', *Times*, 16 March.

Tischner, Józef 1984. *The Spirit of Solidarity*. San Francisco: Harper & Row.

    1987. *Marxism and Christianity: The Quarrel and the Dialogue in Poland*. Washington, DC: Georgetown University Press.

    2005 [1981]. *The Ethics of Solidarity [Etyka Solidarności]* (trans. Anna Fraś). Kraków: Znak.

Topmiller, Robert J. 2002. *The Lotus Unleashed: The Buddhist Peace Movement in South Vietnam, 1964–1966*. Lexington: University Press of Kentucky.

Tosini, Domenico 2009. 'A sociological understanding of suicide attacks', *Theory, Culture and Society*, **26**(4): 67–96.

Turkel, Jacob 2010. *Report of the Public Commission to Examine the Maritime Incident of 31 May 2010* (the Turkel Commission) (two parts). Jerusalem: Government Printing Israel.

Turner, Bryan S. 2008. *The Body and Society* (3rd edn). London: Sage.

Turner, Victor 1967. *The Forest of Symbols: Aspects of Ndembu Ritual*. Ithaca, NY: Cornell University Press.

    2008 [1969]. *The Ritual Process: Structure and Anti-Structure* (2nd edn). London: Aldine Transaction.

United Nations 1948. 'Universal declaration of human rights', United Nations, adopted by the General Assembly on 10 December; available at www.un.org/en/documents/udhr/history.shtml.

    2010. 'Israeli action against Gaza flotilla "unlawful" – UN Human Rights Council panel', UN News Centre, 23 September; available at www.un.org/apps/news/story.asp?NewsID=36086&Cr=flotilla&Cr1.

US Department of State 1954. 'The final declaration on Indochina', in John P. Glennon (ed.), *Foreign Relations of the United States, 1952–1954*, vol. XIII, *Indochina*, part 2, 1541. Washington, DC: US Government Printing Office.

Van Gennep, Arnold 1909. *The Rites of Passage*. University of Chicago Press.

Vuori, Juha 2008. 'Illocutionary logic and strands of securitization: applying the theory of securitization to the study of non-democratic political orders', *European Journal of International Relations*, **14**(1): 65–99.

Wæver, Ole 1995. 'Securitization and desecuritization', in Ronnie D. Lipschutz (ed.), *On Security* , 46–86. New York: Columbia University Press.

Wæver, Ole 2000. 'The EU as a security actor: reflections from a pessimistic constructivist on post-sovereign security orders', in Morten Kelstrup and Michael C. Williams (eds.), *International Relations Theory and European Integration: Power, Security and Community*, 250–94. Florence: Routledge.

Walker, R. B. J. 1993. *Inside/Outside: International Relations as Political Theory.* Cambridge University Press.

Walker, R. K. 2006. *The Hunger Strikes.* Belfast: Lagan Books.

Waltz, Kenneth 1979. *Theory of International Politics.* Reading, MA: Addison-Wesley.

Walzer, Michael 1977. *Just and Unjust Wars: A Moral Argument with Historical Illustrations.* London: Penguin Books.

Welsh, Jennifer M. (ed.) 2004. *Humanitarian Intervention and International Relations.* Oxford University Press.

Wendt, Alexander 1987. 'The agent–structure problem in international relations theory', *International Organization*, 41(3): 335–70.

1992. 'Anarchy is what states make of it: the social construction of power politics', *International Organization* 46(2): 391–425.

1999. *Social Theory of International Relations.* Cambridge University Press.

2003. 'Why a world state is inevitable', *European Journal of International Relations*, 9(4): 491–542.

2004. 'The state as person in international theory', *Review of International Studies*, 30(2): 289–316.

Weschler, Lawrence 1982. *Solidarity: Poland in the Season of Its Passion.* New York: Simon Schuster.

Wheeler, Nicholas J. 2002. *Saving Strangers: Humanitarian Intervention in International Society.* Oxford University Press.

2009. 'Beyond Waltz's nuclear world: more trust may be better', *International Relations*, 23(3): 428–45.

Whitbeck, John V. 2012. 'A plan to recover momentum for Palestine', *Huffington Post*, 24 February.

Wiegel, George 1992. *The Final Revolution: The Resistance Church and the Collapse of Communism.* Oxford University Press.

2005. *Witness to Hope: The Biography of John Paul II*, updated edn. London: HarperCollins.

Wiener, Antje 2008. *The Invisible Constitution of Politics: Contested Norms and International Encounters.* Cambridge University Press.

Williams, Paul 1997. 'Some Mahāyāna Buddhist perspectives on the body', in Sarah Coakley (ed.), *Religion and the Body*, 205–30. Cambridge University Press.

2009. *Mahāyāna Buddhism: The Doctrinal Foundations*, 2nd edn. London: Routledge.

Wittgenstein, Ludwig 1922. *Tractatus Logico-Philosophicus* (trans. C. K. Ogden). London: Routledge & Kegan Paul.

1958. *Philosophical Investigations*, 3rd edn. Oxford: Basil Blackwell.

Wolf, Reinhard 2011. 'Respect and disrespect in international politics: the significance of status recognition', *International Theory*, 3(1): 105–42.

Wood, Kristin 2011. 'Terror's power failure in the Middle East', CNN.com, 9 March.

Young, Allen 1995. *The Harmony of Illusions: Inventing Post-Traumatic Stress Disorder.* Princeton University Press.

Yuval-Davis, Nira 2011. *The Politics of Belonging: Intersectional Contestations.* London: Sage.

Zagacki, Kenneth S. 2001. 'Pope John Paul II and the crusade against communism: a case study in secular and sacred time', *Rhetoric and Public Affairs*, 4(4): 689–710.

Zaroulis, Nancy, and Gerald Sullivan 1984. *Who Spoke Up? American Protest against the War in Vietnam 1963–1975.* New York: Doubleday.

Zevnik, Andreja 2009. 'Sovereign-less subject and the possibility of resistance', *Millennium – Journal of International Studies*, 38(1): 83–106.

Zuziak, Wladyslaw (ed.) 2001. *Idea solidarności dzisiaj.* Kraków: Wydawnictwo Naukowe PAT.

## Archival documents

### *Northern Ireland*

The following documents are from the archives of the Northern Ireland Collection of the Linenhall Library in Belfast. G1 refers to documents found in H-Block/Hungerstrike, Box, General; 1CR to Hunger Strike, Box 1 (Material from Chris Ryder); 2CR to Hunger Strike (Material on the 1981 Hunger Strike from Chris Ryder, Box 2); IM10 to Hunger Strike (International Material); IM12 to Hunger Strike, Box 2 (International Material). It should be noted that many of the newspaper articles were not properly referenced in the archival material. Blank spaces have been filled in when possible.

Address to Charter 80 no date. Address to Charter 80 from the H-blocks; in 1CR.

*An Phoblacht/Republican News* 1981a. 'Blanket men start new hunger strike: the only road open', *An Phoblacht/Republican News*, 28 February; in 2 CR.

    1981b. 'Political status now!', *An Phoblacht/Republican News*, 7 March; in 2CR.

    1981c. 'Campaign gains momentum', *An Phoblacht/Republican News*, 21 March; in 2CR.

    1981d. 'Easter statement', *An Phoblacht/Republican News*, 28 March; in 2CR.

    1981e. 'Political recognition', *An Phoblacht/Republican News*, 11 April; in 2CR.

1981f. 'Laying down their life', *An Phoblacht/Republican News*, 18 April; in 2CR.

1981g. 'There will be fire and there will be fury', *An Phoblacht/Republican News*, 25 April; in 2CR.

Arnlis, Peter 1981a. 'Daly gives Brits ammunition', *An Phoblacht/Republican News*, 7 March; in 2CR.

1981b. 'Fermanagh and South Tyrone Westminster elections', *An Phoblacht/Republican News*, 11 April; in 2CR.

1981c. 'Expediency halts expulsion moves: Brits back down', *An Phoblacht/Republican News*, 18 April; in 2CR.

1981d. 'Rapid developments: British resist peaceful resolution of prison crisis', *An Phoblacht/Republican News*, 25 April; in 2CR.

Beake, David 1980. 'Memo to Chris Ryder', *Sunday Times* Newsroom, 3 December; in 1CR.

Beresford, David 1981a. 'Retired loyalist's stand against hunger striker', 7 April; in G1.

1981b. 'Deathbed tape row angers Ulster Catholics', *Guardian*, 25 May; in 1CR.

Breig, Gordon, Noreen Erskine and Roger Scott 1981. 'IRA ready to burn Belfast', *Daily Mail*, 1 May; in 1CR

Campbell, Jim 1981. 'Catholics warned by UDA leader "Back off!"', *Sunday World*, 3 May; in 1CR.

Commonwealth of Massachusetts 1981. 'Resolutions memorializing the president of the United States to urge the government of Great Britain to recognize Bobby Sands as a political prisoner', adopted by the House of Representatives 22 April.

Cowley, Martin 1980. 'Nothing new offered to prisoners – Atkins', 20 December, in 1CR.

1981. 'NI secretary unmoved on prison issue', 6 February, in 1CR.

Delaney, Sean 1981. 'Blanket of press silence shredded', *An Phoblacht/Republican News*, 18 April.

Department of Social Studies, Queen's University Belfast 1980. Letter in response to Chris Ryder's article on the H-blocks, 26 October; in 1CR.

Devlin, Bernadette no date. 'Trial or torture? Where else in the Western world but North Ireland would this be a question?', in IM12.

Ellsworth-Jones, Will, and Chris Ryder 1981. 'Belfast waits for the flashpoint', *Sunday Times*, 10 May; in 2CR.

Fallon, Beth 1981. 'Funeral preparations for Bobby Sands underway in Belfast', *New York Daily News*, 6 May.

Holland, Mary 1980. 'Dying men who stir the boiling pot', *New Statesman*, 5 December; in 1CR.

Howe, Marie 1981. Press release, House of Representatives, Massachusetts, 16 April.

Hunger strike 1980. 'Showdown with imperialism', 3 November, in 1CR. 1981. 'Hunger strike: the facts', 9 January, in 1CR.

Malone, Padraig 1981. 'Sinn Féin – Limerick', speech given in Toronto, 20 March; in IM10.

McCartan, Desmond 1980. 'Human pleads but talks bid fails', 5 December, in 1CR.

McKittrick, David 1980a. 'Starving to death: what it really means and how it was avoided', *Irish Times*, 20 December; in 1CR.
   1980b. 'Special rights whittled down at Maze', *Irish Times*, 23 December; in 1CR.
   1981. 'Provo politics more effective than the gun', *Irish Times*, 9 May; in 2CR.

Moloney, Ed 1980. 'We have worn down their will', *Magill*, September, 5–6; in 1CR.

National H-Block/Armagh Committee 1981. 'Hunger strike: break the wall of silence', in G1.

National Smash H-Block Committee no date. 'H-block: an affront to dignity', in G1.

Northern Ireland Information Service 1981. Press release, 5 February; in 1CR.

Northern Ireland Office 1980. 'Threatened hunger strike at HM Prison Maze', 23 October, in 1CR.

O Duill, Piaras 1981. 'Hunger strike: the children of '69', issued by the National H-Block/Armagh Committee, 12 April; in G1.

Parry, Gareth 1981. 'The dilemma of doctor and priest', *Guardian*, 1 May; in 1CR.

*Times* 1981. Prime minister's questions: 'Political status a licence to kill', *Times*, 6 May; in 1CR.

Republican prisoners of war 1976. Letter to relative action groups, all areas: Long Kesh concentration camp, 22 November.

Ryder, Chris 1980. 'Provos launch propaganda war: Thatcher is victor in Maze confrontation', 21 December, in 1CR.

Thomas, Christopher 1981. 'Maze prisoners issue veiled threat to resume hunger strike after deadlock over reforms "offer"', *Times*, 3 January; in 1CR.

Thomas, Christopher, and John Witherow 1981. 'Battalion flown in for Belfast funeral', *Times*, 7 May; in 1CR.

Whale, John 1980. 'Ethics of a hunger strike', 7 December; in 1CR.

Witherow, John 1981a. 'Depression and despair of the man who chose to die', 20 April, in 2CR.
   1981b. 'Why the Irish use hunger strikes', 6 May, in 2CR.

Zimbabwe H-Block/Armagh Committee 1981. *Action Bulletin* no. 2, Harare, 29 March; in IM12.

*Poland*

The documents below, particularly relating to Popiełuszko, come from the
    Charta Archives in Warsaw. The documents relating to Solidarity come
    from the author's private archive, which were collected in the early
    1990s; these are marked 'AA' for 'author's archive'.
Bogucki, Teofel 1984a. 'Msza sw za Ojczyzne' [Mass of the fatherland],
    Warsaw, 25 November, Charta.
    1984b. 'List do paragian z' (letter sent after Popiełuszko's kidnapping,
    from the hospital to parishioners), 21 October, Charta.
Boyes, Roger, and John Moody 1986. *The Priest Who Had to Die*. London:
    Gollancz.
Bujak, Zbigniew 1982. Interview, 'The aim of the underground', *Labour
    Focus on Eastern Europe*, 5(1/2): 36; AA.
Canine, Craig, and Debbie Seward 1984. 'The making of a martyr',
    *Newsweek*, 12 November; Charta.
CPSU 1981. Letter to Polish party, 'Poland has reached a "critical point"',
    *Current Digest of the Soviet Press*, 33(24): 1.
Fox, John 1985. 'Murder of a Polish priest' , *Reader's Digest*, December;
    archive ref.: TEC ZKA.A0IV/207.2 .
Herold, Jozef (ed.) 2004. *Ostatni dzien ks. Jerzego Popiełuszki*. Bydgoszcz:
    Instytut Wydawniczy 'Swiadectwo'.
Kołakowski, Leszek 1971. 'Hope and hopelessness', *Survey* **17**(3): 37–52.
Kuroń, Jacek 1979. 'The situation in the country and the programme of the
    opposition', *Labor Focus on Eastern Europe*, 3(3): 12–13; AA.
Kuroń, Jacek, Zbigniew Bujak and Wiktor Kulerski 1982. 'Solidarity
    debates strategy', *Labor Focus on Eastern Europe*, 5(3/4):
    17–22; AA.
*Labour Focus on Eastern Europe* 1982. Documents of the resistance
    (13 December 1981), *Labour Focus on Eastern Europe*, 5(1/2): 35–6; AA.
Michnik, Adam 1981. 'What we want to do and what we can do', *Telos*, 47:
    66–77.
    1985. *Letters from Prison and Other Essays* (trans. Maya Latynski).
    Berkeley: University of California Press; AA.
Murphy, Jamie 1985. 'Keeping the lid on murder', *Time*, 2 January; Charta.
*Newsweek* 1984. 'The making of a martyr', *Newsweek*, 12 November, 12;
    Charta.
Pick, Hella 1984a. 'Pope urges forgiveness of priest's murderers', *Guardian*,
    1 November; Charta.
    1984b. 'Message of hope on Polish priest's grave', *Guardian*, 6 November;
    607/4, Charta.

Polska Agencja Prasowa [Polish Press Agency] 1984. 'Nie będzie pobłażania dla anarchii i terroryzmu: Oświadczenia KC PZPR', 27/28 October, Polska Agencja Prasowa; Pol 26 Popiełuszko 607/4, Charta.

Popiełuszko, Jerzy 1984. 'Das Vermächtnis des toten Priesters', *Stern*, 11 August; Charta.

    1986. *The Way of My Cross: Masses at Warsaw* (trans. Michael J. Wrenn). Chicago: Regency Books; AA.

PUWP Central Committee 1981. Plenary session resolution, 11 February, *Current Digest of the Soviet Press*, **33**(6): 12.

Solidarity 1982. Appeal to the public, *Labour Focus on Eastern Europe*, **5**(1/2): 37; AA.

Uniwersytet Warszawski 1984. Uchwała uczelnianego przedstawicielstwa studentów Uniwersytetu Warszawskiego 31 October (statement of students at Warsaw University); AOIV/26.7, Charta.

Urban, Jerzy 1984. Press conference, 'Doprowadzono do ujawnienia przypuszczalnych sprawców porwania ks. Jerzego Popiełuszki', 26 October, Polska Agencja Prasowa; Pol 26 Popiełuszko 607/4, Charta.

Yermolovich, Nadezhda 1984a. 'Growing influence of "militant", anti-regime Catholic clergy decried', *Izvestia*, 7 April (reprinted in *Current Digest of the Soviet Press*, **32**(14): 3).

    1984b. 'A word from the pulpit: from the pages of Polish newspapers', *Izvestia*, 30 November (reprinted in *Current Digest of the Soviet Press*, **38**(48): 17).

# Index

# Cambridge Studies in International Relations